Security Risk Management – The Driving Force for Operational Resilience

The importance of businesses being 'operationally resilient' is becoming increasingly important, and a driving force behind whether an organization can ensure that its valuable business operations can 'bounce back' from or manage to evade impactful occurrences is its security risk management capabilities.

In this book, we change the perspective on an organization's operational resilience capabilities so that it changes from being a reactive (tick box) approach to being proactive. The perspectives of every chapter in this book focus on risk profiles and how your business can reduce these profiles using effective mitigation measures.

The book is divided into two sections:

1. Security Risk Management (SRM).
   All the components of security risk management contribute to your organization's operational resilience capabilities, to help reduce your risks.
   • Reduce the probability/likelihood.
2. Survive to Operate.
   If your SRM capabilities fail your organization, these are the components that are needed to allow you to quickly 'bounce back.'
   • Reduce the severity/impact.

Rather than looking at this from an operational resilience compliance capabilities aspect, we have written these to be agnostic of any specific operational resilience framework (e.g., CERT RMM, ISO 22316, SP 800-160 Vol. 2 Rev. 1, etc.), with the idea of looking at operational resilience through a risk management lens instead.

This book is not intended to replace these numerous operational resilience standards/frameworks but, rather, has been designed to complement them by getting you to appreciate their value in helping to identify and mitigate your operational resilience risks.

Unlike the cybersecurity or information security domains, operational resilience looks at the risks from a business-oriented view, so that anything that might disrupt your essential business operations are risk-assessed and appropriate countermeasures identified and applied.

Consequently, this book is not limited to cyberattacks or the loss of sensitive data but, instead, looks at things from a holistic business-based perspective.

Security, Audit and Leadership Series

Series Editor: Dan Swanson, Dan Swanson and Associates, Ltd., Winnipeg, Manitoba, Canada.

The *Security, Audit and Leadership Series* publishes leading-edge books on critical subjects facing security and audit executives as well as business leaders. Key topics addressed include Leadership, Cybersecurity, Security Leadership, Privacy, Strategic Risk Management, Auditing IT, Audit Management, and Leadership.

Security Risk Management – The Driving Force for Operational Resilience

The Firefighting Paradox

Jim Seaman and Michael Gioia

CRC Press
Taylor & Francis Group
Boca Raton London New York

CRC Press is an imprint of the
Taylor & Francis Group, an **informa** business

Cover image © Shutterstock

First edition published 2024
by CRC Press
6000 Broken Sound Parkway NW, Suite 300, Boca Raton, FL 33487-2742

and by CRC Press
4 Park Square, Milton Park, Abingdon, Oxon, OX14 4RN

© 2024 Jim Seaman and Michael Gioia

CRC Press is an imprint of Taylor & Francis Group, LLC

Library of Congress Cataloging-in-Publication Data
Names: Seaman, Jim (Writer on data protection), author. | Gioia, Michael, author.
Title: Security risk management : the driving force for operational resilience :
the firefighting paradox / Jim Seaman and Michael Gioia.
Description: First edition. | Boca Raton : CRC Press, 2024. |
Series: Security, audit and leadership | Includes bibliographical references.
Identifiers: LCCN 2023004592 (print) | LCCN 2023004593 (ebook) |
ISBN 9781032263885 (hardback) | ISBN 9781032263892 (paperback) |
ISBN 9781003288084 (ebook)
Subjects: LCSH: Organizational resilience. | Business planning. |
Industries–Security measures. | Risk management. | Crisis management.
Classification: LCC HD58.9 .S436 2024 (print) | LCC HD58.9 (ebook) |
DDC 658.4/013–dc23/eng/20230614
LC record available at https://lccn.loc.gov/2023004592
LC ebook record available at https://lccn.loc.gov/2023004593

ISBN: 9781032263885 (hbk)
ISBN: 9781032263892 (pbk)
ISBN: 9781003288084 (ebk)

DOI: 10.1201/9781003288084

Typeset in Sabon
by Newgen Publishing UK

Contents

About the Authors

Jim Seaman honed his skills and craft during a 22-year career in the Royal Air Force Police, with the final decade being employed on counterintelligence, computer security, counterterrorism and risk management duties. On completion of his 22 years of military service, he sought the new challenge of transferring his specialist skills and knowledge across to the corporate sector. In the decade since transitioning across to the corporate environment, he has fulfilled roles within Payment Card Industry Data Security Standard (PCI DSS) compliance, data protection, information security, industrial systems security, and risk management. In the past few years, he has sought to further develop his knowledge and to rise to the challenge of authoring two books, one on the subject of PCI DSS (published May 2020) and the other on protective security (published April 2021).

Michael Gioia is an information security leader with over 18 years' experience of delivering security solutions across several industries. He has served as an officer in the United States Air Force and worked in higher education, the Department of Defense, retail food services, and security consulting. He has performed most of his information security work within higher education, currently, as the Chief Information Security Officer for Babson College and formerly as the Information Security Officer at Eastern Illinois University, Rose-Hulman Institute of Technology, and Bentley University. He retains various professional certifications that include a Certified Information Security Manager and Certified Data Privacy Solutions Engineer from ISACA, Certified Information System Security Professional from ISC2, GIAC Security Leadership Certification from SANS, and Payment Card Industry Professional from the PCI Security Standards Council.

Introduction

All too frequently, businesses do not focus enough on the value that security risk management (SRM) can bring to the defense of their organization. Instead, they will all too often regard SRM as an afterthought and as something that should only be conducted after something has happened or something has gone wrong. The authors of this book will argue that the driving force for operational resilience should and must be leveraged, as the result of the proactive application of SRM practices.

Would you ever imagine teaching a child the safe way to navigate across a busy road, without them first risk-assessing the conditions?

Imagine what the situation would be like if parents and schoolteachers applied the same approach that many business leadership teams appear to have adopted:

- Before stepping out into the road, the child does not need to look for hazards (threats) or consider the weather conditions, or even worry about the speed or type of vehicles traveling along the road.

In its place, the child only needs to consider conducting a risk assessment after they have been hit by a speeding vehicle. As a result (if they live), they can understand the risks of what mistakes they made and the damage caused, to help them apply the lessons learned.

As presented in the analogy above, reactive–rather than proactive–risk assessment can be incredibly costly. The authors of this book will present the concept that SRM should be behind every decision made and every implemented security measure, so that the business leadership teams have a better understanding of why these (often expensive) measures are implemented, which valued business operations/assets they are helping to mitigate, and what the associated risks are.

In today's modern business operations, it seems common sense that the leadership teams would want to ensure that their valued operations remain robust and able to quickly bounce back from impactful occurrences.

DOI: 10.1201/9781003288084-1

However, this does not appear to be the case, meaning that some areas of the globe have seen a need to bring in legislation (e.g., DORA (*Regulation of the European Parliament and of the Council on Digital Operational Resilience for the Financial Sector and Amending Regulations (EC) No 1060/2009, (EU) No 648/2012, (EU) No 600/2014 and (EU) No 909/2014*[1]) so that some regulators (e.g., (Financial Conduct Authority (FCA), "FCA Handbook: SYSC 15A.2 Operational Resilience Requirements"[2]) have powers to enable them to 'encourage' the financial services sector to consider how they can maintain their operational resilience.

In addition to the FCA's guidance, under the topic of operational risk, the Basel Committee (Basel Committee on Banking Supervision[3]) and the Bank of England[4] have created a comprehensive guide on the subject of Operational Resilience. This is stringently enforced within the Saudi Arabian banking rules (Saudi Arabian Monetary Authority[5] and this area is starting to gather pace, Internationally, (Price Waterhouse Cooper (PWC)[6]).

The UK FCA's, "Operational Resilience"[7]) has defined operational resilience as being: "*The capability of firms, financial market infrastructures and the financial sector to prevent, adapt and respond to, recover and learn from operational disruption.*"

This book is delivered through two distinct sections:

1. Security Risk Management
   Some of the SRM considerations and the supporting mitigation measures that are needed to help forge operationally resilient business operations.
   • Reducing the probability/likelihood.
2. 'Survive to Operate'
   Let's face it, no business operation can ever truly be 100% operational and secure 100% of the time. People will make mistakes or let their guards down, and risk can never be fully eradicated.
   • Reducing the impacts/consequences.

Notes

1 Regulation of the European Parliament and of the Council on Digital Operational Resilience for the Financial Sector and Amending Regulations (EC) No 1060/2009, (EU) No 648/2012, (EU) No 600/2014 and (EU) No 909/2014. 24 Sept. 2020.
2 Financial Conduct Authority (FCA). "FCA Handbook: SYSC 15A.2 Operational Resilience Requirements." Financial Conduct Authority (FCA), 31 Mar. 2022, www.handbook.fca.org.uk/handbook/SYSC/15A/2.html?date=2022-03-31. Accessed 25 Aug. 2022.
3 Basel Committee on Banking Supervision. Principles for Operational Resilience. Bank for International Settlements, Mar. 2021.

4 Bank of England (BoE). "Operational Resilience." www.bankofengland.co.uk, Mar. 2021, www.bankofengland.co.uk/prudential-regulation/publication/2021/march/operational-resilience-sop. Accessed 26 Aug. 2022.
5 Saudi Arabian Monetary Authority. Cyber Security Framework Saudi Arabian Monetary Authority. 2017.
6 Price Waterhouse Cooper (PWC). "Comparing International Expectations on Operational Resilience." Apr. 2021.
7 UK Financial Conduct Authority. "Operational Resilience." 17 May 2017, www.fca.org.uk/firms/operational-resilience

Section One

Security Risk Management

Reducing the Likelihood/Probability

Chapter 1

Finagling Your Business

Think of this approach as being like snowflakes...

If you allow snowflakes to continue to fall, land and settle without being noticed, they get deeper and deeper with no risks being perceived and no protective measures being prepared.

Then something causes these large accumulations of snowflakes to be disturbed and before you know it...

Avalanche!!!!

1.1 THE FINAGLE ANALOGY

Imagine that you are the owner and the driver of a motor vehicle. The local laws require that this vehicle must remain road legal and safe. Annually, your vehicle must undergo a government safety test to obtain a certificate for its roadworthiness.

Now, when buying the vehicle, you did not consider how much it might cost to support the vehicle's roadworthiness. Consequently, when the annual road safety test comes around, you realize that the tires' tread depth does not meet the smallest expected standards to pass the annual road safety test.

However, you need the car to be operational. As a result, you decide to 'finagle' the annual roadworthiness test by borrowing the wheels (with road-legal tires) from your friend's identical car. Hey presto! You get through the annual roadworthiness evaluation and obtain the annual certificate. Afterwards, you change the wheels back so that your friend gets his wheels back. However, your motor vehicle now has its old threadbare tires back.

The short-term gain of having achieved the annual roadworthiness certificate does not negate the fact that your vehicle is unsafe and is likely to lose traction or will have its stopping distance, under braking, severely affected.

- Does this not sound like the actions of desperation?
- Can you understand the risks of such a strategy?

DOI: 10.1201/9781003288084-3

1.2 INTRODUCTION

Throughout our professional careers, we have been astounded by the attitudes of some of our peers and, more importantly, business leaders. Increasingly there are companies that look to adopt a similar approach to the analogy when running their own businesses. If you think of the business as being like a motor vehicle, it has many moving parts that interact and support each other. For the business to remain successful, these moving parts need to remain operational. This is what is needed for the business to remain operationally resilient.

Gartner[1] defines operational resilience:

> As initiatives that expand business continuity management programs to focus on the impacts, connected risk appetite and tolerance levels for disruption of product or service delivery to internal and external stakeholders (such as employees, customers, citizens and partners).
>
> These initiatives coordinate management of risk assessments, risk monitoring and execution of controls that impact workforce, processes, facilities, technology (IT, OT, IoT, physical and cyber-physical) and third parties across the following risk domains used in the business delivery and value realization process:
> * Security (cyber and physical),
> * Safety,
> * Privacy,
> * Continuity of operations,
> * Reliability.

The difference between running a motor vehicle and keeping an operationally resilient company is that in a corporate environment this may be extremely complex, with many moving parts and processes being involved, and the things 'that could go wrong' may be extremely varied and the threats may be considerable in both type and volume.

Just a single failure of a critical asset or process could have catastrophic implications for the business. Such issues can also be caused by a plethora of causes; for example, IT system outage, IT software failure, human error, cyberattack, natural disaster, malware, etc.

To address this issue, it is vital for business leadership to stop thinking in isolated terms, such as:

* Cybersecurity
  Looking into the origins of this term, the constructs are broken down in the Etymology Online Dictionary ("Cyber- | Search Online Etymology Dictionary"[2]), as follows:

Word-forming component, ultimately from cybernetics (q.v.). It became a 'buzz word' with the rise of the internet early 1990s. One researcher (Nagel) counted 104 words formed from it by 1994. Cyberpunk (by 1986) and cyberspace (1982) were among the earliest. The OED 2nd edition (1989) has only cybernetics and its related forms, and cybernation "theory, practice, or condition of control by machines" (1962).

Security, (Online Etymology Dictionary[3]):

Early 15c., securite, "state or condition of being safe from danger or harm;" mid-15c., "freedom from care or anxiety" (a sense now archaic), from Old French securite and directly from Latin securitas "freedom from care," from securus "free from care" (see secure (adj.)).

Cybersecurity (Merriam-Webster Dictionary[4]):

"Mitigation measures taken to help protect a computer or computer system (as on the Internet) against unauthorized access or attack."
    Should you only be concerned about those company assets that are internet-facing?

- Information Security (The Free Dictionary (Information Security)[5])
  The protection of information and information systems against unauthorized access or modification of information, whether in storage, processing, or transit, and against denial of service to authorized users.
      Information security includes those measures necessary to detect, document, and counter such threats. Information security includes computer security and communications security.

- Network security (Cisco[6])
  "Network security is the protection of the underlying networking infrastructure from unauthorized access, misuse, or theft. It involves creating a secure infrastructure for devices, applications, users, and applications to work in a secure manner."
      What about those assets that have no connectivity to any network infrastructures?

- Physical Security (What Is Physical Security? – Definition from Techopedia[7])
  The measures designed to ensure the physical protection of IT assets like facilities, equipment, personnel, resources and other properties from damage and unauthorized physical access. Physical security

measures are taken to protect these assets from physical threats including theft, vandalism, fire and natural disasters.

All these security industry terms are measures that, when used in combination, can help an organization to increase its operational resilience and reduce its risks. Consequently, it is important for corporations to move away from using these isolated terms and to adopt a more holistic risk-focused approach, to identify what their potential risks are and how the construct of these terms can help the business to reduce these risks to within acceptable parameters.

The title of the book, this chapter, and the security operations chapters are the limited places that you will read the term 'security,' as the focus of the content is on helping the reader to appreciate the value of being more directly risk-focused to enhance your organization's ability to continue operating through adverse events, or to have the ability to quickly 'bounce back' from unexpected, impactful events or incidents.

1.3 THE IMPORTANCE OF EFFECTIVE SECURITY RISK MANAGEMENT

Rather than thinking in terms of security or compliance, if an organization can move to a risk-focused approach everything else tends to fall into place.

- **Compliance** (Compliance | Etymology, Origin and Meaning of Compliance by Etymonline[8]):
  "1640s, 'act of complying; disposition to yield to others,' from comply + -ance. Related: Compliancy."
- **Security** (Security | Search Online Etymology Dictionary[9]):
  "Mid-15c., 'condition of being secure,' from Latin *securitas*, from *securus* 'free from care' (see secure). Replacing *sikerte* (early 15c.), from an earlier borrowing from Latin; earlier in the sense 'security' was *sikerhede* (early 13c.); *sikernesse* (c. 1200)."
- **Assurance** (Assurance | Etymology, Origin and Meaning of Assurance by Etymonline[10]).
  "Late 14c., 'formal or solemn pledge, promise,' also 'certainty, full confidence,' from Old French *asseurance* 'assurance, promise; truce; certainty, safety, security' (11c., Modern French assurance), from *asseurer* 'to reassure, to render sure' (see assure). Meaning 'self-confident' is from 1590s."

In fact, by finding and mitigating the risks to your business operations, you are significantly closer to achieving your compliance or security objectives. For example, if your business is seeking to achieve ISO/IEC 27001 or PCI

DSS compliance, the focus is to find and apply suitable mitigation security controls to mitigate the risks to your business operations and/or assets.

In ISO/IEC 27001, this is based upon your defined scope for the valued business assets and/or operations that you want to protect. Whereas, in PCI DSS, the scope is defined for you, with this being against any asset involved in the processing, storage, or transmission of cardholder data (or anything that could affect, or is connected to, these assets), and the valued assets are those that support the cardholder data operations.

To truly appreciate the value of SRM and how it differs from security or compliance, you need to be able to recognize that security and compliance are reactive strategies, while when applied effectively SRM can be proactive. However, it is important to note that SRM is not an exact science but rather a means of forecasting that something 'might' happen and what the potential impact might be.

The objective of an effective SRM practice should be to articulate to the business a realistic risk scenario, so that the forecasted risks can be calculated, and the key stakeholders and/or risk owners can make an informed decision on, should the forecasted risk occur, whether the business is suitably prepared and whether they are comfortable with these risks or not.

The output of a risk assessment should lead the business to create and document a suitable risk response (National Institute of Standards and Technology (NIST)[11]), as detailed in Table 1.1.

The risk response stage follows the risk assessment and is a critical part of any SRM process, as detailed in the NIST Risk Management Framework (NIST, Risk Management Framework for Information Systems and Organizations[12]).

Table 1.1 Risk Response

Traditional	5 T's	Description
Accept	Tolerate	This consists in identifying the risks and documenting all the risk management information about it, but being comfortable that no action is required, unless the risk occurs.
Avoid	Terminate	Ending the threat by any means available.
Mitigate	Treat	Applying a proper level of risk treatment options that bring the risks to a level that the business risk owners are comfortable with.
Transfer	Transfer	Utilize a third party to take the responsibility for reducing the risk. However, you will still have accountability for ensuring that the third party continues to reduce the risk to within acceptable tolerances.
	Take the opportunity	Finding risk and, rather than resolving it, using this to gain a short-term advantage.

1. Prepare to execute the risk management framework (RMF) from an organization- and a system-level perspective by establishing a context and priorities for managing security and privacy risk.
2. Categorize the system and the information processed, stored, and transmitted by system, based on an analysis of the impact of loss.
3. Select an initial set of controls for the system and tailor the controls as needed to reduce risk to an acceptable level based on an assessment of risk.
4. Implement the controls and describe how the controls are employed within the system and its environment of operation.
5. Assess the controls to determine whether the controls are implemented correctly, operating as intended, and producing the desired outcomes with respect to satisfying the security and privacy requirements.
6. Authorize the system or common controls based on a determination that the risk to organizational operations and assets, individuals, other organizations, and the nation is acceptable.
7. Monitor the system and the associated controls on an ongoing basis to include assessing control effectiveness, documenting changes to the system and environment of operation, conducting risk assessments and impact analyses, and reporting the security and privacy posture of the system.

1.4 TO FINAGLE OR NOT TO FINAGLE? THAT IS THE QUESTION

If I had a £1 or $1 for each time that I heard a business key stakeholder or subject matter expert (SME) suggest the advantages of avoiding doing something to save themselves time, effort, or investment, I would be an extremely rich man.

It had been exceedingly difficult to understand and appreciate why these people would suggest such a thing if the thing they were suggesting would be potentially detrimental to the business or would significantly increase the risks for the organization.

That was until I had dealings with an individual who was in a very senior position within a highly respected IT services company and whose role was to supply specialist governance, risk, and compliance support to the organization's key stakeholders and to supply assurances to their many customers.

While working with this individual (to help prepare the business for an annual 'roadworthiness' check), during a pre-check discussion with one of the SMEs, the SME stated that a mitigation measure was not in place and, as far as they knew, had never been in place. Subsequently, they asked how the company had managed to pass previous 'roadworthiness' assessments.

This individual's response blew my mind: "We finagled it!"

He used a term that I had never heard before and was one that I had to look up in the dictionary ("Definition of Finagle | Dictionary.com"[13]): "To trick, swindle, or cheat (a person) (often followed by out of): He finagled the backers out of a fortune."

Of course, this should not be confused with the term 'Finagle's Law' (Bureman)[14]: "In its most general form, is the idea that anything that can go wrong will go wrong, and usually in the most disastrous way imaginable."

No doubt you have had days when you have felt as if you have been subject to Finagle's Law. However, in an organization that supports the finagling of the business, rather than adopting a risk-focused and balanced approach, Finagle's Law can often become a common part of daily business operations, which, of course, it should never be!

How often have you heard a security SME use the sentence, "It feels like all I do is fight fires!"?

1.5 THE FIREFIGHTING PARADOX

No matter the size or type of your business, no doubt you will face periods when you feel as if you are constantly fighting fires in response to the company's demands. At the same time, you are expected to manage the risks and keep all critical systems and operations safe, while defending against opportunist attackers, as well as protecting the business from the insider risk (deliberate or accidental actions of employees that present a danger to the business).

The 'firefighting' paradox is a term that is well known beyond the security industry and extends well into the business environment. The problem with having a 'firefighting' approach is that, without incorporating a risk management strategy to it, the business has a limited knowledge of which fires need to be prioritized and, as a result, the more impactful fires can be neglected by individuals that are responding to those fires that are more visible to the business. Consequently, the less visible fires that are associated with the more critical parts of the business remain unquenched, leading to significantly more impact and damage to the business.

In the July–August 2000 *Harvard Business Review* magazine, there was a useful article that described the need to 'Stop Fighting Fires,' (Bohn[15]). In this article, the author explains what the term means but then goes on to describe a simple model of firefighting in which the author supplies a depiction of something that most of us will have experienced at first hand: How problems flow through an organization, as depicted in Figure 1.1.

I would be incredibly surprised if no one reading this book has experienced those occasions when you might be expected to tear yourself into several pieces, so that you can solve everyone's problems that are clearly the most important and should be prioritized over anyone else's.

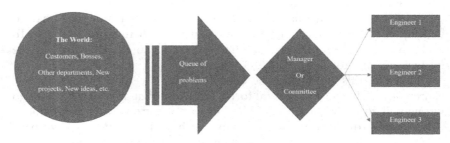

Figure 1.1 Organization problem flows.

$$\text{Traffic intensity} = \frac{\text{(Days to solve) X (Number of new problems per day)}}{\text{Number of engineers}}$$

Figure 1.2 Traffic intensity equation.

This article then tries to explain the value of understanding the traffic intensity, so that a better appreciation can be formulated, based upon the number of days needed to resolve the problem, the number of the latest problems per day and the amount of resources, as depicted in their equation in Figure 1.2.

Without a clear understanding of the potential traffic intensity, it is unlikely that your business will ever stop employing firefighting strategies, which can become increasingly detrimental to your business and can lead to a pressure cooker of working conditions. This, in turn, could result in increased stress to the business teams, which leads to higher sickness or levels of staff turnover.

All of this increases the insider threat, where employees can become disillusioned with the company or, due to increased pressures and workloads, have an increased likelihood of taking shortcuts or making mistakes.

The NIST[16] defines insider risk as being:

> The threat that an insider will use her/his authorized access, wittingly or unwittingly, to do harm to the security of organizational operations and assets, individuals, other organizations, and the Nation. This threat can include damage through espionage, terrorism, unauthorized disclosure of national security information, or through the loss or degradation of organizational resources or capabilities.

In risk-managing operational resilience capabilities, a 'firefighting' approach can prove to be extremely detrimental, as while you are constantly jumping from one fire to another, you are given limited time to take stock and reflect on what went well, and what areas could be improved (lessons learned). As a result, you increase the risks of an impactful incident reoccurring and potentially being more harmful to the company if a more critical asset or process is affected on the repeat occasion.

In addition, you do not have the time to investigate any emerging threats so that you can adapt your defensive strategy, so that it still is current and effective.

By having a risk-focused approach to your operational resilience strategies, you will be better able to triage your responses. This is especially relevant to those businesses that use a 'lean' business model, ("What Is a Lean Business Model? – Definition | Meaning | Example"[17]): "How do you run an effective operationally resilient business, using the Lean Business Model, if you don't understand the risks or what resources are needing to keep the business roadworthy, safe and operational?"

1.6 THE PSYCHOLOGY OF FINAGLING

Knowing how detrimental finagling can be to a business, why is it that so many business leaders and information security SMEs lean toward a finagled approach to reporting the 'State of the Nation'?

This all comes down to human psychology and an individual's natural leaning to employ their ego defense mechanisms. In the 1890s, Sigmund Freud found that human beings had ten ego defense mechanisms that they unconsciously use to protect themselves from anxiety rising through undesirable thoughts or feelings. These ten defense mechanisms consist of the following, (Mcleod[18]), as depicted in Table 1.2.

Often it is said that security requires a 'top-down' approach so that we obtain senior management, or C-Level ("Definition of C-Level | Dictionary. com"[19]) executive buy-in and support. However, what if the C-Level or the person responsible for communicating the risks to the C-Level are unconsciously employing these defensive mechanisms?

Within an organization it is extremely likely that you are going to have several of the nine Belbin team roles, and each can be complementary to each other to create an effective business culture (Team Roles and Organisational Culture[20]), when they are evenly dispersed across an organization. Belbin named nine individual team roles, as depicted in Table 1.3 (Belbin[21]).

As you can imagine, each of these team roles naturally lends itself to the individuals adopting one or more of these defensive mechanisms to help them survive and be successful in their professional career. As a result, you may find that these individuals and their defensive mechanisms have opposite effects on the way that risks are communicated and mitigated against.

For example, let's take a situation where a C-Suite member is a natural 'implementer.' Such an individual is known as action-oriented, with a tendency to lack flexibility and to be very rigid in their approach. Now, if your

Table 1.2 Ten Defense Mechanisms

1. Denial	An individual does not report or accept any reports that there are any issues, problems, or concerns. By not accepting the facts, they are trying to absolve themselves of the consequences or the potential impact on the organization. *Ignore it and hope it will go away or not happen.*
2. Repression	This is when an individual experiences or think things may be threatening but may choose to repress them instead of dealing with the issue or problem. *Bury your head in the sand.*
3. Projection	Rather than acknowledging threatening traits in themselves, the individual points these same traits out in others instead. *Displacing personal feelings onto others.*
4. Displacement	Displacement is the redirection of an impulse (usually aggression) onto a powerless substitute target. *The blame game.*
5. Regression	This is where an individual reverts to display age-inappropriate behavior and adopt immature traits and emotions. *Acting like a child.*
6. Sublimation	This is like displacement; however, this takes place when an individual manages to displace their unacceptable emotions into constructive and socially acceptable behaviors. *Channeling emotions.*
7. Rationalization	This a cognitive distortion of 'the facts' to make an event or an impulse less threatening. *Lying to oneself.*
8. Reaction Formation	This is when an individual goes beyond denial and acts in a manner that is the opposite to the way they think or feel. *Faking it.*
9. Introjection	This is when an individual adopts the personality characteristics of another, to help solve an emotional difficulty. *Mirroring.*
10. Identification with the Aggressor	This is where an individual adopts the behavior of someone who is more powerful and hostile toward them. *Becoming the bully.*

information security manager happens to be a 'teamworker,' rather than being a good thing for the business this could turn out to be the complete opposite. The 'teamworker' is known for being people-oriented and may be very sensitive and avoid hard decisions. As a result, they tend to have calm temperaments and are often extremely diplomatic in their approach.

This combination of natural team roles and their adopted defensive mechanisms can become extremely obstructive, with any significant risks either not being reported or the risk reports falling on deaf ears.

Imagine if the C-Suite member ('implementer') has adopted the denial defense mechanism and the information security manager (teamworker) has adopted the rationalization defense mechanism:

Table 1.3 Belbin Team Roles

Team Role	Description
Resource Investigator	Uses their inquisitive nature to find ideas to bring back to the team. Strengths: Outgoing, enthusiastic. Explores opportunities and develops contacts. Allowable weaknesses: Might be over-optimistic and can lose interest once the initial enthusiasm has passed. Do not be surprised to find that: They might forget to follow up on a lead.
Teamworker	Helps the team to gel, using their versatility to identify the work required and complete it on behalf of the team. Strengths: Cooperative, perceptive, and diplomatic. Listens and averts friction. Allowable weaknesses: Can be indecisive in crunch situations and tends to avoid confrontation. Do not be surprised to find that: They might be hesitant to make unpopular decisions.
Coordinator	Needed to focus on the team's objectives, draw out team members, and delegate work appropriately. Strengths: Mature, confident, identifies talent. Clarifies goals. Allowable weaknesses: Can be seen as manipulative and might offload their own share of the work. Do not be surprised to find that: They might over-delegate, leaving themselves little work to do.
Plant	Tends to be highly creative and good at solving problems in unconventional ways. Strengths: Creative, imaginative, free-thinking, generates ideas, and solves difficult problems. Allowable weaknesses: Might ignore incidentals and may be too preoccupied to communicate effectively. Do not be surprised to find that: They could be absent-minded or forgetful.
Monitor Evaluator	Provides a logical eye, making impartial judgments where required and weighs up the team's options in a dispassionate way. Strengths: Sober, strategic, and discerning. Sees all options and judges accurately. Allowable weaknesses: Sometimes lacks the drive and ability to inspire others and can be overly critical. Do not be surprised to find that: They could be slow to come to decisions.
Specialist	Brings in-depth knowledge of a key area to the team. Strengths: Single-minded, self-starting, and dedicated. They provide specialist knowledge and skills. Allowable weaknesses: Tends to contribute on a narrow front and can dwell on the technicalities. Do not be surprised to find that: They overload you with information.

(Continued)

Table 1.3 (Continued)

Team Role	Description
Shaper	Provides the necessary drive to ensure that the team keeps moving and does not lose focus or momentum. Strengths: Challenging, dynamic, thrives on pressure. Has the drive and courage to overcome obstacles. Allowable weaknesses: Can be prone to provocation and may sometimes offend people's feelings. Do not be surprised to find that: They could risk becoming aggressive and bad-humored in their attempts to get things done.
Implementer	Needed to plan a workable strategy and carry it out as efficiently as possible. Strengths: Practical, reliable, efficient. Turns ideas into actions and organizes work that needs to be done. Allowable weaknesses: Can be a bit inflexible and slow to respond to new possibilities. Do not be surprised to find that: They might be slow to relinquish their plans in favor of positive changes.
Completer Finisher	Most effectively used at the end of tasks to polish and scrutinize the work for errors, subjecting it to the highest standards of quality control. Strengths: Painstaking, conscientious, anxious. Searches out errors. Polishes and perfects. Allowable weaknesses: Can be inclined to worry unduly, and reluctant to delegate. Do not be surprised to find that: They could be accused of taking their perfectionism to extremes.

- **Denial:** "Adopting a mode of defense which consists of the subject's refusing to recognize the reality of a traumatic perception." (Laplanche and Pontalis[22]).
- **Rationalization:** "Occurs when a person has performed an action and then concocts the beliefs and desires that would have made it rational. Then, people often adjust their own beliefs and desires to match the concocted ones." (Brody and Costa[23]).

The information security manager, being the natural diplomat, will lend themself to make life easier by only presenting positive spin/news to the C-Suite implementer. Therefore, the business becomes complacent, believing that it is facing few or no risks.

With a great deal of luck, this does not present any issues to the business leaders, who continue oblivious to the dangers that they might face, and any potential exploitable vulnerabilities remain untracked and are not risk-prioritized for remediation. However, the reality in an ever-increasing digital and internet-connected world, where the risks of a cyberattacks

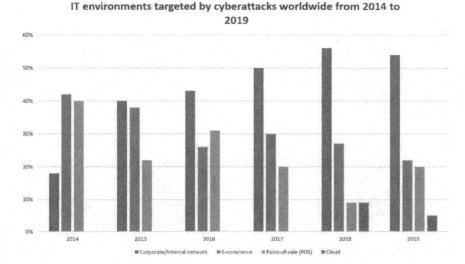

IT environments targeted by cyberattacks worldwide from 2014 to 2019

■ Corporate/internal network ■ E-commerce ■ Point-of-sale (POS) ■ Cloud

Figure 1.3 Cyberattack trends, 2014 to 2019.

grow exponentially, as shown in Figure 1.3 ("Cyber Attacks: Targeted IT Environments 2019"[24]) and Figure 1.4 ("Successful Cyber Attacks Launched Against Global Businesses 2021"[25]), relying on luck to safeguard your business becomes a very dangerous strategy.

1.7 EFFECTIVE RISK COMMUNICATION

Given individual character traits and their subconscious adoption of defensive mechanisms, as well as business pressures and the lack of technical knowledge, this can make the communication of risk extremely difficult to achieve. As a result, this might be an area where the risk reports are 'finagled,' and the produced risk reports may not be achieving the desired effects to help the business reduce prioritized risks, and you may only be going through the motions to tick an expected box.

- Are your risk reports being reviewed?
- Does the receiving audience ever ask questions on the content?
- Do the reports help to drive business decision-making decisions?

Cybersecurity/information security SMEs tend to want to prove how knowledgeable they are (worth their salaries), so they adopt the practice of making their risk messages too long and complex. As a result, the receiving audience does not understand the risks.

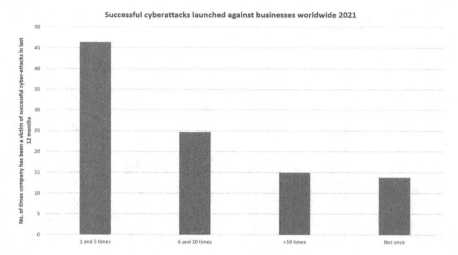

Figure 1.4 2021 successful cyberattacks.

Another factor to consider is whether you have prioritized the reported risks. You need to avoid sounding like 'Chicken Little,' ("The Story of Chicken Little: The Sky Is Falling"[26]) and sending out messages that articulate that the business world is falling in.

Another problem is that the receiving audience members got to where they are because they are proficient in their role responsibilities and not because they understand technology or threat profiles. Consequently, the risk messages need to be simplified so that they answer the 'so what?' question, and that the audience clearly understands the urgency and potential impacts that the risks present.

It is also important to remember that the receiving audience is extremely busy and has limited time availability. Consequently, it is extremely important to develop risk reports that easily convey the risk messages, in a clear easy-to-read format. Remember that a picture paints a thousand words, so consider the benefits of using graphs. You can gain exceptional value by periodically asking the receiving audience for some feedback on your risk reports.

- Do they find the risk reports easy to read and understand?
- Do the risk reports supply the information they need to make informed risk decisions?
- What improvements can be made to the risk reports?

1.8 WHEN SECURITY RISK MANAGEMENT BITES BACK

When a business does not focus on risk and, instead, focuses on 'ticking a box' for compliance or security assurance needs, they are faced with an increasing number of plates that need to be kept spinning and, ultimately, they can pay the price of focusing on keeping the wrong plate spinning, while a far more valuable plate falls to the ground and breaks.

For instance, look at British Airways (BA) and Claire's Accessories. Both being high-volume e-commerce merchants, they would have needed to have been annually assessed as being PCI DSS compliant. In fact, BA took security assurance and PCI DSS compliance so seriously that they even paid the PCI Security Standards Council (PCI SSC) a fee to be a 'participating organization,' as seen in the captured image on Wayback Machine for 21:23:06, on 14th September 2017, as depicted in Figure 1.5, ("Official PCI Security Standards Council Site – Verify PCI Compliance, Download Data Security and Credit Card Security Standards"[27]).

Over one year previously (6th October 2016) RiskIQ was reporting that e-commerce websites were victims of malicious script injections, (Spruell[28]). These types of attacks would serve as a man-in-the middle (MITM) style of attack, enabling the attacker to redirect the customers' payment journeys so that the customers went from the merchant's website, through the attacker's clandestine infrastructure, to the PCI DSS-compliant payment service provider (PSP)'s interface. As a result, when the customer typed their cardholder details into the PSP's interface, the attackers were able to electronically skim the customers' cardholder details.

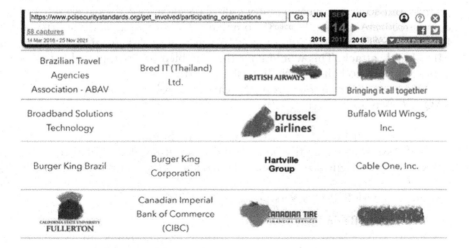

Figure 1.5 Wayback machine screen capture.

Despite this increased risk to e-commerce merchants, few risk-assessed their payment processes and, before long, despite the fact that BA had transferred the risk from payment process, through the use of a redirect or iFrame to a PCI DSS-compliant PSP, between 22:58 BST, 21st August 2018 until 21:45 BST, 5th September 2018 they were the victims of a Magecart group ("All You Need to Know about Magecart Hacking Groups"[29]) cyberattack, ("How Did Hackers Get into British Airways?"[30]). During this time, the Magecart Group 6, (Klijnsma[31]), managed to skim around 500,000 customer credit cards.

Magecart Group 6

Modus operandi
Group 6 was first observed using web-skimmers in 2018 but has a long history in the underground. Group 6 is perhaps the most high-profile Magecart group, and its impact has been huge. The group's approach is to be selective, only going for top-tier targets such as British Airways and Newegg, so that even if they only manage to hold the skimmer in place for a short period, the sheer volume of transactions on the victim website will yield a high return on investment.

The skimmer
Group 6's skimmer is very simple compared to those of the other groups. While the concept is the same as other Magecart skimmers, Group 6 operatives have a good knowledge of how their victim processes payments, which allows them to integrate their skimmer in a much more elegant – and less detectable – way.

Had BA been more risk-focused (proactive) and less motivated by compliance and security assurance, it would have identified that, despite its e-commerce website being PCI DSS compliant (reactive) against the shortened PCI SSC's SAQ A[32] security controls, it was still at risk from this type of MITM-style attack. This would have then enabled BA to apply added mitigation controls to help reduce this risk yet further.

There follows an extract from the earlier October 2018 version of the SAQ A ("Wayback Machine"[33]):

Payment Card Industry (PCI) Data Security Standard
Self-Assessment Questionnaire A and Attestation of Compliance
Card-not-present Merchants, All Cardholder Data Functions Fully
    Outsourced
For use with PCI DSS Version 3.2.1, June 2018

Before You Begin
SAQ A has been developed to address requirements applicable to merchants whose cardholder data functions are completely outsourced

to validated third parties, where the merchant retains only paper reports or receipts with cardholder data.

SAQ A merchants may be either e-commerce or mail/telephone-order merchants (card-not-present), and do not store, process, or transmit any cardholder data in electronic format on their systems or premises.

SAQ A merchants confirm that, for this payment channel:

- Your company accepts only card-not-present (e-commerce or mail/telephone-order) transactions.
- All processing of cardholder data is entirely outsourced to PCI DSS validated third-party service providers.
- Your company does not electronically store, process, or transmit any cardholder data on your systems or premises, but relies entirely on a third party(s) to handle all these functions.
- Your company has confirmed that all third-party(s) handling storage, processing, and/or transmission of cardholder data are PCI DSS compliant; and
- Any cardholder data your company retains is on paper (for example, printed reports or receipts), and these documents are not received electronically.

Additionally, for e-commerce channels:

- All elements of the payment page(s) delivered to the consumer's browser originate only and directly from a PCI DSS validated third-party service provider(s).

This SAQ is not applicable to face-to-face channels.

This shortened version of the SAQ includes questions that apply to a specific type of small merchant environment, as defined in the above eligibility criteria. If there are PCI DSS requirements applicable to your environment that are not covered in this SAQ, it may be an indication that this SAQ is not suitable for your environment. Additionally, you must still comply with all applicable PCI DSS requirements in order to be PCI DSS compliant.

Note: For this SAQ, PCI DSS Requirements that address the protection of computer systems (for example, Requirements 2, 6, and 8) apply to e-commerce merchants that redirect customers from their website to a third party for payment processing, and specifically to the merchant web server upon which the redirection mechanism is located. Mail order/telephone order (MOTO) or e-commerce merchants that have completely outsourced all operations (where there is no redirection mechanism from the merchant to the third party) and therefore do not have any systems in scope for this SAQ, would consider these requirements to be "not applicable." Refer to guidance on the following pages for how to report requirements that are not applicable.

Unfortunately, for BA and any e-commerce retailer, such as NewEgg (Lukic[34]), TicketMaster (Dunn[35]), Claire's Accessories (Scroxton[36]), etc. that employs an embedded iFrame or a redirect to a PCI DSS-compliant PSP to qualify for PCI DSS against the shortened SAQ, this leaves them wide open to a Magecart MITM-style attack. The shortened SAQ did not include essential security controls, such as:

6.1 Establish a process to identify security vulnerabilities, using reputable outside sources for security vulnerability information, and assign a risk ranking (for example, as "high," "medium," or "low") to newly discovered security vulnerabilities.

12.2 Implement a risk-assessment process that:

- Is performed at least annually and upon significant changes to the environment (for example, acquisition, merger, relocation, etc.),
- Identifies critical assets, threats, and vulnerabilities, and
- Results in a formal, documented analysis of risk.

With a focus on compliance and not on the risks to their e-commerce business operations, they were not required to keep track of any new vulnerabilities or to carry out risk assessments. As a result, the threat from the Magecart group cyberattacks went unnoticed, so no additional mitigation controls were applied to help protect their e-commerce operations from this new threat.

This clearly shows that, at the time, the card brands (Visa, Mastercard, Amex, JCB and Discovery) and the PCI SSC were comfortable with the convenience and the reduction of scope and effort that transferring the risk to a PCI DSS-compliant PSP provided. It was this convenience and lack of SRM that allowed the opportunist criminals to exploit this online payment journey.

1.9 THE SECURITY RISK MANAGEMENT ENABLER

Both information and IT systems have become the life support (e.g., Information Systems = Blood; Information/IT Systems = Vital organs; Intrusion Detection Systems = Nerve System, etc.) for most businesses and, as a result, it is important for organizations to remain vigilant to potential hazards and to have first aid and contingency plans to ensure that these systems remain healthy and operational. However, frequently, business risk and security practices are addressed in isolation rather than as being complementary to one another, much like an industrial or manufacturing business might do with health and safety (H&S) (Health & Safety Authority, "Hazards and Risk"[37]):

What is a Hazard?

When we refer to hazards in relation to occupational safety and health the most commonly used definition is "A Hazard is a potential source of harm or adverse health effect on a person or people."

The terms Hazard and Risk are often used interchangeably but this simple example explains the difference between the two.

If there was a spill of water in a room then that water would present a slipping hazard to persons passing through it. If access to that area was prevented by a physical barrier, then the hazard would remain though the risk would be minimized.

What is Risk?

When we refer to risk in relation to occupational safety and health the most commonly used definition is "Risk is the likelihood that a person may be harmed or suffers adverse health effects if exposed to a hazard."

In such an organization, the business proactively encourages all its employees to report hazards. These hazards are then risk-assessed and prioritized for remediation, as part of the company's risk management practices. This should be the same for SRM, which should focus on the following:

1. What are the valuable assets of the business?
2. What vulnerabilities have been identified to these valued assets?
   - What are the vulnerability risk ratings?
3. What threat actors are likely to exploit these identified vulnerabilities?
4. What is the forecasted impact if these threat actors exploit the identified vulnerabilities?
5. Is the business comfortable with these risks?
   - Have you documented these risks and obtained the risk owners sign off?
   - What additional control measures are available to help treat any identified risk?

1.10 DECODING SECURITY RISK MANAGEMENT

Unfortunately, the value of security and compliance to an organization can be reduced by a lack of risk-focused practices. As a result, security- and compliance-driven approaches become reactive practices, with a lack of teamwork and visible return on investments.

Consequently, unlike H&S practices, a 'bare acceptable minimum' approach is adopted, whereby the business either becomes increasingly comfortable with the hazards that it may face or is unaware of the risks that it faces and the potential impact that might occur as a result.

- Can you imagine a construction company director not investing in safety helmets for their construction workers, or a police officer not being issued body protection?

Much like the terms hazard and risk are interchangeable, the control measures are implemented/applied to help mitigate these hazards or risks. However, often, in the business environment the risk assessment for the company's life support systems are not given the same importance, and rather than applying proper defensive measures to any identified hazards or risks, these impactful risks are often not identified or risk-assessed, so are left untreated.

These untreated risks can present an opportunity for exploitation, which can lead to a compromise of the business's life support systems. This can then affect the health of the business operations or lead to a data breach (severed artery).

Much like H&S, SRM does not show a tangible return on investment; however, employers that invest in SRM can expect to reduce their risks from accidental or deliberate actions that result in a breach of data confidentiality, integrity, or availability, or IT system integrity or availability (outages). This will result in benefits in a variety of areas, such as reduced regulatory penalties, increased company reputation, and customer confidence. In addition, employers often find that changes made to improve SRM can result in significant improvements to their organization's productivity and financial performance, while creating a cohesive enterprise-wide risk culture.

In fact, in Gartner's Top 8 Cybersecurity Predictions for 2021–2022, it is forecasting that threat actors will be cause physical harm (Gartner, Panetta[38]), meaning that SRM could soon become more akin to H&S:

8. By 2025, threat actors will have weaponized operational technology environments successfully enough to cause human casualties.

As malware spreads from IT to OT, it shifts the conversation from business disruption to physical harm with liability likely ending with the CEO. Focus on asset-centric cyber-physical systems, and make sure there are teams in place to address proper management.

Notes

1 Gartner. "Operational Resilience." 2012. www.gartner.com/en/information-tec hnology/glossary/operational-resilience
2 "Cyber- | Search Online Etymology Dictionary." www.etymonline.com, www.ety monline.com/search?q=cyber-&ref=searchbar_searchhint. Accessed 7 Jan. 2022.

3 Online Etymology Dictionary. "Security | Origin and Meaning of Security by Online Etymology Dictionary." www.etymonline.com, 2022, www.etymonline.com/word/security#etymonline_v_30368. Accessed 23 July 2022.

4 Merriam-Webster Dictionary. "Definition of CYBERSECURITY." Merriam-Webster.com, 2019, www.merriam-webster.com/dictionary/cybersecurity. Accessed 23 July 2022.

5 "Information Security." TheFreeDictionary.com, www.thefreedictionary.com/information+security.

6 Cisco. "What Is Network Security?" Cisco, 2019, www.cisco.com/c/en/us/products/security/what-is-network-security.html

7 "What Is Physical Security? – Definition from Techopedia." Techopedia.com, 2020, www.techopedia.com/definition/14514/physical-security

8 "Compliance | Etymology, Origin and Meaning of Compliance by Etymonline." www.etymonline.com, www.etymonline.com/word/compliance#etymonline_v_28480. Accessed 7 Jan. 2022.

9 "Security | Search Online Etymology Dictionary." www.etymonline.com, www.etymonline.com/search?q=security

10 "Assurance | Etymology, Origin and Meaning of Assurance by Etymonline." www.etymonline.com, www.etymonline.com/word/assurance#etymonline_v_26630. Accessed 7 Jan. 2022.

11 NIST, CSRC Content. "Risk Response – Glossary | CSRC." Csrc.nist.gov, csrc.nist.gov/glossary/term/risk_response. Accessed 7 Jan. 2022.

12 NIST. Risk Management Framework for Information Systems and Organizations: Dec. 2018, nvlpubs.nist.gov/nistpubs/SpecialPublications/NIST.SP.800-37r2.pdf, 10.6028/nist.sp.800-37r2

13 "Definition of Finagle | Dictionary.com." www.dictionary.com, www.dictionary.com/browse/finagle. Accessed 7 Jan. 2022.

14 Bureman, Liz. "Finagle's Law: A Writer's Guide." The Write Practice, 26 Aug. 2014, thewritepractice.com/finagles-law. Accessed 7 Jan. 2022.

15 Bohn, Roger. "Stop Fighting Fires." *Harvard Business Review*, 1 July 2000, hbr.org/2000/07/stop-fighting-fires

16 NIST. "Security and Privacy Controls for Information Systems and Organizations." *Security and Privacy Controls for Information Systems and Organizations*, 5 (23), Sept. 2020, nvlpubs.nist.gov/nistpubs/SpecialPublications/NIST.SP.800-53r5.pdf, 10.6028/nist.sp.800-53r5. Accessed 22 Aug. 2022.

17 "What Is a Lean Business Model? – Definition | Meaning | Example." My Accounting Course, 2019, www.myaccountingcourse.com/accounting-dictionary/lean-business-model

18 Mcleod, Saul. "Defense Mechanisms." Simplypsychology.org, *Simply Psychology*, 10 Apr. 2019, www.simplypsychology.org/defense-mechanisms.html

19 "Definition of C-Level | Dictionary.com." www.dictionary.com/browse/c-level. Accessed 7 Jan. 2022.

20 "Team Roles and Organisational Culture." www.belbin.com/resources/blogs/team-roles-and-culture. Accessed 7 Jan. 2022.

21 Belbin. "Belbin Team Roles." Belbin.com, Belbin, www.belbin.com/about/belbin-team-roles.

22 Laplanche, Jean, and Pontalis, Jean-Bertrand. The Language of Psycho-Analysis. London, The Hogarth Press, 1973.

23 Brody, Stuart, and Costa, Rui. (2020). Rationalization is a suboptimal defense mechanism associated with clinical and forensic problems. *Behavioral and Brain Sciences*, 43.

24 "Cyber Attacks: Targeted IT Environments 2019." Statista, www.statista.com/statistics/434764/it-environment-cyber-crime-attack

25 "Successful Cyber Attacks Launched Against Global Businesses 2021." Statista, www.statista.com/statistics/221394/successful-cyber-attacks-launched-against-businesses-worldwide. Accessed 7 Jan. 2022.

26 "The Story of Chicken Little: The Sky Is Falling." www.dltk-Teach.com, www.dltk-teach.com/fairy-tales/chicken-little/story.htm

27 "Official PCI Security Standards Council Site – Verify PCI Compliance, Download Data Security and Credit Card Security Standards." web.archive.org, 14 Sept. 2017, web.archive.org/web/20170914212306/www.pcisecuritystandards.org/get_involved/participating_organizations. Accessed 7 Jan. 2022.

28 Spruell, Darren. "Compromised E-Commerce Sites Lead to 'Magecart'" | RiskIQ. 6 Oct. 2016, www.riskiq.com/blog/labs/magecart-keylogger-injection. Accessed 7 Jan. 2022.

29 "All You Need to Know about Magecart Hacking Groups." Reflectiz, 4 May 2021, www.reflectiz.com/blog/magecart-hacking-groups-how-they-are-expanding-their-limits-beyond-the-regular-e-commerce-websites. Accessed 7 Jan. 2022.

30 "How Did Hackers Get into British Airways?" BBC News, 7 Sept. 2018, www.bbc.co.uk/news/technology-45446529

31 Klijnsma, Yonathan. "Virus Bulletin: VB2019 Paper: Inside Magecart: The History Behind the Covert Card-Skimming Assault on the E-Commerce Industry." www.virusbulletin.com, 2019, www.virusbulletin.com/virusbulletin/2019/10/vb2019-paper-inside-magecart-history-behind-covert-card-skimming-assault-e-commerce-industry. Accessed 7 Jan. 2022.

32 Payment Card Industry (PCI) Data Security Standard Self-Assessment Questionnaire A and Attestation of Compliance Card-Not-Present Merchants, All Cardholder Data Functions Fully Outsourced for Use with PCI DSS Version 3.2.1. 2018.

33 "Wayback Machine." web.archive.org. www.pcisecuritystandards.org/documents/PCI-DSS-v3_2_1-SAQ-A.pdf. Accessed 7 Jan. 2022.

34 Lukic, David. "Is Newegg Safe? The Story of Newegg Hack." IDStrong, 20 Oct. 2020, www.idstrong.com/sentinel/the-newegg-data-breach. Accessed 7 Jan. 2022.

35 Dunn, John. "The Ticketmaster Breach – What Happened and What to Do." Naked Security, 28 June 2018, nakedsecurity.sophos.com/2018/06/28/ticketmaster-breach-what-happened-and-what-to-do. Accessed 7 Jan. 2022.

36 Scroxton, Alex. "Accessories Store Claire's Hit by Magecart Credit Card Fraudsters." ComputerWeekly.com, 15 June 2020, www.computerweekly.com/news/252484652/Accessories-store-Claires-hit-by-Magecart-credit-card-fraudsters

37 "Hazards and Risk." Health and Safety Authority, www.hsa.ie/eng/Topics/Hazards

38 Panetta, Kasey. "The Top 8 Cybersecurity Predictions for 2021–2022." Gartner, 21 Oct. 2021, www.gartner.com/en/articles/the-top-8-cybersecurity-predictions-for-2021-2022

Chapter 2

Business Impact Analysis

2.1 A VEHICLE WHEEL AND TIRE ANALOGY

Much the same as the analogy that you will read in Chapter 3, if you think of your business as being like a vehicle, then there are numerous distinct parts, but some are more important to keeping the vehicle operational.

Before setting off on a long journey, you might consider reviewing the vehicle and finding which parts would be most impactful on the vehicle's operability, should they become compromised or inoperable, and to analyze whether the risks to any high-impact parts are acceptable, or what contingency plans might be considered.

For a vehicle, you would be highly likely to find the wheels and tires as being of high importance to the continued operability of the vehicle, so you would check the wear and tear on these vehicle parts. Additionally, you might consider the impact on the vehicle, should the wheels and tires become compromised (e.g., cracked wheel rim, puncture, etc.). This is where the business impact analysis (BIA) feeds into your incident management, business continuity, and disaster recovery practices (Section 2 of this book). For example:

- Do you have run flats?
- Do you have a spare tire?
- Do you have a suitable jack?
- Do you have a wheel brace?
- Do you have the locking wheel nut?
- Is the spare tire in good condition?
- Do you have an instant puncture repair kit?
- Do you need roadside recovery?
- Do you need a mobile phone?
- Do you have a charger for the mobile phone?
- Do you have a roadside warning triangle?

What might be the impact of your vehicle wheels/tires being compromised?

- High-speed blowout.
- Puncture on the highway.
- Puncture in a remote/rural location.
- Puncture at night.
- Two tires being punctured.
- Run flats limit top speed (limp mode).
- The spare is a space-saver wheel that has a limited top speed.
- Coming to a stop in a dangerous location.

All of these might appear to be common sense. However, in business do you find and analyze the vulnerabilities to your higher-impact assets, and risk-assess these vulnerabilities so that higher-risk remediation efforts can be prioritized? What about any contingency plans being driven by vulnerability management activities?

2.2 INTRODUCTION TO BUSINESS IMPACT ANALYSIS/ ASSESSMENT

BIA should be the primary driver of any business's security defensive strategies, ensuring that you have a good appreciation of what operations/ processes are important to the business's key stakeholders and to value and to categorize the supporting assets.

Without effective BIA, how can you be sure that the defensive efforts are reducing the risks to within your risk appetites and tolerances and ensure that the cost of the defensive measures are not exceeding the perceived value of the assets needing protection.

Although often associated with SRM, the terms risk appetite, risk tolerance, and risk thresholds (Usmani[1]) are often used within other business environments (e.g., project management, H&S, etc.). Consequently, it is important to understand these terms as they are often used to describe the same things but, in fact, have unique differences.

2.2.1 Risk Appetite

Wordnik[2] supply three different definitions for the term 'risk appetite':

> The degree of uncertainty that an investor is willing to accept in respect of negative changes to its business or assets. (Generic).
> The amount of risk, on a broad level, an entity is willing to accept in pursuit of value. (COSO).
> Amount and type of risk that an organization is prepared to pursue, keep or take. (ISO31000).

Whereas Workiva[3] describes this term as being: "A broad description of the amount and types of risk an organization is willing to accept to achieve its objectives. Companies often talk about operational risk and strategic risk."

CSRC NIST Glossary[4] describes risk appetite as: "The types and amount of risk, on a broad level, an organization is willing to accept in its pursuit of value."

This is a high-level statement on the level of risk that an organization (or one of its departments) is willing to accept. In mature risk practices it is not uncommon to see a hierarchy of multiple risk appetite statements (Gartner)[5].

Your risk appetite statements should be aligned with the business's mission statement and should start by supporting the business goals and aims. If your risk appetite statements are constrictive of the business's mission statement, they will ultimately become worthless.

Additionally, any risk appetite statements should be treated as live content and should be subject to periodic reviews and updated to meet any changes to the business strategy or key stakeholders' beliefs.

2.2.2 Risk Tolerance

The Committee of Sponsoring Organizations (COSO)[6] defines 'risk tolerance' as being (NC State University[7]):

> *The acceptable level of variation relative to achievement of a specific objective. This variation is often measured using the same units as its related objective. In setting risk tolerance, management considers the relative importance of the related objective and aligns risk tolerances with risk appetite. Therefore, an entity operating with its risk tolerances is operating within its risk appetite.*

This supports the 'risk appetite' statement but supplies an agreed and acceptable range of diversification.

2.2.3 Risk Threshold

Koenraad Van Brabant defines 'risk threshold' and shows how this fits into a SRM framework (Koenraad Van Brabant and Overseas Development Institute (London, England). Humanitarian Practice Network[8]), as depicted in Figure 2.1: "The point beyond which the risk is considered too high to continue operating; influenced by the probability that an incident will occur, and the seriousness of the impact if it occurs."

If you think of these terms against the analogy of a vehicle's tire integrity management, it is easier to appreciate these differences:

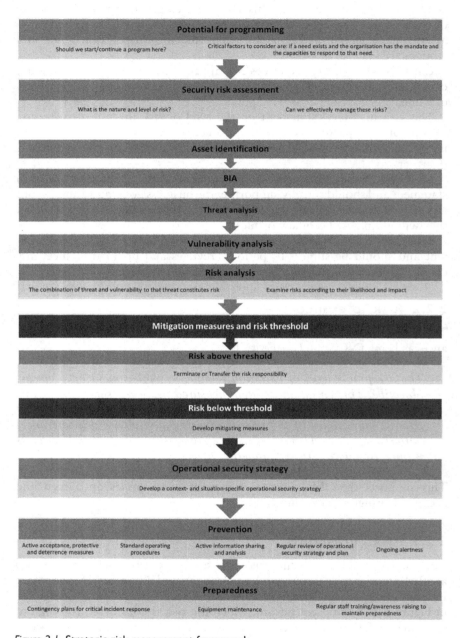

Figure 2.1 Strategic risk management framework.

- Risk Appetite
  - All the vehicle's tires must remain road legal.
  - All the tires must remain adequately inflated.
- Risk Tolerance
  - It is acceptable for tire tread depth to be within 1.6mm to 1.8mm throughout a continuous band in the center three-quarters of the tread and around the entire circumference of the tire (Automobile Association[9]).
  - During the winter months the tire tread should remain within 1.8mm to 2.0mm throughout a continuous band in the center three-quarters of the tread and around the entire circumference of the tire.
  - The tire should maintain an inflation rate of 28 to 32 PSI.
- Risk Threshold
  - When the tire tread depth is at 1.6mm, the tire must be changed.
  - In winter, when the tire tread depth is at 1.8mm, the tire must be changed.
  - When the amber tire inflation warning light is illuminated, the driver must take the next opportunity to stop and check the integrity of the tires.
  - When the red tire inflation warning light is illuminated, the driver should stop at the next available safe location to check the integrity of the tires.
  - The vehicle must not continue to be driven when the tire tread is below 1.6mm.
  - The vehicle must not continue to be driven when the tire pressures are below 20 PSI.

Armed with a better understanding (and differences between) of some of the key risk management terms, it is easier to appreciate the importance that the BIA plays within risk management practices. This is looking at your business operations and evaluating their different importance so that they can be appropriately categorized and prioritized, based upon their perceived importance to your organization.

No risk management practice can be exact without effective and continual BIA operations, to help ensure that informed decision-making can be applied to any risk response choices.

As you are likely already aware, an effective SRM strategy will focus on reducing the risks associated with the information security triad (as defined in NIST's SP800-12 Rev 1 (Nieles et al.[10]) key terms):

Information – Facts or ideas, which can be represented (encoded) as various forms of data: Knowledge (e.g., data, instructions) in any medium or form that can be communicated between system entities.

Information Security – The protection of information and information systems from unauthorized access, use, disclosure, disruption, modification, or destruction in order to ensure confidentiality, integrity, and availability.

Confidentiality – Preserving authorized restrictions on information access and disclosure, including means for protecting personal privacy and proprietary information.

Integrity – Guarding against improper information modification or destruction and ensuring information non-repudiation and authenticity.

Data Integrity – The property that data has not been altered in an unauthorized manner. Data integrity covers data in storage, during processing, and while in transit.

System Integrity – The quality that a system has when it performs its intended function in an unimpaired manner, free from unauthorized manipulation of the system, whether intentional or accidental.

Availability – Ensuring timely and reliable access to and use of information.

Security Controls – The management, operational, and technical controls (i.e., safeguards or countermeasures) prescribed for a system to protect the confidentiality, availability, and integrity of the system and its information.

Gartner defines BIA as being (Gartner Glossary[11]):

The process of determining the criticality of business activities and associated resource requirements to ensure operational resilience and continuity of operations during and after a business disruption.

The BIA quantifies the impacts of disruptions on service delivery, risks to service delivery, and recovery time objectives (RTOs) and recovery point objectives (RPOs). These recovery requirements are then used to develop strategies, solutions and plans.

2.3 UNDERSTANDING RECOVERY POINT OBJECTIVES

Defining your business's recovery point objectives (RPO) involves key stakeholders finding the largest acceptable amount of data that can be lost from the point in time that a data loss event occurs, or the largest acceptable amount of downtime of a particular IT system. Knowing the RPO is an essential part of risk management and BIA practices, as the greater the amount of lost data or time that an IT system is unavailable, the greater the potential impact and risk.

The Indeed Editorial Team[12] supplies further guidance to help businesses to understand how to calculate their RPOs and describe the RPO as being:

A measurement of time from when a system failure, disaster or loss-causing event takes place, like a power outage, ransomware attack, data corruption event or user error instance. RPOs return to a previous point when your data existed in a usable format, most often from a recent save or backup.

In business, IT leaders in an organization or company often set the desired timeframe for which data loss is acceptable, or not causing extreme harm, and program an RPO accordingly.

2.4 UNDERSTANDING RECOVERY TIME OBJECTIVES

When estimating the impact from lost data or IT systems downtime, recovery time objectives (RTO) help you to estimate the potential costs associated with the time taken to recover any lost data (e.g., from backups) or to get IT systems operational once again. RTO is defined as (Techopedia[13]):

The maximum desired length of time allowed between an unexpected failure or disaster and the resumption of normal operations and service levels.

The RTO defines the point in time after a failure or disaster at which the consequences of the interruption become unacceptable.

Additionally, other disaster recovery considerations that can help you to calculate the potential impact (Garn[14]) are, for example:

- Mean time between failure (MTBF).
- Mean time to failure (MTTF).
- Mean time to recovery (MTTR).

Wherever valued assets are compromised, there is an impact on the business, and it is important to have an estimated calculation of these associated costs. Helpfully, there are some online resources that can help you to calculate these costs; for example:

- RTO Calculator (allCare IT Technology Solutions[15]).
- RPO Calculator (Quick Backup Recovery[16]).
- MTBF & MTTR Calculator (Olofsson[17]).
- MTTF Calculator (RF Wireless World[18]).

2.5 IDENTIFYING POTENTIAL LOSS/IMPACT

Think back to the vehicle wheel and tire analogy that introduced this chapter. There are numerous risk scenarios that could arise from a compromise of the vehicle's wheels or tires and just as many (if not more) potential impact scenarios; for example:

- Tire blowout at high speed
  Severe injury or death to driver passengers and other road users.

- Puncture
  Delay to journey.

- Damaged wheel
  Unable to change damaged wheel with the spare wheel.

- Shredded tire
  Vehicle stopping in a dangerous location.

All these scenarios have different cost implications and, therefore, different impact ratings. The same applies when trying to calculate the costs and impacts associated with the compromise to a business's valued assets/operations.

2.6 PRIORITIZING BUSINESS ASSETS/PROCESSES/ OPERATIONS

Imagine your business as being like a motor vehicle, constructed of numerous working parts and operations to ensure that it works as expected. However, these working parts and operations do not have an equal importance to operability of the vehicle and do not have the same amount of impact should they stop working.

Think about it. If the interior light or the 12v power socket stop working, it might be annoying or be an inconvenience, but it would not affect the operability or safety of the vehicle. However, you would not think the same of other vehicle components, such as:

- Braking system
- Gearbox
- Cooling system
- Engine oil
- Ignition system
- Cam belt
- Fan belt

Consequently, vehicle manufacturers have identified the importance of their vehicle components and have accordingly prioritized the components that need to be checked during the maintenance/service schedules, as depicted in the Fiat 500 Service Plan Schedule, Table 2.1. (FIAT Workshop[19]).

A poorly maintained vehicle increases the risks of a critical part failing and causing the vehicle to become unsafe, unserviceable, or breaking down.

You should approach your business in the same manner as vehicle manufacturers do for their vehicles. Everything is comprehensively designed

Table 2.1 Fiat 500 Service Schedule Plan

SCHEDULED SERVICING PLAN (petrol engines)

Miles per thousand >	9	18	27	36	45	54	63	72	81	90
Check tire condition/wear including space saver	•	•	•	•	•	•	•	•	•	•
Check operation of ALL lighting	•	•	•	•	•	•	•	•	•	•
Top up ALL fluid levels	•	•	•	•	•	•	•	•	•	•
Check exhaust emissions	•	•	•	•	•	•	•	•	•	•
Check engine management system using examiner	•	•	•	•	•	•	•	•	•	•
Check condition of bodywork, pipes, lines and bushes	•		•		•		•		•	
Check operation of the windscreen wiper/washer system	•		•		•		•		•	
Check condition of locks		•		•		•		•		•
Check handbrake travel and adjust		•		•		•		•		•
Visually inspect the condition of brake pads, disks or drum brake lining	•	•	•	•	•	•	•	•	•	•
Visual check of condition of belts				•				•		
Check tension of auxiliary belt (WITHOUT automatic tensioner)		•		•		•		•		•
Check manual gearbox oil level						•				
We think the oil service intervals are too long, so we change the oil & filter EVERY service										
Replace engine oil and oil filter	•	•	•	•	•	•	•	•	•	•
Replace spark plugs		•		•		•		•		•
Change brake fluid (at extra cost)		•		•		•		•		•
Replace auxiliary belt								•		
Replace cam belt								•		
Replace air filter		•		•		•		•		•
Replace pollen filter		•		•		•		•		•

at the outset and all parts found, documented, and prioritized based upon their importance to the vehicle's continued operability.

- Have you found those assets/processes/operations that are the most valuable/important to the continued operability of your business?
- Have you found those assets that are at a higher risk (e.g., internet-facing, sensitive data processing, etc.)?

- Have you calculated the potential impact if something goes wrong or an asset is compromised or stops working?
  - Primary impacts:
    - Productivity losses
    - Response costs
    - Replacement costs
    - Competitive advantage losses
    - Fines and judgments costs
    - Reputational costs
  - Secondary impacts:
    - Costs associated with secondary stakeholder reactions
      - Productivity losses
      - Response costs
      - Replacement costs
      - Competitive advantage losses
      - Fines and judgments costs
      - Reputational costs

A BIA can be as simple as a single, one page, table as shown in Table 2.2.

Table 2.2 Example Business Impact Analysis Worksheet

Business Impact Analysis Worksheet					
Name of critical function:					
Function description:					
Security controls in place:					
BIA Owner:					
Assessment Date:		Review Date:			
Critical Function Priority:					
Impact on Business:					
Time:		Impact			
• First 24 hours. • 24–48 hours. • Up to 7 days. • Up to 14 days. Requirements for Recovery:					
Time:	People:	Location(s):	Systems:	Data:	Suppliers/Partners
First 24 hours. 24–48 hours. Up to 7 days. Up to 14 days.					

For any business that must follow data privacy regulations (e.g., European Union's General Data Protection Regulation. California Consumer Privacy Act (Office of the Attorney General, California Department of Justice[20]), etc.), there is already a form of this as a legal requirement (Data Protection Impact Assessments (DPIAs), (European Commission[21]), article 35 (GDPR. EU[22]), for any business conducting elevated risk operations involving the processing, storage, or transmission of personal data of EU data subjects. In Table 2.3 I have included an example (based on the Information Commissioner's Officer's (ICO's) guidance) of a DPIA (Information Commissioner's Office[23]).

When combined with your asset management practices, you can understand the value of your assets and their associations, so that you can conduct effective risk data aggregation and risk reporting (Falcon Edufin[24]). Principles for effective risk data aggregation and risk reporting (Basel Committee on Banking Supervision[25]):

BENEFITS OF RISK DATA AGGREGATION

According to the Basel Committee, risk data aggregation means "defining, gathering and processing risk data according to the bank's risk reporting requirements to enable the bank to measure its performance against its risk tolerance/ appetite."

Benefits:

- An increased ability to anticipate problems.
- In times of financial stress, effective risk data aggregation enhances a bank's ability to identify routes to return to financial health.
- Improved resolvability in the event of bank stress or failure.
- By strengthening a bank's risk function, the bank is better able to make strategic decisions, increase efficiency, reduce the chance of loss, and ultimately increase profitability.

To truly appreciate the potential impact of a business operation, process or data store, you need to understand the associated assets and how integral they are to each other, so that you can gain an accurate understanding of the potential risks associated with a break in the chain of systems, or the potential cascade of failed systems. The Basel Committee explain risk data aggregation through the application of the following 11 principles:

PRINCIPLE 1—GOVERNANCE

According to the committee, "a bank's risk data aggregation capabilities and risk reporting practices should be subject to strong governance arrangements consistent with the other principles and guidance established by the Basel Committee."

Table 2.3 Information Commissioner's Office Data Protection Impact Assessment Template

1. Justification
Explain broadly what the project aims to achieve and what type of processing it involves.
You may find it helpful to refer or link to other documents, such as a project proposal.
• Summarise why you identified the need for a DPIA.

2. Processing Operations

Description	Scope	Context	Purpose
Describe the nature of the processing: how will you collect, use, store and delete data? • What is the source of the data? Will you be sharing data with anyone? You might find it useful to refer to a data flow diagram or another way of describing data flows. • What types of processing identified as likely high risk are involved?	Describe the scope of the processing: • What is the nature of the data, and does it include special category or criminal offence data? • How much data will you be collecting and using? • How often? • How long will you keep it? • How many individuals are affected? • What geographical area does it cover?	Describe the context of the processing: • What is the nature of your relationship with the individuals? How much control will they have? • Would they expect you to use their data in this way? • Do they include children or other vulnerable groups? • Are there prior concerns over this type of processing or security flaws? • Is it novel in any way? • What is the current state of technology in this area? • Are there any current issues of public concern that you should factor in? • Are you signed up to any approved code of conduct or certification scheme (once any have been approved)?	Describe the purposes of the processing: • What do you want to achieve? • What is the intended effect on individuals? • What are the benefits of the processing for you, and more broadly?

3. Consultation

Consider how to consult with relevant stakeholders:

Describe when and how you will seek individuals' views – or justify why it's not appropriate to do so.

- *Who else do you need to involve within your organisation?*
- *Do you need to ask your processors to assist?*
- *Do you plan to consult information security experts, or any other experts?*

4. Necessity & Proportionality

Describe compliance and proportionality measures, in particular:

- *What is your lawful basis for processing?*
- *Does the processing actually achieve your purpose?*
- *Is there another way to achieve the same outcome?*
- *How will you prevent function creep?*
- *How will you ensure data quality and data minimisation?*
- *What information will you give individuals?*
- *How will you help to support their rights?*
- *What measures do you take to ensure processors comply?*
- *How do you safeguard any international transfers?*

5. Identify & assess risks

Describe the source of risk and nature of potential impact on individuals. Include associated compliance and corporate risks, as necessary.	Likelihood of harm	Severity of harm	Overall risk
	• *Remote* • *Possible* • *Probable*	• *Minimal* • *Significant* • *Severe*	• *Low* • *Medium* • *High*

(Continued)

Table 2.3 (Continued)

6. Measures to reduce risk

Identify additional measures you could take to reduce or eliminate risks identified as medium or high risk in step 5.

Risk	Options to reduce or eliminate risk	Effect on risk	Residual risk	Measure approved
		• Eliminated • Reduced • Accepted	• Low • Medium • High	• Yes • No

7. Sign off & record outcome

Item	Name/Date	Notes
Measures approved by: Residual risks approved by: DPO advice provided: Summary of DPO advice:		Integrate actions back into project plan, with date and responsibility for completion If accepting any residual high risk, consult the ICO before going ahead DPO should advise on compliance, step 6 measures and whether processing can proceed
DPO advice accepted or overruled by: Comments:		DPO advice accepted or overruled by:
Consultation responses reviewed by: Comments:		If your decision departs from individuals' views, you must explain your reasons
This DPIA will be kept under review by:		The DPO should also review ongoing compliance with DPIA

PRINCIPLE 2—DATA ARCHITECTURE & IT INFRASTRUCTURE

According to the committee, "a bank should design, build and maintain data architecture and IT infrastructure which fully supports its risk data aggregation capabilities and risk reporting practices not only in normal times but also during times of stress or crisis, while still meeting the other Principles."

RISK DATA AGGREGATION CAPABILITIES
PRINCIPLE 3—ACCURACY & INTEGRITY

According to the committee, "a bank should be able to generate accurate and reliable risk data to meet normal and stress/crisis reporting accuracy requirements. Data should be aggregated on a largely automated basis so as to minimize the probability of errors."

PRINCIPLE 4—COMPLETENESS

According to the committee, "a bank should be able to capture and aggregate all material risk data across the banking group. Data should be available by business line, legal entity, asset type, industry, region and other groupings, as relevant for the risk in question, that permit identifying and reporting risk exposures, concentrations and emerging risks."

PRINCIPLE 5—TIMELINESS

According to the committee, "a bank should be able to generate aggregate and up-to-date risk data in a timely manner while also meeting the principles relating to accuracy and integrity, completeness and adaptability. The precise timing will depend upon the nature and potential volatility of the risk being measured as well as its criticality to the overall risk profile of the bank. The precise timing will also depend on the bank-specific frequency requirements for risk management reporting, under both normal and stress/crisis situations, set based on the characteristics and overall risk profile of the bank."

PRINCIPLE 6—ADAPTABILITY

According to the committee, "a bank should be able to generate aggregate risk data to meet a broad range of on-demand, ad hoc risk management reporting requests, including requests during stress/crisis situations, requests due to changing internal needs and requests to meet supervisory queries."

PRINCIPLE 7—ACCURACY

According to the committee, "risk management reports should accurately and precisely convey aggregated risk data and reflect risk in an exact manner. Reports should be reconciled and validated."

PRINCIPLE 8—COMPREHENSIVENESS

According to the committee "risk management reports should cover all material risk areas within the organization. The depth and scope of these reports should be consistent with the size and complexity of the bank's operations and risk profile, as well as the requirements of the recipients."

PRINCIPLE 9—CLARITY & USEFULNESS

According to the committee "risk management reports should communicate information in a clear & concise manner. Reports should be easy to understand yet comprehensive enough to facilitate informed decision-making. Reports should include meaningful information tailored to the needs of the recipients."

PRINCIPLE 10—FREQUENCY

According to the committee, "the board and senior management (or other recipients as appropriate) should set the frequency of risk management report production and distribution. Frequency requirements should reflect the needs of the recipients, the nature of the risks reported, and the speed at which the risks can change, as well as the importance of reports in contributing to sound risk management and effective and efficient decision-making across the bank. The frequency of reports should be increased during times of stress/crisis."

PRINCIPLE 11—DISTRIBUTION

According to the committee, "risk management reports should be distributed to the relevant parties while ensuring confidentiality is maintained."

2.7 WHEN BUSINESS IMPACT ANALYSIS BITES BACK

One company that could have received help from a comprehensive asset management and BIA process was the Colonial Pipeline Company. On 7th May 2021, after receiving a ransom note (Turton and Mehrotra[26]), they discovered that they had become a victim of a cyberattack that involved the use of ransomware (Panettieri[27]).

Their attackers, a Russian hacking group (Darkside), (Baylor[28]), had managed to get unauthorized access to the corporate network through the exploitation of a legacy virtual private network (VPN), which had not been intended for use (The United States Senate Committee on Homeland Security & Governmental Affairs[29]), but which had still been active.

As an organization that is deemed as being critical national infrastructure, delivering 45% of the fuel used along the Eastern Seaboard (Bajak and Bussewitz[30]), including serving critical industries and services in multiple states, including several airports such as Atlanta's Hartsfield Jackson Airport, Nashville, Tenn.; Baltimore-Washington; and Charlotte and Raleigh-Durham, N.C. (OT Cybersecurity Information Sharing and Analysis Center[31]), in addition to paying the $2.3 Million (Bitcoin) ransom (Wilkie and Macias[32]) and having to sustain a six-day shutdown (Egan and Duffy[33]), the impact of this cyberattack must have been considerable (Congressional Research Service[34]).

The root cause of this cyberattack is believed to be this legacy VPN not having the added multifactor authentication (MFA) protection (Novinson[35]).

Okay, so being a critical national infrastructure organization, how could this inactive VPN have been missed? Why wasn't the importance of this asset named to ensure that the added MFA security measures were applied?

- Was the legacy VPN identified as part of the asset management practices?
- Was the legacy VPN subject to a BIA?
- If so, what was the justification for accepting the risk of having a single-factor authentication measure in place for an asset that gave access to the corporate network and enabled DarkSide to launch a successful ransomware attack?

I can only imagine that if this asset was named as part of the asset management practices, its value must not have been named and the asset categorized during the BIA process.

- Can you imagine any member of their senior management team signing off a BIA?

To see what the BIA should have looked like, I have compiled an example for this legacy VPN, as shown in Table 2.4.

2.8 LESSONS LEARNED FROM HEALTH AND SAFETY

If you work for an organization that is heavily regulated for H&S, you will be able to appreciate how risk and reporting is embedded into the business operations and how everyone works as a team to help protect the safety and welfare of others.

According to the Health and Safety at Work etc. Act 1974 (Gov.uk[36]), this is:

An Act to make further provision for securing the health, safety and welfare of persons at work, for protecting others against risks to health or safety in connection with the activities of persons at work, for controlling the keeping and use and preventing the unlawful acquisition, possession and use of dangerous substances, and for controlling certain emissions into the atmosphere; to make further provision with respect

Table 2.4 Legacy Virtual Private Network – Example Business Impact Analysis

Business Impact Analysis Worksheet	
Name of critical function: Function description	Internet-facing legacy VPN This is a legacy VPN that is not intended for use but that when live supplies access to the corporate network and, if compromised, could give access to large volumes of sensitive data.
Security controls in place	• Complex password. • Single Sign-On (No MFA).
BIA Owner:	Joe Smith
Assessment Date:	15 Jan 2021 Review Date: 14 Jan 2022
Critical function priority:	Critical
Impact on Business:	Critical

Time:	Impact
• First 24 hours.	Moderate
• 24–48 hours.	High
• Up to 7 days.	Severe
• Up to 14 days.	Critical

Requirements for recovery:

Time:	People:	Location(s):	Systems:	Data:	Suppliers/Partners
First 24 hours.	Bronze team	Site A	Legacy VPN Corporate Network	100 gigabytes	Atlanta's Hartsfield Jackson Airport, Nashville, Tenn.; Baltimore-Washington. Charlotte and Raleigh-Durham, N.C.
24–48 hours.	Silver team Senior Management Mandiant (Part of FireEye)	Site A	Legacy VPN Corporate Network	100 gigabytes	Atlanta's Hartsfield Jackson Airport, Nashville, Tenn.; Baltimore-Washington. Charlotte and Raleigh-Durham, N.C.
Up to 7 days.	Gold Team C-Suite Mandiant (Part of FireEye)	Site A	Legacy VPN Corporate Network	100 gigabytes	Atlanta's Hartsfield Jackson Airport, Nashville, Tenn.; Baltimore-Washington. Charlotte and Raleigh-Durham, N.C.
Up to 14 days.	Gold Team C-Suite Mandiant (Part of FireEye)	Site A	Legacy VPN Corporate Network	100 gigabytes	Atlanta's Hartsfield Jackson Airport, Nashville, Tenn.; Baltimore-Washington. Charlotte and Raleigh-Durham, N.C.

to the employment medical advisory service; to amend the law relating to building regulations, and the Building (Scotland) Act 1959; and for connected purposes.

Safety, Health and Welfare at Work Act 2005 (Electronic Irish Statute Book (eISB)[37]) includes the following:

Hazard identification and risk assessment.
19.—(1) Every employer shall identify the hazards in the place of work under his or her control, assess the risks presented by those hazards and be in possession of a written assessment (to be known and referred to in this Act as a "risk assessment") of the risks to the safety, health and welfare at work of his or her employees, including the safety, health and welfare of any single employee or group or groups of employees who may be exposed to any unusual or other risks under the relevant statutory provisions.
(2) For the purposes of carrying out a risk assessment under subsection (1), the employer shall, taking account of the work being carried on at the place of work, have regard to the duties imposed by the relevant statutory provisions.
(3) The risk assessment shall be reviewed by the employer where—
    (a) there has been a significant change in the matters to which it relates, or
    (b) there is another reason to believe that it is no longer valid, and, following the review, the employer shall amend the risk assessment as appropriate.
(4) In relation to the most recent risk assessment carried out by an employer, he or she shall take steps to implement any improvement considered necessary relating to the safety, health and welfare at work of employees and to ensure that any such improvement is implemented in respect of all activities and levels of the place of work.
(5) Every person to whom sections 12 or 15 applies shall carry out a risk assessment in accordance with this section to the extent that his or her duties under those sections may apply to persons other than his or her employees.

The Health Impact Assessments (International Council on Mining and Metals[38]) states: "HIAs are used to: identify and maximize the positive and avoid and minimize the negative community health and wellbeing impacts, and identify opportunities that a mining and metals project can bring."

Within such an organization, individuals often receive periodic H&S refresher training (via different mediums, such as face to face, poster campaigns, email campaigns, department training, etc.), are encouraged (and even rewarded) to report risk-ranked events or incidents through an electronic ticketing system, and this receives senior management support.

For example, if you were to visit a manufacturing facility, you would expect to receive a H&S brief, to be issued the H&S rules, and any supporting personal protection equipment, and it would be expected that any employee would challenge anyone that did not adhere to the company's H&S rules.

2.9 DECODING BUSINESS IMPACT ANALYSIS

Many an organization's risk management activities are fundamentally flawed through the lack of effective asset management and BIA activities. As a result, risk decisions are made without having a comprehensive understanding of the context or asset associations. Consequently, they either underestimate or overestimate the asset(s)/process(es)/operation(s) being risk-assessed and, as a result, may underinvest or overinvest in their chosen countermeasures, to help reduce the risks to within the acceptable risk appetite levels.

To enhance your risk management practices, you need to ensure that you are investing enough time and resources into asset management and BIA, so that you have a comprehensive understanding of what is being risk-assessed. Do not hesitate to request additional supporting reference documentation (e.g., asset inventory, network diagrams, data flow diagrams, etc.) so that you are able to truly make an informed decision on the risk exposure.

When conducting your BIA/assessments, you should always insist on referencing any support documentation from the asset management practices, enabling you to appreciate what category of assets are included in the item(s) being analyzed for impact. Additionally, you should always ensure that you speak with any key stakeholders that have an association with the item(s) to be analyzed.

Both the asset management and BIA/assessment activities are critical components for a successful and correct risk assessment and need to be assigned proper importance so that sufficient effort is made to make them a useful resource input for the risk management operations.

Effective BIA/assessments (supported by effective asset management) can really help to bring everything into context so that, based on the context and value of the item(s) being risk-assessed, you can truly make an informed decision as to what measures are proportionate to bring the risks down to acceptable levels and to help prevent you from applying unnecessary and needless countermeasures. As a result, your risk-making decisions will be balanced and could reduce your costs, while increasing the accuracy of your risk assessments.

Notes

1 Usmani, Fahad. "Risk Appetite, Risk Tolerance, and Risk Threshold I." PM Study Circle, 28 Oct. 2021, pmstudycircle.com/risk-appetite-risk-tolerance-and-risk-threshold. Accessed 7 Mar. 2022.

2 Wordnik. "Risk Appetite Definition." Wordnik, www.wordnik.com/words/risk%20appetite. Accessed 7 Mar 2022.
3 Workiva. "Writing a Risk Appetite Statement | Workiva." www.workiva.com, 17 Feb. 2022, www.workiva.com/blog/writing-risk-appetite-statement
4 CSRC NIST Glossary. "Risk Appetite – Glossary | CSRC." Csrc.nist.gov, csrc.nist.gov/glossary/term/Risk_Appetite
5 Gartner. "Sample Risk Appetite Statements Collection." Gartner, 16 Sept. 2021, www.gartner.com/en/documents/4005850/sample-risk-appetite-statements-collection. Accessed 7 Mar. 2022.
6 The Committee of Sponsoring Organizations' (COSO). "Guidance on Enterprise Risk Management." 2019. www.coso.org/Pages/erm.aspx
7 NC State University. "COSO's Enterprise Risk Management – Integrated Framework – ERM – Enterprise Risk Management Initiative | North Carolina State Poole College of Management." Erm.ncsu.edu, 1 Sept. 2004, erm.ncsu.edu/library/article/coso-erm-framework
8 Koenraad Van Brabant, and Overseas Development Institute (London, England). Humanitarian Practice Network. Operational Security Management in Violent Environments. London, Humanitarian Practice Network, 2010.
9 Automobile Association (AA). "What Is the Minimum Legal Tyre Tread Depth? UK Tyre Law Guide | the AA." 2019. www.theaa.com/driving-advice/legal/tyres
10 Nieles, Michael, et al. "An Introduction to Information Security." An Introduction to Information Security, June 2017, nvlpubs.nist.gov/nistpubs/SpecialPublications/NIST.SP.800-12r1.pdf, 10.6028/nist.sp.800-12r1
11 Gartner Glossary. "Definition of Business Impact Analysis (BIA) – Gartner Information Technology Glossary." Gartner, www.gartner.com/en/information-technology/glossary/bia-business-impact-analysis
12 Indeed Editorial Team. "How to Calculate a Recovery Point Objective." Indeed Career Guide, 19 Jan. 2022, www.indeed.com/career-advice/career-development/recovery-point-objective. Accessed 7 Mar. 2022.
13 Techopedia. "What Is Recovery Time Objective (RTO)? – Definition from Techopedia." Techopedia.com, 2020, www.techopedia.com/definition/24250/recovery-time-objective--rto
14 Garn, Damon. "5 IT Disaster Recovery Measurements to Know." Default, 26 Jan. 2022, www.comptia.org/blog/disaster-recovery-measurements. Accessed 7 Mar. 2022.
15 allCare IT Technology Solutions. "Recovery Time Calculator." AllCare IT, 2022, www.allcareit.com/rto. Accessed 7 Mar. 2022.
16 Quick Backup Recovery. "RTO / RPO Calculator." www.quick-Backup-Recovery.com, www.quick-backup-recovery.com/rtc. Accessed 7 Mar. 2022.
17 Olofsson, Oskar. "MTBF and MTTR Calculator." World-Class-Manufacturing.com, 2019, world-class-manufacturing.com/KPI/mtbf.html
18 RF Wireless World. "MTBF Calculator | MTTF Calculator | Online." www.rfwireless-World.com, www.rfwireless-world.com/calculators/MTBF-MTTF-Calculator.html. Accessed 7 Mar. 2022.
19 FIAT Workshop. "Fiat 500 Service Schedules." www.fiatworkshop.co.uk, www.fiatworkshop.co.uk/fiat_500_service_schedule.shtml. Accessed 8 Mar. 2022.
20 Office of the Attorney General, California Department of Justice. California Consumer Privacy Act (CCPA) FACT SHEET CALIFORNIA DEPARTMENT

of JUSTICE OFFICE of the ATTORNEY GENERAL the CCPA Grants New Rights to California Consumers.

21 European Commission. "Guidelines on Data Protection Impact Assessment (DPIA) (Wp248rev.01)." Europa.eu, 2022, ec.europa.eu/newsroom/just/document.cfm?doc_id=47711. Accessed 8 Mar. 2022.

22 GDPR.EU. "Art. 35 GDPR – Data Protection Impact Assessment." GDPR.eu, 14 Nov. 2018, gdpr.eu/article-35-impact-assessment. Accessed 8 Mar. 2022.

23 Information Commissioner's Office (ICO). Sample DPIA Template Step 1: Identify the Need for a DPIA. 9 Feb. 2018.

24 Falcon Edufin. "C03 PRINCIPLES for EFFECTIVE RISK DATA AGGREGATION & RISK REPORTING – FRM Prep Providers." Falcon Edufin, falconedufin.com/book/frm-part-i-short-notes-2022/book-1-foundations-of-rm/c03-principles-for-effective-risk-data-aggregation-risk-reporting. Accessed 9 Mar. 2022.

25 Basel Committee on Banking Supervision. Basel Committee on Banking Supervision Principles for Effective Risk Data Aggregation and Risk Reporting. 2013.

26 Turton, William, and Kartikay Mehrotra. "Hackers Breached Colonial Pipeline with One Compromised Password." www.aljazeera.com, 4 June 2021, www.aljazeera.com/economy/2021/6/4/hackers-breached-colonial-pipeline-with-one-compromised-password. Accessed 8 Mar. 2022.

27 Panettieri, Joe. "Colonial Pipeline Cyberattack: Timeline and Ransomware Attack Recovery Details." MSSP Alert, 8 June 2021, www.msspalert.com/cybersecurity-breaches-and-attacks/ransomware/colonial-pipeline-investigation. Accessed 8 Mar. 2022.

28 Baylor, Ramarcus. "DarkSide Ransomware Gang: An Overview." Unit42, 12 May 2021, unit42.paloaltonetworks.com/darkside-ransomware. Accessed 8 Mar. 2022.

29 The United States Senate Committee on Homeland Security & Governmental Affairs. Hearing before the United States Senate Committee on Homeland Security & Governmental Affairs. 2021.

30 Bajak, Frank, and Cathy Bussewitz. "Colonial Pipeline Hack: Who's behind the Breach and What Does It Mean for Gas Prices and Fuel Supplies?" NBC New York, 11 May 2021, www.nbcnewyork.com/news/national-international/colonial-pipeline-hack-what-we-know-and-how-will-it-impact-gas-prices/3048422. Accessed 8 Mar. 2022.

31 OT Cybersecurity Information Sharing and Analysis Center (OT-ISAC). "OT-ISAC Resources." OTISAC, 21 May 2021, www.otisac.org/ot-isac-resources. Accessed 8 Mar. 2022.

32 Wilkie, Christina, and Macias, Christina. "U.S. Recovers $2.3 Million in Bitcoin Paid in the Colonial Pipeline Ransom." CNBC, 7 June 2021, www.cnbc.com/2021/06/07/us-recovers-some-of-the-money-paid-in-the-colonial-pipeline-ransom-officials-say.html

33 Egan, Matt, and Duffy, Clare. CNN Business. "Colonial Pipeline Launches Restart after Six-Day Shutdown." CNN, 13 May 2021, edition.cnn.com/2021/05/12/business/colonial-pipeline-restart/index.html

34 Congressional Research Service. CRS INSIGHT Prepared for Members and Committees of Congress INSIGHTi Colonial Pipeline: The DarkSide Strikes. 2021.

35 Novinson, Michael. "Colonial Pipeline Hacked via Inactive Account without MFA." CRN, 5 June 2021, www.crn.com/news/security/colonial-pipeline-hac ked-via-inactive-account-without-mfa
36 Gov.uk. "Health and Safety at Work Etc. Act 1974." Legislation.gov.uk, 2019, www.legislation.gov.uk/ukpga/1974/37
37 Electronic Irish Statute Book (eISB). "Electronic Irish Statute Book (EISB)." www.irishstatutebook.ie, 2005, www.irishstatutebook.ie/eli/2005/act/10/enac ted/en/print#sec19. Accessed 9 Mar. 2022.
38 International Council on Mining and Metals. "ICMM: Good Practice Guidance on Health Impact Assessment." www.icmm.com, www.icmm.com/en-gb/guida nce/health-safety/guidance-hia. Accessed 9 Mar. 2022.

Chapter 3

Asset Management

3.1 THE U.S. AIR FORCE MISSION STATEMENT ANALOGY

Asset management is essential in supporting an organization's mission statement, objectives, values, etc. A good example would be to investigate the U.S. Air Force's mission statement ("U.S. Air Force – Mission"[1]) and the importance asset management plays in this.

> The mission of the United States Air Force is to fly, fight and win – airpower anytime, anywhere.
>
> Whether full time, part time, in or out of uniform, everyone who serves plays a critical role in helping us achieve mission success.

There are several different assets that are involved with the maintenance of this mission statement, so I will investigate a single critical asset type.

It is well known that the F35 Lightning II Strike Fighter, as depicted in Figure 3.1 (Wilson[2]), plays a pivotal role in the U.S. Air Force's mission statement. The F35 Strike Fighter is a single complex piece of machinery that is constructed from a plethora of component parts (assets) that need to be maintained and protected.

However, to ensure that these Strike Fighters remain operational, it is extremely important to look beyond just the aircraft and its component parts and to identify, understand, categorize, and prioritize any asset that is essential to the continued operability of the aircraft.

Consequently, the asset management of an F35 Strike Fighter stretches beyond the aircraft itself:

- Aircraft fuselage
- Ejector seat system
- Undercarriage system
- Jet propulsion system
- Radar system

DOI: 10.1201/9781003288084-5

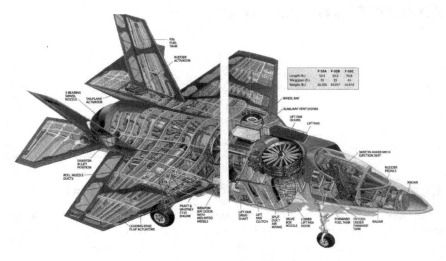

Figure 3.1 F-35B STOVL (U.S. Marine corps variant) joint strike fighter.

What are the ancillary assets that could affect the aircraft's continued operability?

- Pilots and Navigators
  - Flying clothing
  - Flight simulator
  - Briefing facilities
  - Officers' mess
  - Married accommodation
  - Catering staff
  - Food supplies
  - Medical services
  - Gym facilities
- Fuel
  - Fuel depot
  - Refueling bowsers
- Ground crew
  - Sergeants' mess
  - Single-living accommodation
  - Married accommodation
  - Catering staff
  - Food supplies

- Medical services
- Gym facilities
- Hardened aircraft shelter
  - Locking mechanism
  - Electricity
  - Lighting
  - Heating
- Airfield
  - Airfield support teams
  - Airfield support vehicles
- Aircraft Servicing Team
  - Aircraft servicing facilities
  - Tools and equipment
- Air Traffic Control (ATC) team
  - Air traffic control tower
  - Radar
  - Radio
  - GPS

This list could grow further, should the environmental factors change; for example, overseas deployments (Republic World[3]):

- All the supporting, associated assets
- A foreign airfield

Although not an exhaustive list, you start to appreciate the number of assets that need to be protected to keep just one jet aircraft operational. A compromise of any of these associated assets could affect the continued operations of the F35 Strike Fighter; for example:

- The Covid-19 pandemic affecting the availability of the pilots, navigator, or support teams.
- The breakage of a specialist tool needed to service the aircraft.
- An interruption to the supply chain.
- A foggy or frozen airfield.
- Contaminated fuel.

Equally, in business, there will be complex systems and processes that need to be maintained and protected to help keep the business operational. Like the F35 Strike Fighter, these business systems and processes will have complex asset systems, with supporting/associated assets, which need to be appropriately managed.

3.2 INTRODUCTION

In Chapter 1 we introduced the idea of finagling, and in Chapter 2 we described the importance of appreciating the business impact. Without effective BIA and asset management practices, you increase the chance of finagling your business and decreasing the value of your risk management procedures. You need to start by engaging the business stakeholders to understand what business operations are important to them and which assets (and their associated assets) are critical to these operations, in support of the business's mission statement.

Without effective asset management, every supporting defensive strategy will be undermined. It is important to start by understanding which plates are the most valuable to the organization, which need to be kept spinning for the continued success of the business, and which need less focus, so that if they fall to the ground and break, their impact on the business can be absorbed.

It is important to remember that, in the modern digital business, still being operationally resilient requires your business assets to be categorized so that the efforts can be prioritized, based upon the assets' perceived business values.

Without this, you will increasingly feel like you are 'boiling the ocean' or constantly 'firefighting,' as you try to equally secure all your assets. The reality is that some of your assets need to be given a lower prioritization, in favor of those assets that are more critical to your company. Remember that the compromise of an asset only takes one negligent or missed action. However, not all the consequences of these negligent or missed actions are the same, so without asset categorization and the prioritization of your business assets, you may end up focusing on securing or maintaining lower value assets at the detriment to your more impactful assets.

3.3 WHAT IS AN ASSET?

For both SRM and operational resilience, understanding and appreciating the context of a situation or issue is vitally important. However, without effective asset management the context is difficult to define. Consequently, before doing anything else you should conduct reconnaissance of your business and engage with your business stakeholders to understand what is important to the business and what assets support this. However, to effectively do this, you need to define what your business considers to be an asset, and there are several definitions available to help guide you in defining what an asset means to your business.

> noun
> 1. a useful and desirable thing or quality:
>   Organizational ability is an asset.
> 2. a single item of ownership having exchange value:
>   Our summer home is an asset we're not willing to sell.

3. (in intelligence) a person followed or spied upon to obtain information: as a participant in an operation, an asset may be consenting, forced, as by blackmail, or unaware of being used:

It was a catalog of virtually every CIA asset within the Soviet Union. Compare confidential informant.

assets

a. Finance. Items of ownership convertible into cash; total resources of a person or business, as cash, notes and accounts receivable, securities, inventories, goodwill, fixtures, machinery, or real estate (opposed to liabilities).
b. Accounting. The items detailed on a balance sheet, especially in relation to liabilities and capital.
c. Law. All property available for the payment of debts, especially of a bankrupt or insolvent firm or person.
d. Law. Property in the hands of an heir, executor, or administrator, that is sufficient to pay the debts or legacies of a deceased person.
(Source: The Dictionary.com ("Definition of Asset | Dictionary.com"[4]))

Assets can be both tangible and intangible and are far more than just IT systems. The National Institute of Standards Technology (NIST) has a number of definitions for the term asset, e.g.,

a. A major application, general support system, high-impact program, physical plant, mission critical system, personnel, equipment, or a logically related group of systems.
b. An item of value to achievement of organizational mission/business objectives.
   • Note 1: Assets have interrelated characteristics that include value, criticality, and the degree to which they are relied upon to achieve organizational mission/business objectives. From these characteristics, appropriate protections are to be engineered into solutions employed by the organization.
   • Note 2: An asset may be tangible (e.g., physical item such as hardware, software, firmware, computing platform, network device, or other technology components) or intangible (e.g., information, data, trademark, copyright, patent, intellectual property, image, or reputation).
c. An item of value to achievement of organizational mission/business objectives.
   • Note 1: Assets have interrelated characteristics that include value, criticality, and the degree to which they are relied upon to achieve organizational mission/business objectives. From these

characteristics, appropriate protections are to be engineered into solutions employed by the organization.

- Note 2: An asset may be tangible (e.g., physical item such as hardware, software, firmware, computing platform, network device, or other technology components) or intangible (e.g., information, data, trademark, copyright, patent, intellectual property, image, or reputation).

d. An item of value to stakeholders. An asset may be tangible (e.g., a physical item such as hardware, firmware, computing platform, network device, or other technology component) or intangible (e.g., humans, data, information, software, capability, function, service, trademark, copyright, patent, intellectual property, image, or reputation). The value of an asset is determined by stakeholders in consideration of loss concerns across the entire system life cycle. Such concerns include but are not limited to business or mission concerns.

e. Anything that has value to an organization, including, but not limited to, another organization, person, computing device, information technology (IT) system, IT network, IT circuit, software (both an installed instance and a physical instance), virtual computing platform (common in cloud and virtualized computing), and related hardware (e.g., locks, cabinets, keyboards).

(Source: NIST Glossary (NIST[5]))

An asset is a resource owned or controlled by an individual, corporation, or government with the expectation that it will generate a positive economic benefit. Common types of assets include current, non-current, physical, intangible, operating, and non-operating. Correctly identifying and classifying the types of assets is critical to the survival of a company, specifically its solvency and associated risks.

(Source: Corporate Financial Institute ("Types of Assets"[6]))

An asset is a resource that is owned or controlled by a company and will provide a benefit in current and future periods for the business. In other words, it's something that a company owns or controls and can use to generate profits today and in the future.

(Source: My Accounting Course ("What Is an Asset? – Definition | Meaning | Example"[7]))

An IT asset is a piece of software or hardware within an information technology environment. Tracking of IT assets within an IT asset management system can be crucial to the operational or financial success of an enterprise. IT assets are integral components of the organization's systems and network infrastructure.

(Source: Techopedia ("What Is an IT Asset? – Definition from Techopedia"[8])).

By investigating the origins of the term, you can get a better appreciation of what the definition of an asset should incorporate:

asset (n.)
a 19c. artificial singular of assets (q.v.).

assets (n.)
1530s, "sufficient estate," from Anglo-French assetz, asetz (singular), from Old French assez "sufficiency, satisfaction; compensation" (11c.), noun use of adverb meaning "enough, sufficiently; very much, a great deal," from Vulgar Latin *ad satis "to sufficiency," from Latin ad "to" (see ad-) + satis "enough," from PIE root *sa- "to satisfy."
At first a legal word meaning "sufficient estate" (to satisfy debts and legacies), it passed into a general sense of "property," especially "any property that theoretically can be converted to ready money" by 1580s. Figurative use from 1670s. Asset is a 19c. artificial singular. Corporate asset stripping is attested from 1972.
(Source: Online Etymology Dictionary ("Asset |
Etymology, Origin and Meaning of Asset by Etymonline"[9])

For me, the definition is:

Assets can be tangible or intangible (e.g., IT hardware, IT software, buildings, rooms, infrastructure, data, people, third-party suppliers, documentation (policies, standard operating procedures, etc.).
An asset is anything that supplies support to the continued safe and secure operations for important business functions and if compromised could affect the continued operations or reputation of the business.

Your valuable business operations/processes are likely to rely on many differing asset types (as depicted in Figure 3.2) to remain operational.
Every asset has a unique value to your business, and when these assets are connected or in a grouped environment their value can increase, due to the aggregation principle.

Data Aggregation
Data Aggregation is the ability to get a more complete picture of the information by analyzing several different types of records at once.
(Source: SANS[10])

Aggregation
As government employs greater sharing and reuse of commoditized ICT solutions as well as shifting public services delivery to online channels, there is potential for large volumes of data objects to be concentrated in

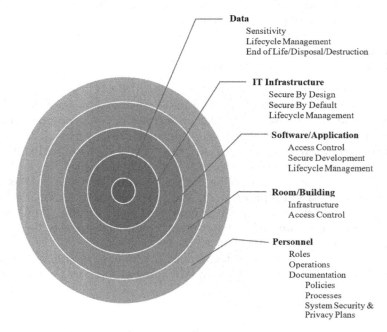

Data
Sensitivity
Lifecycle Management
End of Life/Disposal/Destruction

IT Infrastructure
Secure By Design
Secure By Default
Lifecycle Management

Software/Application
Access Control
Secure Development
Lifecycle Management

Room/Building
Infrastructure
Access Control

Personnel
Roles
Operations
Documentation
Policies
Processes
System Security &
Privacy Plans

Figure 3.2 Asset types.

a small number of systems or services, or for a single system to provide a large number of government services.

(Source: UK Government Cabinet Office[11])

Understanding the business value of an individual, connected or group of assets is essential to understand the value of the risk exposure and to ensure that the costs associated with any mitigation measures does not exceed the perceived values of these assets.

Without effective asset management and context, there is an increased probability for finagling and firefighting, as personnel subconsciously enact their defense mechanisms, or when an issue arises they frantically run around trying to identify any affected business assets and to gain an understanding of the context.

Let's face it, without effective asset management any defensive strategy and compliance activities will have an element of 'finagling,' with most industry security standard frameworks or standards having a component of asset management; for example,

ISO/IEC 27001:2013 (ISO[12]).

Having identified the scope of your ISO/IEC 27001:2013 and risks, the entity then applies the mitigation controls. The annex A controls include an element for asset management:

A.8 Asset management
A.8.1 Responsibility for assets
Objective: To identify organizational assets and define appropriate protection responsibilities.

(Source: PCI DSS, ("Official PCI Security Standards
Council Site – Verify PCI Compliance, Download
Data Security and Credit Card Security Standards"[13])

In PCI DSS, the focus is on naming the scope, which incorporates any asset that is directly involved with the processing, storage, or transmission of cardholder data or any asset that can indirectly impact or is connected to any asset that processes, stores, or transmits cardholder data.

Scope of PCI DSS Requirements
The PCI DSS security requirements apply to all system components included in or connected to the cardholder data environment. The cardholder data environment (CDE) is comprised of people, processes and technologies that store, process, or transmit cardholder data or sensitive authentication data. "System components" include network devices, servers, computing devices, and applications. Examples of system components include but are not limited to the following:

- Systems that provide security services (for example, authentication servers), facilitate segmentation (for example, internal firewalls), or may impact the security of (for example, name resolution or web redirection servers) the CDE.
- Virtualization components such as virtual machines, virtual switches/routers, virtual appliances, virtual applications/desktops, and hypervisors.
- Network components including but not limited to firewalls, switches, routers, wireless access points, network appliances, and other security appliances.
- Server types including but not limited to web, application, database, authentication, mail, proxy, Network Time Protocol (NTP), and Domain Name System (DNS).
- Applications including all purchased and custom applications, including internal and external (for example, Internet) applications.
- Any other component or device located within or connected to the CDE.

The first step of a PCI DSS assessment is to accurately determine the scope of the review. At least annually and prior to the annual assessment, the assessed entity should confirm the accuracy of their PCI DSS scope by identifying all locations and flows of cardholder data, and identify all systems that are connected to or, if compromised, could impact the CDE (for example, authentication servers) to ensure they are included in the PCI DSS scope. All types of systems and locations should be considered as part of the scoping process, including backup/recovery sites and failover systems.

To confirm the accuracy of the defined CDE, perform the following:

- Identify and document the existence of all cardholder data in their environment, to verify that no cardholder data exists outside of the currently defined CDE.
- Verify that PCI DSS scope is appropriate (for example, the results may be a diagram or an inventory of cardholder data locations).
- The entity considers any cardholder data found to be in scope of the PCI DSS assessment and part of the CDE. If the entity identifies data that is not currently included in the CDE, such data should be securely deleted, migrated into the currently defined CDE, or the CDE redefined to include this data."

(Source: Center for Internet Security (CIS) 18 Critical Security Controls ("The 18 CIS Controls"[14])

The Center for Internet Security has identified the need to maintain asset inventories for any tangible assets as being their number one and number two critical security controls:

CIS Critical Security Control 1: Inventory and Control of Enterprise Assets

Overview
Actively manage (inventory, track, and correct) all enterprise assets (end-user devices, including portable and mobile; network devices; non-computing/Internet of Things (IoT) devices; and servers) connected to the infrastructure physically, virtually, remotely, and those within cloud environments, to accurately know the totality of assets that need to be monitored and protected within the enterprise. This will also support identifying unauthorized and unmanaged assets to remove or remediate.

CIS Critical Security Control 2: Inventory and Control of Software Assets

Overview
Actively manage (inventory, track, and correct) all software (operating systems and applications) on the network so that only authorized software is installed and can execute, and that unauthorized and unmanaged software is found and prevented from installation or execution.

(Source: NIST Cyber Security Framework (CSF), ("Framework for Improving Critical Infrastructure Cybersecurity"[15])

In support of the NIST Risk Management Framework (NIST, "About the RMF – NIST Risk Management Framework | CSRC | CSRC"[16]), the application of the CSF commences with asset management, as depicted in Table 3.1.

3.4 THE COMPONENTS OF EFFECTIVE ASSET MANAGEMENT

Let's face it, for any business to remain operationally resilient requires continually functioning operational processes and business services. These operational processes and business services have a reliance on assets, such as:

- Technology
- Data
- People
- Facilities
- Outsourced services

These assets need to be identified, prioritized, documented, inventoried, and assigned an asset owner.

The importance of asset management has been recognized by both NIST and the Carnegie Mellon University's Software Engineering CERT Division ("The CERT Division | Software Engineering Institute"[17]).

For the management of your IT assets, NIST have created:

- NIST SP 1800-5B: IT Asset Management (Stone et al.[18]).

The CERT Division has an excellent guide (CERT RMM – Asset Definition and Management (ADM), (Caralli et al.[19])), as depicted in Table 3.2, to help you develop an effective asset management practice, which I will explain in further detail.

This guide has even been endorsed by the Cybersecurity and Infrastructure Security Agency (CISA), ("CRR Supplemental Resource Guide Asset Management"[20]) in support of an entity's development of effective operational resilience practices. It has even included a cross-mapping to the NIST CSF, (Cyber Resilience Review (CRR) NIST Cybersecurity Framework Crosswalks[21]).

3.4.1 ADM:SG1 Establish Organizational Assets

Organizational assets (people, information, technology, and facilities) are identified, and the authority and responsibility for these assets are established.

Table 3.1 NIST ID.AM

Function	Category	Subcategory	Informative References
IDENTIFY (ID)	**Asset Management (ID.AM):** The data, personnel, devices, systems, and facilities that enable the organization to achieve business purposes are identified and managed consistent with their relative importance to business objectives and the organization's risk strategy	**ID.AM-1:** Physical devices and systems within the organization are inventoried	• **CCS CSC 1** • **COBIT 5** BAI09.01, BAI09.02 • **ISA 62443-2-1:2009** 4.2.3.4 • **ISA 62443-3-3:2013** SR 7.8 • **ISO/IEC 27001:2013** A.8.1.1, A.8.1.2 • **NIST SP 800-53 Rev. 4** CM-8
		I D.AM-2: Software platforms and applications within the organization are inventoried	• **CCS CSC 2** • **COBIT 5** BAI09.01, BAI09.02, BAI09.05 • **ISA 62443-2-1:2009** 4.2.3.4 • **ISA 62443-3-3:2013** SR 7.8 • **ISO/IEC 27001:2013** A.8.1.1, A.8.1.2 • **NIST SP 800-53 Rev. 4 CM-8**
		ID.AM-3: Organizational communication and data flows are mapped	• **CCS CSC 1** • **COBIT 5** DSS05.02 • **ISA 62443-2-1:2009** 4.2.3.4 • **ISO/IEC 27001:2013** A.13.2.1 • **NIST SP 800-53 Rev. 4** AC-4, CA-3, CA-9, PL-8
		ID.AM-4: External information systems are cataloged	• **COBIT 5** AP002.02 • **ISO/IEC 27001:2013 A.11.2.6** • **NISI SP 800-53 Rev. 4** AC-20, SA-9
		ID.AM-5: Resources (e.g., hardware, devices, data, and software) are prioritized based on their classification, criticality, and business value	• **COBIT 5** AP003.03, AP003.04, BAI09.02 • **ISA 62443-2-1:2009** 4.2.3.6 • **ISO/IEC 27001:2013** A.8.2.1 • **NIST SP 800-53 Rev. 4** CP-2, RA-2, SA-14
		ID.AM-6: Cybersecurity roles and responsibilities for the entire workforce and third-party stakeholders (e.g., suppliers, customers, partners) are established	• **COBIT 5** AP001.02, DSS06.03 • **ISA 62443-2-1:2009** 4.3.2.3.3 • **ISO/IEC 27001:2013** A.6.1.1

Table 3.2 ADM Goals and Practices

Goals	Practices
ADM:SG1 Establish Organizational Assets	ADM: SG1.SP1 Inventory Assets ADM: SG1.SP2 Establish a Common Understanding ADM: SG1.SP3 Establish Ownership and Custodianship
ADM:SG2 Establish the Relationship Between Assets and Services	ADM: SG2.SP1 Associate Assets with Services ADM: SG2.SP2 Analyze Asset-Service Dependencies
ADM:SG3 Manage Assets	ADM: SG3.SP1 Identify Change Criteria ADM: SG3.SP2 Maintain Changes to Assets and Inventory

ADM: SG1.SP1 Inventory Assets: Organizational assets are identified and inventoried.

The first phase of your asset management program starts with engagement. Reach out to the business to understand the context of the business and to gain an understanding of what is important to the company. With this knowledge at hand, next you need to collaborate with the stakeholders to reconnaissance these operational processes and services to find and start to inventory which assets support them.

The typical output you can expect from this exercise:

1. Critical assets register (of all high-value assets of each type).
2. Standard assets register or database(s).

Contributing to these outputs you can expect to enable the following sub-practices:

1. Identify and catalog vital staff.
2. Identify and inventory high-value information assets.
3. Identify and portfolio high-value technology components.
4. Identify and list high-value facilities.
5. Develop and maintain critical asset register(s) for all high-value assets.

    All information relevant to the asset should be contained with the asset in its entry in the right asset database(s). Operational access to and integrity of the inventory information is the main factor, whether there is one or more than one primary repository or database for all assets.

6. Develop and maintain standard asset register(s) for any ancillary assets.
   This could include any assets that are required for contingency plans, supporting, or lower-value assets. Such assets, if compromised, will have a limited short-term direct impact on the identified business processes or services.

7. In addition to maintaining asset registers, visualize these assets and their connectivity in network diagrams (layer 2 and layer 3) and data flow diagrams. These diagrams should be periodically reviewed so that they retain their accuracy.

ADM: SG1.SP2 Establish a Common Understanding: A common and consistent definition of assets is established and communicated.

The language used to describe the assets can often cause confusion between the business leaders, asset owners, and asset custodians. Consequently, it is essential that a common language is used to describe your assets, and consistency is the key to success. You will find that engaging with the stakeholders to develop suitable descriptions and to develop and maintain a support glossary extremely helpful.

A consistent description helps in the development of operational resilience requirements and to ensure alignment to these requirements. This should clearly define the context of the asset(s), stating the boundaries and extent of the asset(s), which is extremely helpful for identifying the ownership and responsibility for the resilience of the assets).

Additionally, an asset's description can be easily communicated within and outside of the business to help facilitate communication of their resilience requirements to both internal communities and external business partners.

The minimal baseline should ensure that a critical asset register is maintained so that all the high-value assets are accurately and clearly defined. It is important to ensure that the business's key stakeholders engage in the development of the asset descriptions, including why the asset has been categorized as a high-value asset to the business. Table 3.3 highlights some common elements that should be considered as a minimum:

The following shows examples of the types of output that you could be expected to produce:

1. Asset profiles (for all high-value assets of each type).
2. Updated asset database(s) (including asset profiles).

This list that follows provides you with an example of some of the practices that would be expected to the establishment of a common language:

Table 3.3 Asset Register – Example Content

Asset Type	Associated Data	Data Format	Category	Location	Owner	Custodian	Backup Location	Dependencies	Lifecycle
People	Cardholder	Electronic	Critical/Very					Services that	Predicted
Data	Customer	Paper	High/High/					are reliant on	end of life
			Moderate/Low					the asset.	(if applicable).
Technology	Personal data								
Facility									
Supplier	Intellectual								
	property								
	Financial								

1. Create asset profiles for each high-value asset (or similar work product) and document a common description.
   - Be sure to address the entire range of information that should be collected for each type of asset, including, as a minimum, the owner and the custodian(s) of the asset.
   - Also, include the resilience requirements of the asset as established or acquired by the organization.
2. Describe and document the 'acceptable use' of the asset.
   - Ensure alignment between acceptable uses and resilience requirements.
3. Categorize information assets as to their level of sensitivity.
4. Update the asset register(s) with asset profile information.

All information relevant to the asset (collected from the asset profile) should be contained with the asset in its entry in the proper asset register.

ADM: SG1.SP3 Establish Ownership and Custodianship: Authority and responsibility for assets are established.

Responsibility, ownership, and accountability for each asset is created, at both asset owner and asset custodial levels.

The output from such an exercise should result in the following types of output:

1. Owners are formally identified.
2. Custodians are formally identified.
3. Asset profiles (including owner and custodian) are updated.
4. Asset registries/database(s) are updated to include the owners and custodians.

The formal product output would include:

1. A description of the owner of each asset on the asset profile (or similar work product) are documented.
2. Group assets that are collectively needed to perform a specific service, with service owners named, if necessary.
3. A description of the physical location of the asset and the custodian of the asset is documented.

3.4.2 ADM:SG2 Establish the Relationship Between Assets and Services

The relationship between assets and the services they support is established and examined.

ADM: SG2.SP1 Associate Assets with Services: Assets are associated with the service or services they support.

Without understanding the linkages or associations of your assets it becomes almost impossible to appreciate any aggregation or risks that the assets may present to the business operations they support.

Typically, the following output should be produced:

1. List of high-value services and associated assets.
2. Asset profiles (including service information) are updated.
3. The asset registry/database (including service information) is updated.
   a) Identify high-value services.
      A list of high-value services is created in the enterprise focus process area. Assets can be associated with services in this practice, but it is best to have a validated list of services to which assets are associated. (Refer to the enterprise focus process area for more information.)
   b) Assign assets in the asset database(s) to one or more services.
   c) Update asset profiles to establish and document associations of assets to services.
      • If an asset is connected to more than one service, ensure this is noted as part of the asset profile.
   d) Update the asset database(s) with asset-to-service association information.
      • All information relevant to the asset (collected from the asset profile) should be contained with the asset in its entry in the asset database.

ADM: SG2.SP2 Analyze Asset-Service Dependencies. Instances where assets support more than one service are identified and analyzed.

This is the analysis for the aggregation principle. Can you identify any inter-business services that are reliant on a handful of assets (or even a solitary asset) to support multiple business operations? What about an asset that provides essential support to another critical business asset?

3.4.3 ADM:SG3 Manage Assets

The lifecycle of assets is managed.

ADM: SG3.SP1 Identify Change Criteria: The criteria that would indicate changes in an asset or its association with a service are established and maintained.

A change to an asset should be carried out with great caution and should be a decision that is made knowing the potential risk or any rollback considerations. Imagine applying a system update to your mainframe, which serves multiple business services and operations. What would be the forecasted impact should the system update stop the mainframe from functioning during a peak period?

To enable effective change management decisions, it is important for the asset owners to understand the change criteria. Consequently, the expected output for this would be:

1. Asset inventory baseline.
2. Asset change criteria.

To achieve this, you would need to:

1. Ensure that an asset inventory baseline is established from which changes will be managed.
2. Develop and document criteria for establishing when a change in asset inventory must be considered.
   - Ensure that the criteria are proportionate to the organization's risk tolerances.

ADM: SG3.SP2 Maintain Changes to Assets and Inventory: Changes to assets are managed as conditions dictate.

In a dynamic business environment it is inevitable that changes will be needed. However, it is imperative that any changes do not increase the risks for an important asset being compromised. Consequently, when changes occur, it is critical that the support asset inventory be updated to reflect any changed states.

The desired output from this would be evidenced through the following:

- Maintenance of asset change documentation.
- Maintenance of the asset inventory (kept current).
- Asset and service resilience requirements are updated.
- Asset and service protection strategies and controls is kept up to date.
- Strategies and continuity plans for sustaining assets and services are maintained.

To achieve this, you would need to ensure that:

1. Asset changes are documented by updating asset profiles and the asset database(s).
2. A requirement change history with the rationale for performing the changes is kept.
3. The impact of asset changes on existing resilience requirements and activities and commitments for protecting and sustaining assets is evaluated.
4. Asset resilience requirements, asset protection strategies, and plans for sustaining assets are updated, as necessary.

5. Communication channels to ensure custodians are aware of changes in assets are established.
6. Service-level agreements (SLAs) with custodians are updated, if necessary, to reflect commitment to changes.

3.5 WHEN SECURITY RISK MANAGEMENT BITES BACK

One of the greatest examples of when poor asset management practices resulted in a compromise of critical business assets, leading to a significant data breach, was the 2017 Equifax cyberattack (U.S. House of Representatives Committee on Oversight and Government Reform the Equifax Data Breach Majority Staff Report 115th Congress[22]), as depicted in the kill chain demonstrated in Figure 3.3.

Equifax is a large global consumer reporting agency and, as such, routinely processes, stores, and transmits consumers' sensitive data (e.g., personal data and cardholder data). Given that it is subject to heavy regulations you might have assumed that Equifax had an effective defensive strategy in place (and who am I to say otherwise!).

Now, it is important to remember that today's cybercriminals (no matter how small or sophisticated) all have one thing in common: They are opportunists, who seek out opportunities that they can exploit.

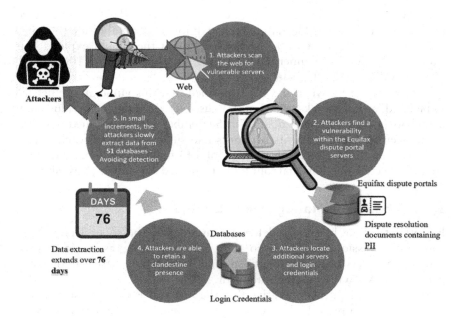

Figure 3.3 Equifax kill chain.

opportunist (n.)
1881, from opportunism (q.v.) + -ist. A word in Italian politics, later in France opportuniste was applied derisively to the moderate Léon Gambetta (1876), leader of the party between the monarchists and the extreme republicans. In English the word was used generally of anyone whose policy or tendency is to seek to profit from the prevailing circumstances or take advantage of opportunities as they occur.

Once seated in the legislature Gambetta argued that all republicans—the old guard, young republicans, and even recent converts—could and should cooperate. He preached compromise and accommodation—Opportunism—in order to achieve the politically possible. He spoke against violent revolution and sought to promote peaceful reforms using legal methods, a stance that pitted him directly against the militant demagogue Henri Rochefort, who latched onto the term Opportunism as a term of abuse. [Robert Lynn Fuller, "The Origins of the French Nationalist Movement, 1886–1914"].

(Source: Online Etymology Dictionary ("Opportunist | Etymology,
Origin and Meaning of Opportunist by Etymonline"[23]))

Your professional cybercriminal gang will deliberately seek out (even create) the opportunities that a rewarding target can present, while the more amateur attacker might only stumble upon them.

In March 2017, Chinese state-sponsored criminals (EPIC[24]) discovered that an internet-accessible database had known vulnerabilities ("CVE – CVE-2017-5638"[25]), (Woo[26]), (Metasploit[27]) that they could exploit. This was a newly identified vulnerability, having been published on 10th March 2017 ("NVD – CVE-2017-5638"[28]).

In fact, the asset owner was never notified that this vulnerability needed to be fixed, and six weeks after Equifax discovered that its high-value database had been compromised, on 7th September 2017, it issued a public announcement stating that its networks had suffered a data breach, which had exposed the personal information of 143 million consumers. Equifax later discovered an additional four million affected consumers (Miyashiro[29]).

3.5.1 The Asset Management Enabler

Essential to your business's defense strategy must be to understand the company's mission statement so that the supporting assets (and their associated assets) can be identified and prioritized, based upon their perceived risks to the mission statement.

To achieve this, it is imperative that the business is engaged so that key stakeholders can provide their valued input. Remember, no one knows the business better than the business itself.

Having identified and categorized your assets, it is extremely important that these are documented and assigned an owner and a custodian.

Finally, your asset management program needs to be continually managed and any changes to these assets or their environments strictly controlled so that the impact and rollback considerations can be made before any changes are actioned.

3.5.2 Decoding Asset Management

Like an F35 Joint Strike Fighter, modern business environments can be extremely complex, relying on numerous connected assets. These assets need to be protected from compromise to ensure that everything remains operational.

The problem with many organizations is the failure to focus on the need to develop effective asset management practices. Consequently, they either try to treat all the assets as being the same value or rely on their compliance activities to identify their high-value assets, which results in them trying to do too much or missing something.

The criminals only need to find a single exploitable vulnerability of a high-value assets for them to see a return on their efforts. Additionally, a poorly maintained high-value asset could result in an impactful outage.

By identifying, documenting, and assigning ownership and custodianship of the business assets (categorized by risks), you will be able to better prioritize your defensive efforts, based upon the perceived balance of risks.

1. Identify your assets.
2. Categorize your asset(s).
   a. Value of the asset(s)
      i. Critical (5)
      ii. Very High (4)
      iii. High (3)
      iv. Moderate (2)
      v. Low (1)
   b. Likelihood that the asset(s) will be targeted.
      i. Extremely likely (5)
      ii. Highly likely (4)
      iii. Somewhat likely (3)
      iv. Likely (2)
      v. Unlikely (1)
   c. Multiply the value and likelihood scores to get an asset risk score; for example:
      i. Critical = 21 to 25
      ii. Very High = 16 to 20
      iii. High = 11 to 15

      iv. Moderate = 6 to 10

      v. Low = 5 or under

3. Understand any asset associations and linkages.

4. Maintain your approved assets.

    a. Asset lifecycles

5. Carefully manage any changes to your approved assets.

6. Knowing your approved assets helps with:

    a. Knowing what NORMAL looks like.

    b. Quickly and effectively identifying the ABNORMAL.

Notes

1 "U.S. Air Force – Mission." Airforce.com, 2019, www.airforce.com/mission.
2 Wilson, Jim. "America's New Strike Fighter: PM Meets the F-35." *Popular Mechanics*, 25 Jan. 2021, www.popularmechanics.com/military/aviation/a35229793/f-35-history-archive. Accessed 20 Jan. 2023.
3 Republic World. "US Air Force Permanently Deploys F-35 Stealth Fighter Jets in Europe to Counter Russia." *Republic World*, 17 Dec. 2021, www.republicworld.com/world-news/us-news/us-air-force-permanently-deploys-f-35-stealth-fighter-jets-in-europe-to-counter-russia.html. Accessed 7 Jan. 2022.
4 "Definition of Asset | Dictionary.com." www.dictionary.com, www.dictionary.com/browse/asset. Accessed 7 Jan. 2022.
5 NIST, CSRC Content. "Asset(S) – Glossary | CSRC." Csrc.nist.gov, csrc.nist.gov/glossary/term/asset
6 "Types of Assets." Corporate Finance Institute, corporatefinanceinstitute.com/resources/knowledge/accounting/types-of-assets. Accessed 7 Jan. 2022.
7 "What Is an Asset? – Definition | Meaning | Example." My Accounting Course, www.myaccountingcourse.com/accounting-dictionary/asset
8 "What Is an IT Asset? – Definition from Techopedia." Techopedia.com, 2019, www.techopedia.com/definition/16946/it-asset
9 "Asset | Etymology, Origin and Meaning of Asset by Etymonline." www.etymonline.com, www.etymonline.com/word/asset#etymonline_v_26613. Accessed 7 Jan. 2022.
10 SANS. "SANS Institute." www.sans.org, 2022, www.sans.org/security-resources/glossary-of-terms. Accessed 21 July 2022.
11 UK Government Cabinet Office. Government Security Classifications. 2018.
12 ISO. "ISO/IEC 27001 Information Security Management." ISO, 2013, www.iso.org/isoiec-27001-information-security.html
13 "Official PCI Security Standards Council Site – Verify PCI Compliance, Download Data Security and Credit Card Security Standards." www.pcisecuritystandards.org, www.pcisecuritystandards.org/document_library#agreement. Accessed 7 Jan. 2022.
14 "The 18 CIS Controls." CIS, www.cisecurity.org/controls/cis-controls-list
15 "Framework for Improving Critical Infrastructure Cybersecurity." 2014.
16 NIST. "About the RMF – NIST Risk Management Framework | CSRC | CSRC." CSRC | NIST, 30 Nov. 2016, csrc.nist.gov/projects/risk-management/about-rmf

17 "The CERT Division | Software Engineering Institute." www.sei.cmu.edu, www.sei.cmu.edu/about/divisions/cert. Accessed 7 Jan. 2022.
18 Stone, Michael, et al. IT Asset Management: Financial Services. Sept. 2018, csrc.nist.gov/publications/detail/sp/1800-5/final, 10.6028/nist.sp.1800-5
19 Caralli, Richard, et al. CERT® Resilience Management Model, Version 1.2 Asset Definition and Management (ADM) CERT Program. 2016.
20 "CRR Supplemental Resource Guide Asset Management." 2016, www.cisa.gov/sites/default/files/publications/CRR_Resource_Guide-AM.pdf
21 Cyber Resilience Review (CRR) NIST Cybersecurity Framework Crosswalks. 2020, www.cisa.gov/uscert/sites/default/files/c3vp/csc-crr-nist-framework-crosswalk.pdf
22 U.S. House of Representatives Committee on Oversight and Government Reform the Equifax Data Breach Majority Staff Report 115th Congress. 2018.
23 "Opportunist | Etymology, Origin and Meaning of Opportunist by Etymonline." www.etymonline.com, www.etymonline.com/word/opportunist#etymonline_v_30959. Accessed 7 Jan. 2022.
24 Electronic Privacy Information Center. "EPIC – Equifax Data Breach." Archive. epic.org, archive.epic.org/privacy/data-breach/equifax. Accessed 7 Jan. 2022.
25 "CVE – CVE-2017-5638." Cve.mitre.org, 2017, cve.mitre.org/cgi-bin/cvename.cgi?name=CVE-2017-5638.
26 Woo, Vex. "Apache Struts 2.3.5 < 2.3.31 / 2.5 < 2.5.10 – Remote Code Execution." Exploit Database, 7 Mar. 2017, www.exploit-db.com/exploits/41570
27 Metasploit. "Apache Struts 2.3.5 < 2.3.31 / 2.5 < 2.5.10 – 'Jakarta' Multipart Parser OGNL Injection (Metasploit)." Exploit Database, 15 Mar. 2017, www.exploit-db.com/exploits/41614. Accessed 7 Jan. 2022.
28 "NVD – CVE-2017-5638." Nvd.nist.gov, 2017, nvd.nist.gov/vuln/detail/CVE-2017-5638#vulnCurrentDescriptionTitle
29 Miyashiro, Irini Kanaris. "Case Study: Equifax Data Breach." Sevenpillarsinstitute. org, 30 Apr. 2021, sevenpillarsinstitute.org/case-study-equifax-data-breach. Accessed 7 Jan. 2022.

Chapter 4

Risk-Based Vulnerability Management

4.1 THE FIRST AID ANALOGY

Let's imagine that you are the first on the scene of a serious, mass-casualty, road traffic collision. Not everyone involved will have life-threatening injuries, so before jumping straight into treating the casualties, you need to analyze the situation and to prioritize those casualties that need to have their injuries treated first.

Just because one casualty is screaming louder than another does not mean that they may be the higher priority. You need to understand the context of each casualty's injuries and the extent to which they might be life-threatening. Based upon the analysis of the situation, you can then prioritize your first-aid activities. Those injuries that are believed to be life-threatening would be identified as a high priority for the application of first aid.

- Do you prioritize a screaming casualty that has a painful broken leg (not an open (compound) fracture ("Open Fractures – OrthoInfo – AAOS"[1])) over a silent, unconscious, casualty who is bleeding out?

As you can see, vulnerability management is remarkably like first aid, as not only do you need to find your 'wounds' (vulnerabilities), but you also need to analyze the situation and triage (prioritize) your first-aid (remediation) activities, based upon the perceived likelihood and impacts (risk).

You cannot ignore these wounds but you, equally, cannot treat everything as being equally as important.

- You need to understand the risks and prioritize accordingly.

4.2 INTRODUCTION TO VULNERABILITY MANAGEMENT

Many organizations really do struggle to manage the risks associated with vulnerability management, almost feeling:

DOI: 10.1201/9781003288084-6

- They are damned if they do, damned if they don't.
- If it isn't broken, then don't try to fix it.

Vulnerability management is a combination of hardening the assets (locking down any unnecessary services, port, or protocols (SPPs)), maintaining antivirus protection, keeping the systems updated and identifying any new vulnerabilities (e.g., vulnerability scanning, penetration testing, etc.). The purpose is to help reduce the risks to any high-value business assets, to keep the essential business cogs turning.

On the one hand, what if the application of a new update requires a business-critical asset to be taken offline, or what if the update affects the operability of the asset? Either of these scenarios could also present an impact to these business operations that without the update would not affect the asset's function.

On the other hand, what if that new update prevents a weakness in the asset from being exploited? If you do not apply the update or harden the asset, then a threat actor could maliciously or accidentally exploit this and compromise the operability of the critical business asset.

- Between a rock and a hard place?

To enable and support effective vulnerability management practices, it is important to work with the business's key stakeholders, asset owners, and risk owners to analyze and risk-assess any newly identified vulnerabilities, and to appropriately manage any remediation activities, so that any updates can be applied with minimal disruption to the business operations, and with the support from the business.

One thing you need to try to avoid is leaving any longstanding high-risk vulnerabilities to remain without any remediation planning.

Start by hardening your important assets so that they only supply the SPPs they need for their role and all unnecessary services are disabled. This will reduce the number of updates that need to be applied for SPPs that are not even needed.

- Imagine that you have an 'out-of-the-box' Microsoft server. This does not ensure access to this computer from the network is set to 'administrators, authenticated users' (MS only). Do you really want to leave this 'out-of-the-box' server susceptible to known attackers' techniques and tactics? For example:
  - TA0008. Lateral Movement ("Lateral Movement, Tactic TA0008 – Enterprise | MITRE ATT&CK®"[2]).
  - T1563. Remote Session Hijacking ("Remote Service Session Hijacking, Technique T1563 – Enterprise | MITRE ATT&CK®"[3]).
  - T1021. Remote Services ("Remote Services, Technique T1021 – Enterprise | MITRE ATT&CK®"[4]).

- The same Microsoft server has unnecessary Adobe software installed, which is never used. If this unused/not needed software is not supported, what added vulnerabilities ("CVE – Search Results"[5]) might this present? For example:
  - ("CVE – CVE-2021-40730"[6]). Adobe Acrobat Reader DC version 21.007.20095 (and earlier), 21.007.20096 (and earlier), 20.004.30015 (and earlier), and 17.011.30202 (and earlier) is affected by a use-after-free that allows a remote attacker to show sensitive information on affected installations of Adobe Acrobat Reader DC. User interaction is needed to exploit this vulnerability in that the target must visit a malicious page or open a malicious file. The specific flaw exists within the parsing of JPG2000 images.
  - ("CVE – CVE-2021-40719"[7]). Adobe Connect version 11.2.3 (and earlier) is affected by a 'deserialization of untrusted data' vulnerability to achieve arbitrary method invocation when action message format messages are deserialized on an Adobe Connect server. An attacker can use this to execute remote code execution on the server.
  - ("CVE – CVE-2021-36004"[8]). Adobe InDesign version 16.0 (and earlier) is affected by an 'out-of-bounds write' vulnerability in the CoolType library. An unauthenticated attacker could use this vulnerability to achieve remote code execution in the context of the current user. Exploitation of this issue requires user interaction in that a victim must open a malicious file.

Effective vulnerability management relies on effective asset management and BIA to help ensure that your organization understands the context of the affected assets and the potential impact of this vulnerability leading to the asset being compromised. The greater the perceived risks, the increased need for the prioritization of remediation of these vulnerabilities.

The longer high-risk vulnerabilities stay against high-impact assets, the greater the likelihood that these vulnerabilities could lead to the compromise of an asset, affecting high-impact business operations.

4.3 WHAT IS VULNERABILITY MANAGEMENT?

If you look at the origins of the terms 'vulnerability' and 'management,' you can gain an appreciation of what this means:

Vulnerability (n.)
1767, noun from vulnerable (q.v.).
Entries linking to vulnerability
Vulnerable (adj.)

c. 1600, from Late Latin vulnerabilis "wounding," from Latin vulnerare "to wound, hurt, injure, maim," from vulnus (genitive vulneris) "wound," perhaps related to vellere "pluck, to tear" (see svelte), or from PIE *wele-nes-, from *wele- (2) "to strike, wound" (see Valhalla).

(Source: Online Etymology Dictionary ("Vulnerability | Etymology,
Origin and Meaning of Vulnerability by Etymonline"[9]))

Management (n.)
1590s, "act of managing by direction or manipulation," from manage + -ment. Sense of "act of man aging by physical manipulation" is from 1670s. Meaning "governing body, directors of an undertaking collectively" (originally of a theater) is from 1739.
Entries linking to management

Manage (v.)
Origin and meaning of manage
1560s, "to handle, train, or direct" (a horse), from the now-obsolete noun manage "the handling or training of a horse; horsemanship" (see manege, which is a modern revival of it), from Old French manège "horsemanship," from Italian maneggio, from maneggiare "to handle, touch," especially "to control a horse," which ultimately from Latin noun manus "hand" (from PIE root *man- (2) "hand").

Extended sense of "control or direct by administrative ability" any sort of business is by 1570s; meaning "to wield (a tool or object) by hand" is from 1580s. Meaning "effect by effort" (hence "succeed in accomplishing") is by 1732. Intransitive sense of "get by, carry on affairs" is suggested by 1650s, in frequent use from mid-19c. Related: Managed; managing. Managed economy was used by 1933.

Manage literally implies handling, and hence primarily belongs to smaller concerns, on which one may always keep his hand: as, to manage a house; to manage a theater. Its essential idea is that of constant attention to details: as, only a combination of great abilities with a genius for industry can manage the affairs of an empire. [Century Dictionary]

(Source: Online Etymology Dictionary ("Management | Etymology,
Origin and Meaning of Management by Etymonline"[10]))

There are several industry definitions for vulnerability management, which include the NISTIR 8011, Volume 1, Automation Support for Security Control Assessments (Dempsey et al.[11]) supported by Volume 5 of the Information Security Continuous Monitoring (ISCM) defines this as follows:

An ISCM capability that identifies vulnerabilities [Common Vulnerabilities and Exposures (CVEs)] on devices that are likely to be used by attackers to compromise a device and use it as a platform from which to extend compromise to the network.

According to Techopedia ("What Is Vulnerability Management? – Definition from Techopedia"[12]):

> Vulnerability management is a security practice specifically designed to proactively prevent the exploitation of IT vulnerabilities that could potentially harm a system or organization.
>
> The practice involves identifying, classifying, mitigating, and fixing known vulnerabilities within a system. It is an integral part of computer and network security and plays an important role in IT risk management.

NIST NICE Framework (NIST[13]) states:

> Where a person: Conducts assessments of threats and vulnerabilities, determines deviations from acceptable configurations, enterprise or local policy, assesses the level of risk, and develops and/or recommends appropriate mitigation countermeasures in operational and non-operational situations.

In essence, vulnerability should not be restricted to the identification and prioritization of remediation efforts for IT systems but should be extended to cover any valued asset and should analyze the context of any identified vulnerabilities against the associated asset(s) and their environments, so that remediation can be triaged based upon the perceived risks to the business operations that they support.

Remember, asset management extends beyond just IT systems and includes any asset that is valuable to the business, including people, software, hardware, data, buildings, etc.

To appreciate the risks that a vulnerability presents to your business assets, it is important to understand how the vulnerability scores have been calculated. The Common Vulnerability Scoring System (NIST[14]), scores are *not* your risk scores but are the perceived ratings of the vulnerability (security impact ratings, as depicted in Table 4.1 ("What Is the CVSS (Common Vulnerability Scoring System)?"[15]) and these do *not* reflect how this vulnerability relates to the risk presented to your asset, as the vulnerability score *cannot* reflect your environment, the role of the asset, or where it might be sited.

The CVSS scoring consist of three types of metrics to help supply the calculation ("NVD – CVSS v3 Calculator"[16]):

Table 4.1 Security Impact Ratings

Score	Rating
0.0	None
0.1–3.9	Low
4.0–6.9	Medium
7.0–8.9	High
9.0–10.0	Critical

1. Base score metrics: Depends on sub-formulas for impact sub-score, impact, and exploitability.
2. Temporal score metrics: Equal to a roundup of base score, exploit code maturity, remediation level, and report confidence.
3. Environmental score metrics: Depends on sub-formulas for modified impact sub-score, modified impact, and modified exploitability.
   • The formula for this is Minimum (1 – [(1 – Confidentiality Requirement Modified Confidentiality), (1 – Integrity Requirement × Modified Integrity), (1 – Availability Requirement, Modified Availability)], 0.915).

Within each set of metrics are the following sub-categories:

• Base score metrics: Attack vector, attack complexity, privileges required, user interaction, scope, confidentiality impact, integrity impact, availability impact.
• Temporal score metrics: Exploitability, remediation level, report confidence.
• Environmental score metrics: Attack vector, attack complexity, privileges required, user interaction, scope, confidentiality impact, integrity impact, availability impact, confidentiality requirement, integrity requirement, availability requirement.

The equations for CVSS calculations are shown in Table 4.2.

The vulnerabilities that exist, and which may be impactful on your valued business operations, can be identified through a variety of means, as depicted in Figure 4.1.

4.4 DIFFERENCE BETWEEN RISK-BASED PATCH MANAGEMENT AND RISK-BASED VULNERABILITY MANAGEMENT

Many individuals confuse patch management with vulnerability management. However, it is important to distinguish between these two terms. Patch management is the prioritization of new system/software updates, while vulnerability

Table 4.2 CVSS Equations

CVSS v3.0 Equations	*CVSS v3.1 Equations*
Base:	Base:
The Base Score is a function of the Impact and Exploitability sub score equations. Where the Base score is defined as:	The Base Score is a function of the Impact and Exploitability sub score equations. Where the Base score is defined as:
If (Impact sub score <= 0) 0 else,	*If (Impact sub score <= 0) 0 else,*
Scope Unchanged₄	*Scope Unchanged₄*
Roundup(Minimum[(Impact + Exploitability), 10])	*Roundup(Minimum[(Impact + Exploitability), 10])*
Scope Changed Roundup(Minimum[1.08 × (Impact + Exploitability), 10])	*Scope Changed Roundup(Minimum[1.08 × (Impact + Exploitability), 10])*
and the Impact sub score (ISC) is defined as:	and the Impact sub score (ISC) is defined as:
Scope Unchanged $6.42 \times ISC_{Base}$	*Scope Unchanged* $6.42 \times ISC_{Base}$
Scope Changed $7.52 \times [ISC_{Base} - 0.029] - 3.25 \times [ISC_{Base} - 0.02]^{15}$	*Scope Changed* $7.52 \times [ISC_{Base} - 0.029] - 3.25 \times [ISC_{Base} - 0.02]^{15}$
Where:	Where:
$ISC_{Base} = 1 - [(1 - Impact_{Cont}) \times (1 - Impact_{Integ}) \times (1 - Impact_{Avail})]$	$ISC_{Base} = 1 - [(1 - Impact_{Cont}) \times (1 - Impact_{Integ}) \times (1 - Impact_{Avail})]$
And the Exploitability sub score is, $8.22 \times AttackVector \times AttackComplexity \times PrivilegeRequired \times UserInteraction$	And the Exploitability sub score is, $8.22 \times AttackVector \times AttackComplexity \times PrivilegeRequired \times UserInteraction$
Temporal:	Temporal:
The Temporal score is defined as:	The Temporal score is defined as:
Roundup(BaseScore × ExploitCodeMaturity × RemediationLevel × ReportConfidence)	*Roundup(BaseScore × ExploitCodeMaturity × RemediationLevel × ReportConfidence)*
Environmental:	Environmental:
The environmental score is defined as:	The environmental score is defined as:
If (Modified Impact Sub score <= 0) 0 else,	If (Modified Impact Sub score <= 0) 0 else,
If Modified Scope is Unchanged Round up(Round up (Minimum [(M.Impact + M.Exploitability),10]) × Exploit Code Maturity × Remediation Level × Report Confidence)	If Modified Scope is Unchanged Round up(Round up (Minimum [(M.Impact + M.Exploitability),10]) × Exploit Code Maturity × Remediation Level × Report Confidence)
If Modified Scope is Changed Round up(Round up (Minimum [1.08 × (M.Impact + M.Exploitability),10]) × Exploit Code Maturity × Remediation Level × Report Confidence)	If Modified Scope is Changed Round up(Round up (Minimum [1.08 × (M.Impact + M.Exploitability),10]) × Exploit Code Maturity × Remediation Level × Report Confidence)
And the modified Impact sub score is defined as:	And the modified Impact sub score is defined as:

(Continued)

Table 4.2 (Continued)

CVSS v3.0 Equations	CVSS v3.1 Equations
If Modified Scope is Unchanged 6.42 × $[ISC_{Modified}]$ If Modified Scope is Changed 7.52 × $[ISC_{Modified} - 0.029]$-3.25× $[ISC_{Modified} - 0.02]$ 15 Where: $ISC_{Modified} = Minimum$ [[1 – (1 – M. IConf × CR) × (1 – M. IInteg × IR) × (1 – M. IAvail × AR)], 0.915] The Modified Exploitability sub score is: 8.22 × M. AttackVector × M. AttackComplexity × M. PrivilegeRequired × M. UserInteractionn 4 Where "Round up" is defined as the smallest number, specified to one decimal place, that is equal to or higher than its input. For example, Round up (4.02) is 4.1; and Round up (4.00) is 4.0.	If Modified Scope is Unchanged 6.42 × $[ISC_{Modified}]$ If Modified Scope is Changed 7.52 × $[ISC_{Modified} - 0.029]$-3.25× $[ISC_{Modified} × 0.9731 - 0.02]$ 13 Where: $ISC_{Modified} = Minimum$ [[1 – (1 – M. IConf × CR) × (1 – M. IInteg × IR) × (1 – M. IAvail × AR)], 0.915] The Modified Exploitability sub score is: 8.22 × M. AttackVector × M. AttackComplexity × M. PrivilegeRequired × M. UserInteractionn 4 Where "Round up" is defined as the smallest number, specified to one decimal place, that is equal to or higher than its input. For example, Round up (4.02) is 4.1; and Round up (4.00) is 4.0.

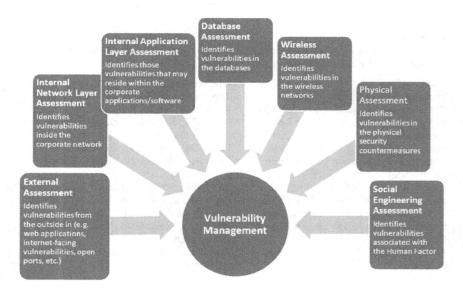

Figure 4.1 Components of vulnerability management.

management is a far broader term (which incorporates patch management), to include systems configuration, user error, antivirus, systems failures, etc.

In NIST's SP800-137: Information Security Continuous Monitoring (ISCM) for Federal Information Systems and Organizations (K. L. Dempsey et al.[17]), patch management is defined as being: "The systematic notification, identification, deployment, installation, and verification of operating system and application software code revisions. These revisions are known as patches, hot fixes, and service packs."

Although patch management is focused on supporting the IT systems and software, it is important to note that a single update/patch may address several vulnerability findings, and the same applies to the hardening of a single asset being able to address multiple identified vulnerabilities.

4.5 APPLYING PROJECT MANAGEMENT TECHNIQUES

One of the easiest approaches to vulnerability management is to apply a formalized project management approach. For me, I apply a Waterfall-based approach, entitled PIE FARM, as depicted in Figure 4.2, (Seaman[18]).

4.5.1 Planning and Preparation

Everything starts with the planning and preparation phase, whereby you work with the business's key stakeholders to gain an understanding of which assets are important to the business (gained from the BIA exercises) and need to have their vulnerabilities managed, so that the perceived risks remain within acceptable tolerances. In this phase you will agree the objectives, the scope, and the strategy of the vulnerability management practice and understand how these fit into and support the overall defensive strategy, as depicted in Figure 4.3 (DoD IACs[19]).

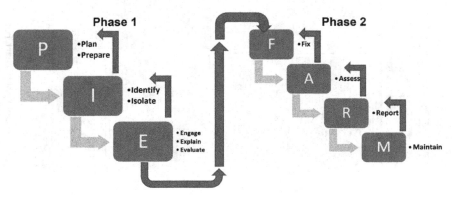

Figure 4.2 PIE FARM.

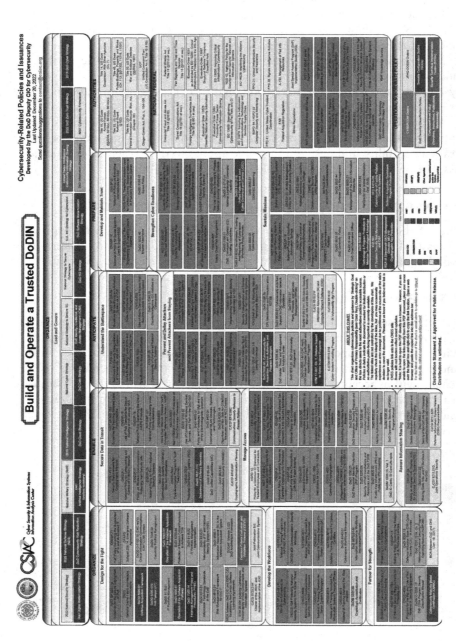

Figure 4.3 DoD policy chart. For a full version of this chart please visit https://dodiac.dtic.mil/wp-content/uploads/2021/09/2021-09-8-csiac-dod-cybersecurity-policy-chart_UpdatedDTIClogo.pdf

4.5.2 Identify

The next phase involves the use of the asset management practice to show all the assets associated with the scope, so that any identified vulnerabilities can have their remediation activities prioritized based on their perceived value to the business.

- Which assets do you need to evaluate for vulnerabilities?
- How often?
- Which tools might you use? For example:
  - Digital footprint scanners.
  - Security Content Automation Protocol Validation Program-approved (Computer Security Division[20]) vulnerability scanners.
  - Network configuration audit scanners.
  - System configuration scanners.
  - Network ports scan ("Port Scanning Basics | Nmap Network Scanning"[21]).
  - Network ports database ("SG TCP/IP Ports Database"[22]).

Criminals will commonly scan for vulnerable ports that they can exploit. Consequently, it is important for you to identify these ports (before they do) and to understand the associated risks. For example:

- An open remote desktop protocol (RDP) port, such as led to be the potential root cause of Honda's ransomware attack (Threat Intelligence Team[23]).
- RDP uses port number 3389 for local area network (internal/private) traffic (as depicted in Figures 4.4 & 4.5) and port 3390 for wide area network (internet/public) traffic. If you need to allow RDP into a firewall policy, then these are the ports you need to use for allowing RDP connections or for blocking.
- The Microsoft Windows – BlueKeep RDP Remote Windows Kernel Use After Free (Metasploit[24]), (NIST, "NVD – CVE-2019-0708"[25]) vulnerability is associated with the port.

4.5.3 Evaluate, Engage, and Explain

Having created the strategy, named the scope, set the objectives, and identified the assets to be covered by the vulnerability management practices, next is the need to engage with the stakeholders to explain the purpose of the vulnerability management evaluation and to define the expectations.

This is all about understanding the context of the environment for which the vulnerabilities are associated, so that the remediation efforts can be better prioritized based upon their perceived risks, such as location on the

Port 3389 Details

threat/application/port search:

[   ] [🔍 SEARCH]

known port assignments and vulnerabilities

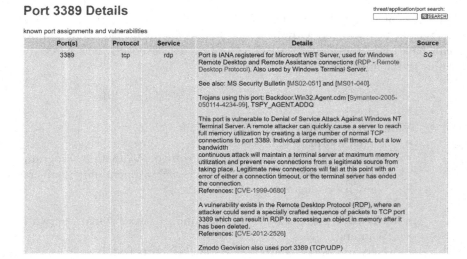

Port(s)	Protocol	Service	Details	Source
3389	tcp	rdp	Port is IANA registered for Microsoft WBT Server, used for Windows Remote Desktop and Remote Assistance connections (RDP - Remote Desktop Protocol). Also used by Windows Terminal Server. See also: MS Security Bulletin [MS02-051] and [MS01-040]. Trojans using this port: Backdoor.Win32.Agent.cdm [Symantec-2005-050114-4234-99], TSPY_AGENT.ADDQ This port is vulnerable to Denial of Service Attack Against Windows NT Terminal Server. A remote attacker can quickly cause a server to reach full memory utilization by creating a large number of normal TCP connections to port 3389. Individual connections will timeout, but a low bandwidth continuous attack will maintain a terminal server at maximum memory utilization and prevent new connections from a legitimate source from taking place. Legitimate new connections will fail at this point with an error of either a connection timeout, or the terminal server has ended the connection. References: [CVE-1999-0680] A vulnerability exists in the Remote Desktop Protocol (RDP), where an attacker could send a specially crafted sequence of packets to TCP port 3389 which can result in RDP to accessing an object in memory after it has been deleted. References: [CVE-2012-2526] Zmodo Geovision also uses port 3389 (TCP/UDP)	SG

Figure 4.4 Port 3389.

Port 3390 Details

threat/application/port search:

[   ] [🔍 SEARCH]

known port assignments and vulnerabilities

Port(s)	Protocol	Service	Details	Source
3390	tcp	trojans	Backdoor.Dawcun [Symantec-2010-040116-0914-99] (2010.04.01) - a trojan horse that steals confidential information and opens a back door on the compromised computer. It opens a back door by connecting to a remote server on TCP ports 2266 and 3390 to send the confidential information and to download, decrypt and then start the updated rootkit driver. Hitachi IP5000 VOIP WIFI Phone 1.5.6 does not allow the user to disable access to (1) SNMP or (2) TCP port 3390, which allows remote attackers to modify configuration using [CVE-2005-3722], or access the Unidata Shell to obtain sensitive information or cause a denial of service. References: [CVE-2005-3723] [SECUNIA-17628] Port is also IANA registered for Distributed Service Coordinator	SG

Figure 4.5 Port 3390.

network (perimeter being a higher risk than the assets residing deep inside the network, e.g., deep inside the network, behind securely configured network security control devices and network segments), the role of the IT system (e.g., domain controller), and/or whether the IT asset is involved with the processing, storage, or processing of sensitive data.

4.5.4 Fix

The output from the vulnerability evaluations will show any known vulnerabilities that need to be prioritized, based upon the perceived risks, to ensure that the vulnerabilities are remediated promptly but with a minimal impact on the affected business operations. In complex environments, this may mean getting the business to agree to the inclusion of prioritized remediation within their maintenance windows/shutdowns.

An important part of this stage is engaging with the system or business owners to create a collaborative approach, whereby mitigation SLAs can be defined and established, with the system/business owners feeling that they are working with the information security teams to effectively minimize the risk exposure from any identified vulnerabilities or missing system updates.

4.5.5 Assess

Following any remediation activities, it is essential that the assets are reassessed to ensure that the activities have been effective. Finding the root cause of a vulnerability can aid the business to ensure that any replication or reoccurrence is avoided or reduced.

4.5.6 Report

Do not let all your efforts go unnoticed. Ensure that effective reporting is created to show which vulnerabilities have been remediated against and which vulnerabilities remain, and the schedule for completing remediation. Where vulnerabilities cannot be remediated against, without affecting business operations, you need to ensure that the asset owners, asset custodians, and risk owners are made aware. This will help to ensure that they remain informed and will allow for risk assessments.

4.5.7 Maintain

The very nature of business means that the supporting infrastructure will be dynamic and will be subject to numerous changes, which could affect the business's important assets and operations. Consequently, it is especially important that continuous operations are applied to help maintain your vulnerabilities estate.

When keeping your vulnerabilities, it is important to be mindful of the disruptive nature that vulnerability and patch management may present. Therefore, you may wish to consider developing a 'pilot group,' using lower-valued (but equivalent) assets. This 'pilot group' can then be used to trial/test the impact of any newly applied updates. However, before rolling out any recent updates, you should risk-assess the updates (consider delaying the rollout of any updates to allow time for any reporting of any issues (e.g., Microsoft Print Spooler problems ("Clarified Guidance for CVE-2021-34527 Windows Print Spooler Vulnerability – Microsoft Security Response Center"[26])) to be included and discuss with the key stakeholders any rollback choices. Once you are suitably assured that the update will present a minimal risk of disruption to their associated business operations, you can confidently schedule the remediation activities.

4.6 WHEN RISK-BASED VULNERABILITY MANAGEMENT BITES BACK

In December 2021, there was a global panic, as businesses across the world entered the 'firefighting paradox' as they became alerted to a new vulnerability ("Apache Log4j Vulnerability Guidance | CISA"[27]). This was related to a remote code executable vulnerability (CVE-2021-44228 ("Offensive Security's Exploit Database Archive"[28]) within the Apache Log4j software ("Log4j – Apache Log4j Security Vulnerabilities"[29]).

The problem was that to ensure these global businesses were not going to become the next victim of this vulnerability, they needed to understand how this vulnerability worked ("CVE-2021-44228: Proof-of-Concept for Critical Apache Log4j Remote Code Execution Vulnerability Available (Log4Shell)"[30]) and which of their business assets/operations used the Apache Log4j software and were vulnerable, as depicted in the CISA flow chart at Figure 4.6 ("Apache Log4j Vulnerability Guidance | CISA"[31]).

Helpfully, the CISA supplied some extensive support material ("CISA Log4j (CVE-2021-44228) Vulnerability Guidance"[32]) and published a list of software and vendors ("CISA Log4j (CVE-2021-44228) Vulnerability Guidance"[33]) that have been identified as being affected by this vulnerability (extract shown in Table 4.3).

However, without effective BIA and asset management practices, the pressure to discover which of the organization's business-valued operations were reliant on any applications that were affected by this vulnerability became increasingly more difficult to evaluate.

- What about those valued business services that have been outsourced?
- Are they using vulnerable applications?

Despite this vulnerability having not been as impactful as the world (Stokel-Walker[34]) and the security industry (Nayyar[35]) had initially imagined, only a limited number of threat actors (e.g., 'script kiddies,' an Iranian hacking group known as APT 35 or "Charming Kitty"(Sganga[36]), Ukraine (Kovacs[37]), etc.) are known to have exploited this particular vulnerability. However, with having the potential to impact a wide variety and large volumes of assets and with the threat actors looking to utilize this vulnerability as a new way of initiating ransomware attacks (Tung[38]), it is predicted that this will impact businesses for many years to come (Gately[39]).

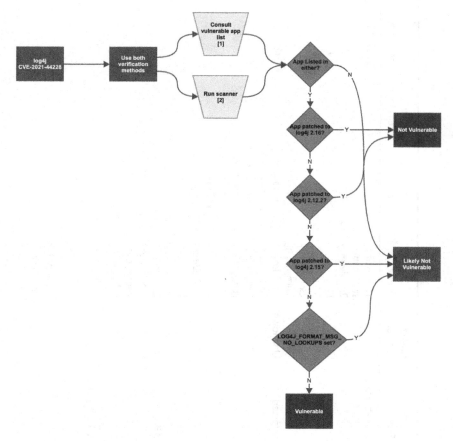

Figure 4.6 CISA log4j flow chart.

4.7 DECODING RISK-BASED VULNERABILITY MANAGEMENT

Through the application of a risk-based approach to vulnerability management, you can gain a better understanding of which 'fires' (vulnerabilities) need to be prioritized ahead of the others to help reduce the risks to your most valued business assets/operations. This will ensure that any identified 'fires' that are the most impactful are extinguished ahead of the others. It is important to appreciate that the feeling of each 'fire' is heavily dependent on the understanding of both the BIAs and the asset management practice. Without this, a CVSS security impact rating might show that a 'fire' is large and needs to be prioritized. However, when evaluated against your business

Table 4.3 Extract from CISA List

Vendor	Product	Version(s)	Status	Update Available	Vendor Link	Notes	Other References	Last Updated
IPassword	All products		Not affected		IPassword statement			12123/2021
2n					2n Advisory Link			
3CX					3CX Community Thread Link			
3M Health Information Systems	CGS		Affected	Unknown	CGS. Log4j Software Updated(login required)	This advisory is available to customer only and has not been reviewed by CISA.		12/15/2021
7-Zip					7Zip Discussion Link			
ABB	ABB Remote Service	ABB Remote Platform (RAP)	Affected		ABB Link			
ABB					Details are shared with active subscribers			
ABB	AlamInsight Cold	AlamInsight KPI Dashboards 1.0.0	Under Investigation					
ABB	B&R Products	See Vendor Advisory			BR-Automation Advisory			

Abbott		Not affected			Abbott Advisory Link	12/15/2021
Abnormal Security	Abnormal Security Accellence				Abnormal Slog	
					ACSAREara Article	
Accellion	Kiteworks	Fixed	v7.6 release	Yes	Kiteworks Statement	12/16/2021
					"As a precaution, Kiteworks released a 7.6.1 Hotfix software update to address the vulnerability. This patch release adds the mitigation for CVE-	

environment and infrastructure, this may be less impactful and smaller 'fires' (lower security-impact vulnerabilities) may need to be prioritized, when they are associated with higher-valued business assets/operations.

This can lead to a failure to appreciate that not all 'fires' are the same and that a risk-based approach is essential to reduce the feeling of this being a 'firefighting paradox' or of this being an impossible situation/task.

Vulnerability management must never be a case of just pointing out to the business's key stakeholders that they have several 'fires' that need to be extinguished, but that the context needs to be provided so that informed risk-based decisions can be made on how these can be prioritized for remediation. Vulnerability management should always be treated as a team effort and never as a 'finger-pointing exercise.'

There will be occasions and situations when high-risk 'fires' cannot be extinguished in line with the corporate policies and procedures. However, a risk balance case should be presented so that the business's key stakeholders can agree on a suitable remediation approach and approve deadlines (temporary risk response options may need to be applied for prolonged periods). This should be treated as a short-term exception and should never become the norm.

By applying a formal and defined project management-style approach to vulnerability management, you will be able to help ensure that a methodical approach is applied for the identification, prioritization, and remediation of the vulnerabilities to your business.

Rather than trying to remediate everything or feeling like this is an unachievable task, the vulnerability efforts will be shown against the context of your business, rather than based upon generic security impact ratings (CVSS).

Notes

1 "Open Fractures – OrthoInfo – AAOS." www.orthoinfo.org, orthoinfo.aaos. org/en/diseases--conditions/open-fractures
2 "Lateral Movement, Tactic TA0008 – Enterprise I MITRE ATT&CK®." Attack. mitre.org, attack.mitre.org/tactics/TA0008. Accessed 7 Jan. 2022.
3 "Remote Service Session Hijacking, Technique T1563 – Enterprise I MITRE ATT&CK®." Attack.mitre.org, attack.mitre.org/techniques/T1563. Accessed 7 Jan. 2022.
4 "Remote Services, Technique T1021 – Enterprise I MITRE ATT&CK®." Attack. mitre.org, attack.mitre.org/techniques/T1021. Accessed 7 Jan. 2022.
5 "CVE – Search Results." Cve.mitre.org, cve.mitre.org/cgi-bin/cvekey. cgi?keyword=adobe. Accessed 7 Jan. 2022.
6 "CVE – CVE-2021-40730." Cve.mitre.org, cve.mitre.org/cgi-bin/cvename. cgi?name=CVE-2021-40730. Accessed 7 Jan. 2022.
7 "CVE – CVE-2021-40719." Cve.mitre.org, cve.mitre.org/cgi-bin/cvename. cgi?name=CVE-2021-40719. Accessed 7 Jan. 2022.

8 "CVE – CVE-2021-36004." Cve.mitre.org, cve.mitre.org/cgi-bin/cvename. cgi?name=CVE-2021-36004. Accessed 7 Jan. 2022.

9 "Vulnerability | Etymology, Origin and Meaning of Vulnerability by Etymonline." www.etymonline.com, www.etymonline.com/word/vulnerability#etymonl ine_v_50006. Accessed 7 Jan. 2022.

10 "Management | Etymology, Origin and Meaning of Management by Etymonline." www.etymonline.com, www.etymonline.com/word/management#etymonline_ v_6770. Accessed 7 Jan. 2022.

11 Dempsey, Kelley, et al. Automation Support for Security Control Assessments. Volume 1: Overview. June 2017, nvlpubs.nist.gov/nistpubs/ir/2017/NIST. IR.8011-1.pdf, 10.6028/nist.ir.8011-1

12 "What Is Vulnerability Management? – Definition from Techopedia." Techopedia.com, www.techopedia.com/definition/16172/vulnerability-man agement

13 NIST. "NICE Framework Resource Center." 13 Nov. 2019, www.nist.gov/itl/ applied-cybersecurity/nice/nice-framework-resource-center

14 NIST. "NVD – Vulnerability Metrics." Nist.gov, 2019, nvd.nist.gov/vuln-metrics/cvss

15 "What Is the CVSS (Common Vulnerability Scoring System)?" SearchSecurity, www.techtarget.com/searchsecurity/definition/CVSS-Common-Vulnerability-Scoring-System

16 "NVD – CVSS v3 Calculator." Nvd.nist.gov, nvd.nist.gov/vuln-metrics/cvss/ v3-calculator

17 Dempsey, K L, et al. Information Security Continuous Monitoring (ISCM) for Federal Information Systems and Organizations. 2011, csrc.nist.gov/ publications/detail/sp/800-137/final, 10.6028/nist.sp.800-137

18 Seaman, Jim. "PIE FARM – a Project Managed Approach to PCI DSS." *PCI DSS*, 2020, pp. 359–384, 10.1007/978-1-4842-5808-8_12. Accessed 7 Jan. 2022.

19 DoD IACs. "DoD Cybersecurity Policy Chart – DoD IACs." Dtic.mil, 2021, dodiac.dtic.mil/dod-cybersecurity-policy-chart. Accessed 7 Jan. 2022.

20 Computer Security Division, Information Technology Laboratory. "SCAP Validated Products and Modules – Security Content Automation Protocol Validation Program | CSRC | CSRC." CSRC | NIST, 6 Nov. 2017, csrc.nist.gov/ projects/scap-validation-program/validated-products-and-modules. Accessed 7 Jan. 2022.

21 "Port Scanning Basics | Nmap Network Scanning." Nmap.org, 2020, nmap.org/ book/man-port-scanning-basics.html

22 "SG TCP/IP Ports Database." SpeedGuide, 2021, www.speedguide.net/ports.php

23 Threat Intelligence Team. "Honda Cyber Attack: Honda & Enel Cyber Attacked by Ransomware." Malwarebytes Labs, 10 June 2020, blog.malwarebytes.com/ threat-analysis/2020/06/honda-and-enel-impacted-by-cyber-attack-suspected-to-be-ransomware. Accessed 7 Jan. 2022.

24 Metasploit. "Microsoft Windows – BlueKeep RDP Remote Windows Kernel Use after Free (Metasploit)." *Exploit Database*, 24 Sept. 2019, www.exploit-db.com/exploits/47416. Accessed 25 Jan. 2022.

25 NIST. "NVD – CVE-2019-0708." Nist.gov, 2019, nvd.nist.gov/vuln/detail/ CVE-2019-0708

26 "Clarified Guidance for CVE-2021-34527 Windows Print Spooler Vulnerability – Microsoft Security Response Center." Msrc-Blog.microsoft.com, 2021, msrc-blog.microsoft.com/2021/07/08/clarified-guidance-for-cve-2021-34527-windows-print-spooler-vulnerability. Accessed 7 Jan. 2022.

27 "Apache Log4j Vulnerability Guidance | CISA." www.cisa.gov, Dec. 2021, www.cisa.gov/uscert/apache-log4j-vulnerability-guidance

28 "Offensive Security's Exploit Database Archive." www.exploit-Db.com, 2021, www.exploit-db.com/search?cve=2021-44228. Accessed 7 Jan. 2022.

29 "Log4j – Apache Log4j Security Vulnerabilities." Logging.apache.org, Dec. 2021, logging.apache.org/log4j/2.x/security.html

30 "CVE-2021-44228: Proof-of-Concept for Critical Apache Log4j Remote Code Execution Vulnerability Available (Log4Shell)." Tenable®, 10 Dec. 2021, www.tenable.com/blog/cve-2021-44228-proof-of-concept-for-critical-apache-log4j-remote-code-execution-vulnerability. Accessed 7 Jan. 2022.

31 "Apache Log4j Vulnerability Guidance | CISA." www.cisa.gov, 2021, www.cisa.gov/uscert/apache-log4j-vulnerability-guidance

32 "CISA Log4j (CVE-2021-44228) Vulnerability Guidance." GitHub, 6 Jan. 2022, github.com/cisagov/log4j-affected-db. Accessed 7 Jan. 2022.

33 "CISA Log4j (CVE-2021-44228) Vulnerability Guidance." GitHub, 6 Jan. 2022, github.com/cisagov/log4j-affected-db/blob/develop/SOFTWARE-LIST.md. Accessed 7 Jan. 2022.

34 Stokel-Walker, Chris. "The FTC Wants Companies to Find Log4j Fast. It Won't Be So Easy." Wired, 10 Jan. 2022, www.wired.com/story/lo4j-ftc-vulnerability. Accessed 22 Jan. 2022.

35 Nayyar, Saryu. "The Log4j Vulnerability Puts Pressure on the Security World." Threatpost.com, 18 Jan. 2022, threatpost.com/log4j-vulnerability-pressures-security-world/177721. Accessed 22 Jan. 2022.

36 Sganga, Nicole. "Nightmare Before Christmas: What to Know About the Log4j Vulnerability." www.cbsnews.com, 17 Dec. 2021, www.cbsnews.com/news/log4j-vulnerability-breach-patch. Accessed 22 Jan. 2022.

37 Kovacs, Eduard. "Ukraine Attacks Involved Exploitation of Log4j, October CMS Vulnerabilities | SecurityWeek.com." www.securityweek.com, 19 Jan. 2022, www.securityweek.com/ukraine-attacks-involved-exploitation-log4j-october-cms-vulnerabilities. Accessed 22 Jan. 2022.

38 Tung, Liam. "Ransomware: Hackers Are Using Log4j Flaw as Part of Their Attacks, Warns Microsoft." ZDNet, 11 Jan. 2022, www.zdnet.com/article/ransomware-warning-hackers-are-using-log4j-flaw-as-part-of-their-attacks-warns-microsoft. Accessed 22 Jan. 2022.

39 Gately, Edward. "Log4j Vulnerabilities Threaten All Industries, Verticals Globally." Channel Futures, 5 Jan. 2022, www.channelfutures.com/mssp-insider/log4j-vulnerabilities-threaten-all-industries-verticals-globally. Accessed 22 Jan. 2022.

Chapter 5

Threat Management

5.1 A FARMING ANALOGY

Imagine that you are a livestock farmer. Your livestock would be a critical asset to your business being profitable and these assets require considerable investment of time, effort, and resources across their lifecycles, before being taken to market to be sold. Should any of these livestock assets be harmed it would have an impact on the profitability of the farmer's business. Consequently, as a farmer, you would naturally be knowledgeable of the threats that could impact on your investments.

A farmer would look at the local environment, as well as any incidents being reported by both the industry ("Antimicrobial Resistance in Livestock: The Invisible Threat | Agrilinks[1]) and other farmers. In addition, you would be keeping abreast of any legislative or regulatory changes ("Proposed Animal Transport Rules a Major Threat to Calf Trade – IFA"[2]) that might impact your business.

Once you understand the threats that are relevant to your farm, you are then able to make informed decisions on whether further mitigation measures are required. For example, if you are a farmer in the UK you would not be worried by the threat presented by wolves (Associated Press[3]). However, you might still be worried about the threat of stray dogs attacking your sheep (MSN[4]), loose livestock being hit by motor vehicles (Linn County Journal[5]), livestock being poisoned (Minot Daily News[6]) or livestock theft (RCW 9A.56.080[7]).

In response to such threats, as the farmer, you are likely to carry out a formal business impact and vulnerability analysis to help you decide your risks and whether you need to formulate a suitable risk response.

This approach should be applied to any type of business and especially any business wishing to safeguard its business essential/valued assets.

DOI: 10.1201/9781003288084-7

5.2 INTRODUCTION TO THREAT MANAGEMENT

Businesses frequently confuse risks with threats, and being that threats are a component of your risks it is particularly important to understand the origins and differences between these two terms.

One of the most suitable definitions for a threat is provided by the Cambridge Dictionary (Cambridge Dictionary[8]): "The possibility that something unwanted will happen, or a person or thing that is likely to cause something unwanted to happen."

5.2.1 Term Origins

risk (n.)
1660s, risqué, "hazard, danger, peril, exposure to mischance or harm," from French risqué (16c.), from Italian risco, riscio (modern rischio), from riscare "run into danger," a word of uncertain origin.

The Englished spelling is recorded by 1728. Spanish riesgo and German Risiko are Italian loan-words. The commercial sense of "hazard of the loss of a ship, goods, or other properties" is by 1719; hence the extension to "chance taken in an economic enterprise."

Paired with run (v.) from 1660s. Risk aversion is recorded from 1942; risk factor from 1906; risk management from 1963; risk-taker from 1892.

risk (v.)
1680s, "expose to chance of injury or loss," from risk (n.), or from French risquer, from Italian riscare, rischaire, from the noun. By 1705 as "venture upon, take the chances of." Related: Risked; risks; risking.
(Source: Etymology Online Dictionary ("Risk | Etymology, Origin and Meaning of Risk by Etymonline"[9]))

Threat (n.)
Old English þreat "crowd, troop," also "oppression, coercion, menace," related to þreotan "to trouble, weary," from Proto-Germanic *thrautam (source also of Dutch verdrieten, German verdrießen "to vex"), from PIE *treud- "to push, press squeeze" (source also of Latin trudere "to press, thrust," Old Church Slavonic trudu "oppression," Middle Irish trott "quarrel, conflict," Middle Welsh cythrud "torture, torment, afflict"). Sense of "conditional declaration of hostile intention" was in Old English.
(Source: Etymology Online Dictionary ("Threat | Etymology, Origin and Meaning of Threat by Etymonline"[10]))

As you can see from the origins of these terms, threats are the circumstances, events, or actions that are perceived to have an impact, whereas risks are the perceptions of the impacts that may be created from any perceived threats and likelihoods. Consequently, these terms have distinctly different definitions.

5.2.2 Term Definitions

Risk:

> The level of impact on organizational operations (including mission, functions, image, or reputation), organizational assets, or individuals resulting from the operation of an information system given the potential impact of a threat and the likelihood of that threat occurring.
>
> (Source: Federal Information Processing Standards (FIPS) 200 (Gutierrez and Jeffrey[11]))

Threat:

> Any circumstance or event with the potential to adversely impact organizational operations (including mission, functions, image, or reputation), organizational assets, individuals, other organizations, or the Nation through an information system via unauthorized access, destruction, disclosure, modification of information, and/or denial of service.
>
> (Source: NIST SP800-37 Rev 2 – Risk Management Framework for Information Systems and Organizations: A System Life Cycle Approach for Security and Privacy (NIST[12]))

This concept is well explained in RiskLens' 'Bald Tire' Risk scenario (Jones[13]), where Jack Jones goes on to break down the risk scenario for a bald car tire. In this White Paper, Jones supplies the following useful definitions:

Threat
A reasonable definition for Threat is anything (e.g., object, substance, human, etc.) that can act against an asset in a manner that can result in harm. A tornado is a threat, as is a flood, as is a hacker. The key consideration is that threats apply the force (water, wind, exploit code, etc.) against an asset that can cause a loss event to occur.

Vulnerability
You may have wondered why "potential" is emphasized when I identified the frayed rope as a potential vulnerability. The reason it's only a potential vulnerability is that we first have to ask the question, "Vulnerable to what?" If our frayed rope still had a tensile strength of 2000 pounds per square inch, its vulnerability to the weight of a tire would, for all practical purposes, be virtually zero. If our scenario had included a squirrel gnawing on the frayed rope, then he also would be considered a threat,

and the rope's hardness would determine its vulnerability to that threat. A steel cable – even a frayed one – would not be particularly vulnerable to our furry friend. The point is that vulnerability is always dependent upon the type and level of force being applied.

Asset

In the context of information risk, we can define Asset as any data, device, or other component of the environment that supports information-related activities, which can be illicitly accessed, used, disclosed, altered, destroyed, and/or stolen, resulting in loss. The question is often asked whether corporate reputation is an asset. Clearly, reputation is an important asset to an organization, yet it doesn't qualify as an information asset given our definition. Yes, reputation can be damaged, but that is a downstream outcome of an event rather than the primary asset within an event. For example, reputation damage can result from public disclosure of sensitive customer information, but the primary asset in such an event is the customer information.

Risk

The following definition applies regardless of whether you're talking about investment risk, market risk, credit risk, information risk, or any of the other commonly referenced risk domains:

Risk – The probable frequency and probable magnitude of future loss

In other words – how often something bad is likely to happen, and how much loss is likely to result. As stated above, these probabilities are derived from the combination of threat, vulnerability, and asset characteristics.

Immediately in this risk scenario you might be drawn into thinking about the threats and risks associated with this bald car tire being fitted to a motor vehicle:

- Asset – vehicle tire
- Threat – loss of traction to the vehicle
- Risk – vehicle crashing
- Impact – serious injury or death of the vehicle occupants

However, for this risk scenario, the bald car tire is not fitted to a vehicle but part of a rope swing. Suddenly, the perceptions of the threats, risks, and impacts are altered.

Consequently, when communicating risk to your business leadership teams, the context of the asset, the threats, its vulnerabilities, and the potential impacts become increasingly important aspects.

Let's look another couple of risk scenarios.

5.2.3 Knife Crime

It has been reported in the UK that there is an increased risk of becoming a victim of a knife attack ("The Consequences of Knife Crime"[14]). This risk is significantly increased if you also carry a knife, but what constitutes the risks associated with knife crime?

- Asset – the person (you, your family, etc.).
- Threat – the person carrying and using the knife (this could be both the aggressor or the defender); being a member of a street gang; carrying valuable and attractive items (e.g., theft); walking through a street gang area.
- Vulnerability – the penetrability of your skin; ability to defend against knife attacks; ability to get to emergency care.
- Impact – the vital organs may be injured, leading to serious injury or even death.

5.3 THREAT MODELING

Toolbox defines threat modeling as being:

> The process of proactively identifying and addressing potential threats to an organization's systems based on inputs from both business and technical stakeholders.
>
> It is usually done while designing a product or a new feature to avoid the costs of security breaches in the future.
>
> (Source: Toolbox ("What Is Threat Modeling? Definition, Process, Examples, and Best Practices"[15]))

This is your attempt to incorporate threat identification and mitigation into the design and build process so that new or known threats are prevented from being built and implemented into the new business systems or software. Additionally, this can be incorporated into the risk assessments of your business's valued operations and assets, ensuring that you investigate and show any known, emerging, or developing threat vectors.

Note: It is important to remember that not all threats originate from outside the organization and that risks can present themselves, caused by occurrence from within your business. In fact, you may even see this as being every risk has a root cause that originates from inside your business: For example:

- A user clicking on a malicious link or downloading a harmful application.
- The IT department falling to patch a valued IT system.

Figure 5.1 Organized criminal group hierarchy.

Table 5.1 Traditional vs Non-Traditional Threats

Traditional	Non-Traditional
Terrorism	Theft
Espionage *(including industrial)*	Loss
Sabotage	Human error *(e.g., data leakages)*
Subversion	Natural disaster *(e.g., fire, flood, earthquake)*
State-sponsored	Failed procedures
Organized crime	Outages
	Amateur hacker
	Fraud
	Criminal damage

Threats can be categorized as being traditional or non-traditional, with the traditional threats being given the TESS(SS)OC acronym ("TESSOC – Terrorism Espionage Subversion Sabotage Organised Crime | AcronymFinder"[16]). You will notice that I have added (SS) to reflect the changing nature of the threat landscapes, where highly skilled and resourced attackers have nation state support.

Traditional threats tend to be those threat actors that are well organized and have found their targets, such as the organized crime move into cyber-crime ("NCSC Publishes New Report on Criminal Online Activity"[17]) and who work as part of a team (as depicted in Figure 5.1).

Non-traditional threats are impactful events or incidents that are caused by unintentional or amateur actions or events, such as the impact caused by an opportunist thief stealing a corporate laptop. "The average value of a lost laptop is $49,246" (Ponemon Institute LLC[18]).

A breakdown of the different category of threats is shown in Table 5.1.

Often, organizations will focus on identifying the traditional threats but will overlook or fail to implement sufficient measures to mitigate the non-traditional threats.

As an example, by looking into the specific threats to a corporate network, you will see that (as depicted in Figure 5.2 (GeeksforGeeks)[19]) these are categorized into two types:

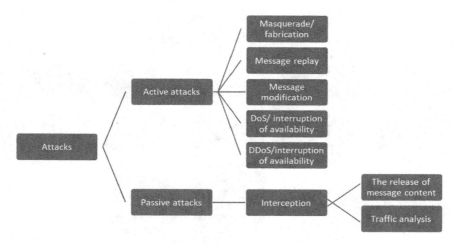

Figure 5.2 Active vs passive attacks.

1. Active Attacks
    This involves the unauthorized change of the system attempted. For example:
    *   Masquerade attacks ("What Is a Masquerade Attack? – Definition from Techopedia"[20]).
    *   Message replay attacks ("Replay Attack"[21]).
    *   Message modification attacks (York, Chapter 3, 41–69[22]).
    *   Denial-of-service attacks (Cybersecurity & Infrastructure Security Agency[23]).
    *   Distributed denial-of-service attacks (Health-ISAC[24]).
2. Passive Attacks
    The interception of sensitive data without the need for any modification.

5.4 ATTACK TREE THREAT ANALYSIS

An attack tree is a method for visualizing your valued business environments against the tactics and techniques employed by the threat actors, who may wish to target and exploit your type of organization.

In such threat analysis, you are seeking to document and visualize the perceived prerequisites of a successful attack (Ingoldsby[25]). An example of an attack tree model is shown at Figure 5.3 ("Attack Tree Diagrams and Application Security Testing | Synopsys"[26]), which shows a simple attack tree based on the Oceans Eleven's plans to rob the Casino:

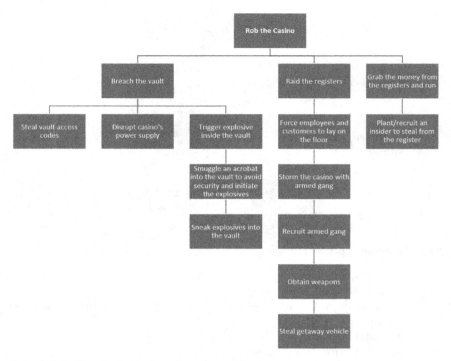

Figure 5.3 Robbing a casino.

Figure 5.4 ("Attack Tree Modeling in AttackTree", Free Trial[27]) shows an example of the potential attack surfaces and vectors related to the unauthorized access to a corporate network.

You are looking to think like your enemies so that you can understand and visualize how an attack might look.

This is something that was articulated by the Chinese military strategist, Sun Tzu (Sun Tzu, 2019[28]): "Though the enemy be stronger in numbers, we may prevent him from fighting. Scheme so as to discover his plans and the likelihood of their success."

For me, this is an area that I believe penetration testing would benefit from, so that rather than just reporting of the identified vulnerabilities, these vulnerabilities are articulated and visualized through an attack tree.

5.5 MITRE ATT&CK® THREAT FRAMEWORK

When looking to understand some of the tactics used by your attackers, there are several paid for as well as free resources that you can use. The MITRE

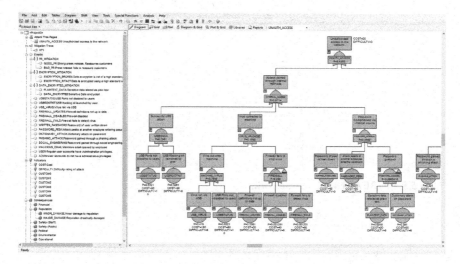

Figure 5.4 Unauthorized access to network attack.

ATT&CK® Threat Matrix ("Matrix – Enterprise | MITRE ATT&CK®"[29]) is a great resource to start with.

5.5.1 Navigating the MITRE ATT&CK® Threat Matrix

Along the top of the website, you will see the following tabulated pages:

- Matrices
- Tactics
  - Enterprise
  - Mobile
- Techniques
  - Enterprise
  - Mobile
- Data Sources
- Mitigations
  - Enterprise
  - Mobile
- Groups
- Software
- Resources
  - General information
  - Getting started.

Figure 5.5 MITRE ATT&CK® framework.

- Training
- ATT&CKcon
- Working with ATT&CK
- FAQ
- Updates
- Versions of ATT&CK
- Related projects
- Blog
- Contribute
- Search

Down the left-hand side, you can filter the matrices based upon your environment, as depicted in Figure 5.5.
For example:

- Enterprise: The tactics and techniques representing the MITRE ATT&CK® Matrix for Enterprise. The matrix contains information for the following platforms: Windows, macOS, Linux, PRE, Azure AD, Office 365, Google Workspace, SaaS, IaaS, Network, Containers.
    - PRE (Pennington[30]): The tactics and techniques representing the MITRE ATT&CK® Matrix for enterprise covering preparatory techniques. The matrix contains information for the PRE platform.
    - Windows: The tactics and techniques representing the MITRE ATT&CK® Matrix for enterprise. The matrix contains information for the Windows platform.
    - macOS: The tactics and techniques representing the MITRE ATT&CK® Matrix for enterprise. The matrix contains information for the macOS platform.

- Linux. The tactics and techniques representing the MITRE ATT&CK® Matrix for enterprise. The matrix contains information for the Linux platform.
- Cloud. The tactics and techniques representing the MITRE ATT&CK® Matrix for enterprise covering cloud-based techniques. The matrix contains information for the following platforms: Azure AD, Office 365, Google Workspace, SaaS, IaaS.
  - Office 365
  - Azure AD
  - Google Workspace
  - SaaS
  - IaaS
  - Network
  - Containers
- Mobile: The tactics and techniques representing the two MITRE ATT&CK® Matrices for mobile. The matrices cover techniques involving device access and network-based effects that can be used by adversaries without device access. The matrices contain information for the following platforms: Android, iOS.
- ICS ("Attackics"[31]). A knowledge base useful for describing the actions an adversary may take while operating within an ICS network. The knowledge base can be used to better characterize and describe post-compromise adversary behavior.

There are two views available to you when investigating the tactics and techniques used by known advanced persistent threat (APT) groups. You can do this manually through the interactive ATT&CK matrices or through the more automated and interactive ATT&CK Navigator ("ATT&CK® Navigator"[32]). In the ATT&CK Navigator, you can filter the matrices based upon your specific environments, as shown in Figures 5.6 & 5.7.

The interactive nature of the MITRE ATT&CK® platforms also allows you to start in the MITRE ATT&CK® matrices and instantly transfer across to view this in the Navigator platform, as shown in Figure 5.8 for APT41 ("APT 41 GROUP"[33]).

A further complementary resource, which aligns the MITRE ATT&CK® Threat Framework to the Center for Internet Security 18 Critical Security Controls (CIS 18 CSCs ("The 18 CIS Controls")[34]), is the CIS attack cards. These are included in the CIS's Community Defense Model ("Blog | CIS Introduces V2.0 of the CIS Community Defense Model"[35]), and with an example shown at Figure 5.9 (e.g., ransomware being mapped to 229 unique ATT&CK (Sub-Techniques)).

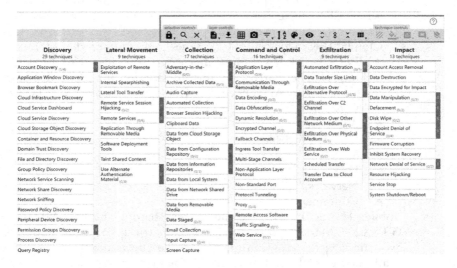

Figure 5.6 MITRE ATT&CK® navigator.

5.6 MITRE'S CAPEC™

Another free resource that is open to you is Mitre's Common Attack Pattern Enumeration and Classification ("CAPEC – Common Attack Pattern Enumeration and Classification (CAPECTM)"[36]). Here you can choose to simply view by:

- Mechanisms of attack ("CAPEC – CAPEC-1000: Mechanisms of Attack (Version 3.4)"[37]).
- Domains of attack ("CAPEC – CAPEC-3000: Domains of Attack (Version 3.3)"[38]).
- Other criteria ("CAPEC – CAPEC List Version 3.6"[39]); for example:
    - External mappings
        - WASC Threat Classification 2.0
        - ATT&CK Related Patterns
        - OWASP Related Patterns
    - Helpful views
        - Mobile Device Patterns
        - Comprehensive CAPEC Dictionary
        - Meta Abstractions
        - Standard Abstractions
        - Detailed Abstractions
        - Deprecated Entries

Figure 5.7 MITRE ATT&CK® navigator (Continued).

As an example, if I wanted to understand the attack patterns originating from the physical security domain (Category ID 514: Attack patterns within this category focus on physical security. The techniques defined by each pattern are used to exploit weaknesses in the physical security of a system to achieve a desired negative technical impact ("CAPEC – CAPEC-514: Physical Security (Version 3.6)[40]"), I would see all the associations with this domain, as shown in Figure 5.10.

Such a resource can prove invaluable for the planning of any internal audit of security awareness activities and is complementary to your vulnerability management practices, as demonstrated in Figure 5.11 (the harmony between Common Weakness Enumeration (CWE), Common

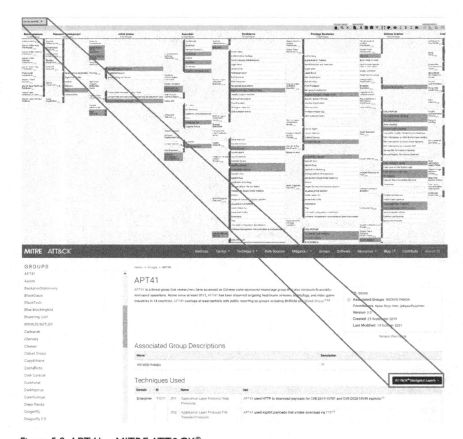

Figure 5.8 APT41 – MITRE ATT&CK®.

Vulnerabilities and Exposures ("CVE – Home"[41]) with Common Attack Pattern Enumeration and Classification ("CAPEC – New to CAPEC?"[42]).

5.7 OPEN-SOURCE INTELLIGENCE

About every cyberattack lifecycle ("Threat-Based Defense"[43]) will include an attacker's attempt to carry out reconnaissance of their intended target. Consequently, it is important that you consider doing the same and there are a several open-source resources that can assist you with this:

- OSINT.Link ("Open Source Intelligence (OSINT) Tools & Resources"[44])
- OSINT Framework ("OSINT Framework"[45])

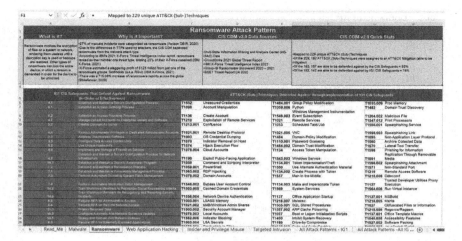

Figure 5.9 CDM ATT&CK cards.

- Qualys SSL Labs ("Qualys SSL Labs"[46])
- Security Headers (Helme[47])
- DNS Dumpster ("DNSdumpster.com – Dns Recon and Research, Find and Lookup Dns Records"[48])
- Virus Total ("VirusTotal"[49])
- Shodan ("Shodan"[50])

5.8 INTERNAL SOURCES/KNOWLEDGE

Additionally, you should also include additional data resources by collecting data on actual incidents, near misses (Cybersecurity Automation[51]) to your own environments and from similar data to those in your industry sector.

5.9 WHEN THREAT MANAGEMENT BITES BACK

The threat from ransomware is real, and the risks for your business having its operational systems and data assets compromised is ever-increasing year on year. Kroll's research into the ransomware threat reported that:

> In Q3 2021, they saw ransomware continue to dominate as the most prominent method of attack.
> Increasing by over 11% on the previous quarter, its share of total incidents has more than doubled this year from 20% in Q1 to around 46% in Q3, giving cyber teams very real cause for concern.
> (Source: Kroll's Q3 2021 Threat Landscape Report ("Q3 2021 Threat Landscape Ransomware in the Supply Chain"[52]))

Figure 5.10 CAPEC ID 514 – Phys Sy.

With such a threat, why is it that so many businesses are still falling victim to such attacks? It may not be through the fault of the efforts being made to fortify their assets but, rather, a lack of understanding of which assets need defending, which mitigation measures need to be prioritized and applied, and which type of ransomware attack they might be vulnerable to.

Darktrace's 2021 Ransomware Threat Report ("2021 Ransomware Threat Report"[53]) provides a comprehensive insight into the difficulties organizations face in trying to mitigate this threat.

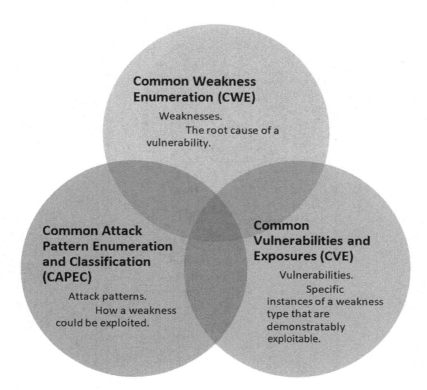

Figure 5.11 The harmonized model.

Although there are several manual measures (e.g., NISTIR 8374 (Barker et al.[54]), CISA ("Ransomware Guide | CISA"[55]), CIS 18 CSCs ("Ransomware Impacts and Defense Controls"[56]) that you can start to put into place, the reality is that corporations may need to enhance their defenses using some automated measures. This approach to create a mixture of manual and automated processes can help to reduce the risks to your valued business assets, across a range of ransomware types ("Live Ransomware Updates"[57]). For example:

- LockBit 2.0 ("LockBit 2.0: Ransomware Attacks Surge after Successful Affiliate Recruitment"[58])
- Hive ("Inside the Hive"[59])
- Conti ("Overview of Conti Ransomware"[60])
- Payload.bin ("PayloadBin Ransomware: Everything You Need to Know"[61])

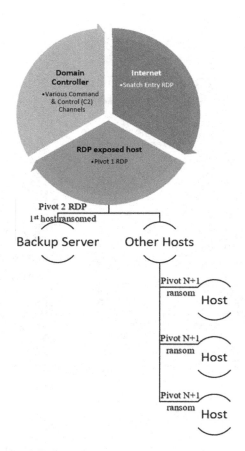

Figure 5.12 Snatch cyber kill chain.

- Snatch ("Snatch Ransomware"[62]) (Cyber Kill Chain depicted in Figure 5.12).

In fact, the Europol Internet Organised Crime Threat Assessment (IOCTA) 2021 ("Internet Organised Crime Threat Assessment (IOCTA) 2021"[63]) revealed that ransomware continues to dominate and proliferate and that with the Covid-19 pandemic, the world has dramatically changed. However, the one constant that has remained is the threat that ransomware poses to financial, public, and even physical safety.

Had Volvo Cars identified that its research and development assets were valuable to them and carried out a risk assessment against the threat presented from the Snatch ransomware, it may have been able to fortify this part of its business operations and avoided becoming a victim of a cyberattack ("Notice of Cyber Security Breach by Third Party"[64]).

- The initial response from Volvo Cars is to refute the claims that they were the victims of a Snatch ransomware attack (Adlam[65]).

5.10 DECODING THREAT MANAGEMENT

Proactive security approaches will incorporate threat management into the vulnerability analysis and remediation activities and will ensure that this is embedded into their risk management practices.

Think of it as employing and embracing the motto: "Forewarned is Forearmed!"

"Definition: Advanced knowledge allows for advanced preparation; knowing about potential problems makes it possible to prepare for them." (Writing Explained ("What Does Forewarned Is Forearmed Mean?"[66]).

Unless you incorporate threat management as a complementary part to your vulnerability management practices, how can you completely understand the risks that you might be exposed to.

A reactive approach will be reliant on your various vulnerability management practices finding any newly published vulnerabilities. However, if you are sporadically or carrying out minimal periodic vulnerability checks (e.g., quarterly requirement for PCI DSS), you are increasing the chances of a high-risk vulnerabilities being discovered and exploited before you have chance to find and remediate them.

Consequently, you should consider embedding threat management into your vulnerability management program so that newly identified threats can instigate ad hoc vulnerability management procedures. This will help to ensure that newly identified threats affecting your valued business operations are found and remediated against promptly, thus reducing the risks to your business.

Incorporating this small amount of added effort will reap a substantial return on your investments.

Notes

1 "Antimicrobial Resistance in Livestock: The Invisible Threat | Agrilinks." Agrilinks.org, agrilinks.org/post/antimicrobial-resistance-livestock-invisible-threat. Accessed 7 Jan. 2022.
2 "Proposed Animal Transport Rules a Major Threat to Calf Trade – IFA." www.farmersjournal.ie, www.farmersjournal.ie/proposed-animal-transport-rules-a-major-threat-to-calf-trade-ifa-666099. Accessed 7 Jan. 2022.

3 Associated Press. "Oregon Expands Wolf Kill due to Threat to Livestock." www. kmvt.com, www.kmvt.com/2021/09/17/oregon-expands-wolf-kill-due-threat-livestock. Accessed 7 Jan. 2022.

4 MSN. "Dog Attacks on Sheep Force Forest Service to Crack down on Leash Law." www.msn.com, www.msn.com/en-us/news/us/dog-attacks-on-sheep-force-forest-service-to-crack-down-on-leash-law/ar-BB1gUefR. Accessed 7 Jan. 2022.

5 Linn County Journal. "Loose Cattle Create Driving Hazards, Problems for Deputies." *Linn County Journal*, 4 Dec. 2021, www.linncountyjournal.com/post/loose-cattle-create-driving-hazards-problems-for-deputies. Accessed 7 Jan. 2022.

6 Minot Daily News "Blister Beetles Danger to People and Livestock, Especially Horses." Minotdailynews.com, www.minotdailynews.com/news/local-news/2021/07/blister-beetles-danger-to-people-and-livestock-especially-horses. Accessed 7 Jan. 2022.

7 "RCW 9A.56.080: Theft of Livestock in the First Degree." Apps.leg.wa.gov, apps.leg.wa.gov/RCW/default.aspx?cite=9A.56.080. Accessed 7 Jan. 2022.

8 Cambridge Dictionary. "THREAT | Meaning in the Cambridge English Dictionary." Cambridge.org, 25 Sept. 2019, dictionary.cambridge.org/dictionary/english/threat

9 "Risk | Etymology, Origin and Meaning of Risk by Etymonline." www.etymonl ine.com, www.etymonline.com/word/risk#etymonline_v_15105. Accessed 7 Jan. 2022.

10 "Threat | Etymology, Origin and Meaning of Threat by Etymonline." www. etymonline.com, www.etymonline.com/word/threat#etymonline_v_13258. Accessed 7 Jan. 2022.

11 Gutierrez, Carlos, and William Jeffrey. FIPS PUB 200 Minimum Security Requirements for Federal Information and Information Systems. 2006.

12 NIST. Risk Management Framework for Information Systems and Organizations: Dec. 2018, nvlpubs.nist.gov/nistpubs/SpecialPublications/NIST. SP.800-37r2.pdf, 10.6028/nist.sp.800-37r2

13 Jones, Jack. BALD TIRE Understanding the Need to Move Information Risk Management from Art toward Science. Feb. 2019.

14 "The Consequences of Knife Crime." Metropolitan Police, www.met.police.uk/cp/crime-prevention/skc/stop-knife-crime/the-consequences-of-crime. Accessed 7 Jan. 2022.

15 "What Is Threat Modeling? Definition, Process, Examples, and Best Practices." Toolbox, www.toolbox.com/it-security/network-security/articles/what-is-threat-modeling-definition-process-examples-and-best-practices. Accessed 7 Jan. 2022.

16 "TESSOC – Terrorism Espionage Subversion Sabotage Organised Crime | AcronymFinder." www.acronymfinder.com, www.acronymfinder.com/Terror ism-Espionage-Subversion-Sabotage-Organised-Crime-(TESSOC).html. Accessed 7 Jan. 2022.

17 "NCSC Publishes New Report on Criminal Online Activity." www.ncsc.gov.uk, www.ncsc.gov.uk/news/ncsc-publishes-new-report-criminal-online-activity

18 The Cost of a Lost Laptop Sponsored by Intel Independently Conducted by Ponemon Institute LLC. 2009.

19 GeeksforGeeks. "Active and Passive Attacks in Information Security." GeeksforGeeks, 5 Sept. 2018, www.geeksforgeeks.org/active-and-passive-attacks-in-information-security. Accessed 16 Jan. 2022.

20 "What Is a Masquerade Attack? – Definition from Techopedia." Techopedia.com, www.techopedia.com/definition/4020/masquerade-attack

21 "Replay Attack." GeeksforGeeks, 18 June 2020, www.geeksforgeeks.org/replay-attack. Accessed 16 Jan. 2022.

22 York, Dan. Seven Deadliest Unified Communications Attacks. Amsterdam Syngress, 2010, pp. 41–69.

23 Cybersecurity & Infrastructure Security Agency. "Understanding Denial-of-Service Attacks | CISA." www.cisa.gov, 4 Nov. 2009, www.cisa.gov/uscert/ncas/tips/ST04-015

24 Health-ISAC. Distributed Denial of Service (DDOS) Attacks. Mar. 2021.

25 Ingoldsby, Terrance. "Attack Tree-Based Threat Risk Analysis." 2021.

26 "Attack Tree Diagrams and Application Security Testing | Synopsys." Software Integrity Blog, 8 Apr. 2015, www.synopsys.com/blogs/software-security/attack-tree-diagram. Accessed 7 Jan. 2022.

27 "Attack Tree Modeling in AttackTree." Isograph, 18 Dec. 2019, www.isograph.com/software/attacktree/creating-an-attack-tree. Accessed 7 Jan. 2022.

28 Sun Tzu. 2019. Chapter 6: Weak Points and Strong. The Art of War. Mineola, New York: Ixia Press.

29 "Matrix – Enterprise | MITRE ATT&CK®." Attack.mitre.org, attack.mitre.org/matrices/enterprise. Accessed 7 Jan. 2022.

30 Pennington, Adam. "Bringing PRE into Enterprise." MITRE ATT&CK®, 27 Oct. 2020, medium.com/mitre-attack/the-retirement-of-pre-attack-4b73ffecd3d3. Accessed 7 Jan. 2022.

31 "Attackics." Collaborate.mitre.org, collaborate.mitre.org/attackics/index.php/Main_Page.

32 "ATT&CK® Navigator." Mitre-Attack.github.io, mitre-attack.github.io/attack-navigator. Accessed 7 Jan. 2022.

33 "APT 41 GROUP." Federal Bureau of Investigation, www.fbi.gov/wanted/cyber/apt-41-group

34 "The 18 CIS Controls." CIS, www.cisecurity.org/controls/cis-controls-list. Accessed 7 Jan. 2022.

35 "Blog | CIS Introduces V2.0 of the CIS Community Defense Model." CIS, 29 Sept. 2021, www.cisecurity.org/blog/cis-introduces-v-2-0-of-the-cis-community-defense-model. Accessed 7 Jan. 2022.

36 "CAPEC – Common Attack Pattern Enumeration and Classification (CAPECTM)." Capec.mitre.org, capec.mitre.org/index.html

37 "CAPEC – CAPEC-1000: Mechanisms of Attack (Version 3.4)." Capec.mitre.org, capec.mitre.org/data/definitions/1000.html

38 "CAPEC – CAPEC-3000: Domains of Attack (Version 3.3)." Capec.mitre.org, capec.mitre.org/data/definitions/3000.html

39 "CAPEC – CAPEC List Version 3.6." Capec.mitre.org, capec.mitre.org/data/index.html

40 "CAPEC – CAPEC-514: Physical Security (Version 3.6)." Capec.mitre.org, capec.mitre.org/data/definitions/514.html. Accessed 7 Jan. 2022.

41 "CVE – Home." Cve.mitre.org, cve.mitre.org/cve/

42 "CAPEC – New to CAPEC?" Capec.mitre.org, capec.mitre.org/about/new_to_ capec.html. Accessed 7 Jan. 2022.

43 "Threat-Based Defense." The MITRE Corporation, 25 July 2013, www.mitre. org/capabilities/cybersecurity/threat-based-defense

44 "Open Source Intelligence (OSINT) Tools & Resources." Osint.link, 26 Mar. 2018, osint.link. Accessed 7 Jan. 2022.

45 "OSINT Framework." osintframework.com

46 "Qualys SSL Labs." www.ssllabs.com

47 Helme, Scott. "Analyse Your HTTP Response Headers." securityheaders.com

48 "DNSdumpster.com – Dns Recon and Research, Find and Lookup Dns Records." dnsdumpster.com

49 "VirusTotal." Virustotal.com, VirusTotal, 2019, www.virustotal.com/gui/home/ upload

50 "Shodan." www.shodan.io, www.shodan.io

51 Cybersecurity-Automation com. "Cybersecurity near Miss Definition." Cybersecurity Automation, 3 July 2021, www.cybersecurity-automation.com/ cybersecurity-near-miss-definition. Accessed 17 Jan. 2022.

52 Kroll. "Q3 2021 Threat Landscape Ransomware in the Supply Chain." Duff & Phelps, www.kroll.com/en/insights/publications/cyber/q3-2021-threat-landsc ape-ransomware-in-the-supply-chain. Accessed 7 Jan. 2022.

53 "2021 Ransomware Threat Report." DarkTrace, 2021, www.darktrace.com/en/ resources/wp-ransomware-threat-report.pdf. Accessed 7 Jan. 2022.

54 Barker, William, et al. "Cybersecurity Framework Profile for Ransomware Risk Management (Preliminary Draft)." Csrc.nist.gov, 9 June 2021, csrc.nist.gov/ publications/detail/nistir/8374/draft

55 "Ransomware Guide | CISA." www.cisa.gov, 2020, www.cisa.gov/stopransomw are/ransomware-guide

56 "Ransomware Impacts and Defense Controls." CIS, 31 July 2019, www.cisecur ity.org/blog/ransomware-impacts-and-defense-controls. Accessed 7 Jan. 2022.

57 "Live Ransomware Updates." Ransomware Database, 7 Jan. 2022, www.ran som-db.com/real-time-updates. Accessed 7 Jan. 2022.

58 "LockBit 2.0: Ransomware Attacks Surge after Successful Affiliate Recruitment." Security Intelligence, 2021, securityintelligence.com/posts/lockbit-ransomware-attacks-surge-affiliate-recruitment. Accessed 7 Jan. 2022.

59 "Inside the Hive." Group-IB, 2021, blog.group-ib.com/hive. Accessed 7 Jan. 2022.

60 "Overview of Conti Ransomware." Cybersecurity and Infrastructure Agency, 25 May 2021, www.cisa.gov/sites/default/files/publications/202105251 512_Analyst%20Note_Conti%20Ransomware_TLP%20WHITE.pdf. Accessed 7 Jan. 2022.

61 "PayloadBin Ransomware: Everything You Need to Know." MUD, 24 Nov. 2021, www.makeuseof.com/payloadbin-ransomware-all-you-need-to-know

62 "Snatch Ransomware." The DFIR Report, 21 June 2020, thedfirreport.com/ 2020/06/21/snatch-ransomware. Accessed 7 Jan. 2022.

63 "Internet Organised Crime Threat Assessment (IOCTA) 2021." Europol, www. europol.europa.eu/publications-events/main-reports/internet-organised-crime-threat-assessment-iocta-2021. Accessed 7 Jan. 2022.

64 "Notice of Cyber Security Breach by Third Party." www.media.volvocars.com, www.media.volvocars.com/global/en-gb/media/pressreleases/292817/notice-of-cyber-security-breach-by-third-party-1. Accessed 7 Jan. 2022.

65 Adlam, Stephanie. "Volvo Cars under Snatch Attack." Gridinsoft Blogs, 4 Jan. 2022, gridinsoft.com/blogs/volvo-cars-under-snatch-attack. Accessed 7 Jan. 2022.

66 "What Does Forewarned Is Forearmed Mean?" Writing Explained, writingexplained.org/idiom-dictionary/forewarned-is-forearmed. Accessed 7 Jan. 2022.

Chapter 6

Risk Scenarios

What is a risk scenario?
The concept of risk scenario building is present in one form or another in all major risk frameworks, including NIST Risk Management Framework (RMF), ISACA's Risk IT, and COSO ERM. The above frameworks have one thing in common: the purpose of risk scenarios is to help decision-makers understand how adverse events can affect organizational strategy and objectives.

The secondary function of risk scenario building, according to the above frameworks, is to set up the next stage of the risk assessment process: risk analysis. Scenarios set up risk analysis by clearly defining and decomposing the factors contributing to the frequency and the magnitude of adverse events.

(Source: Martin-Vegue. "How to Write Strong
Risk Scenarios and Statements."[1])

6.1 THE 'BIG BAD WOLF' ANALOGY

Once upon a time, there were three little pigs who were qualified and employed as building architects. Each had been given the task of designing a house that would meet the goal of supplying suitable shelter from the elements and that incorporated the 'secure by design' principles.

The first little pig used a lean operating model and designed a house that was lightweight and easy to construct, and which was cost-effective.

- His design was constructed with straw.

The second little pig wanted to create a design that supplied more longevity and to be made of more substantial material, while still being an easy to construct and affordable choice.

- His design was constructed with sticks.

DOI: 10.1201/9781003288084-8

The third little pig was more thorough with his design and incorporated a risk scenario into the planning phase. During the development of the risk scenarios, he found the threat presented by the 'Big Bad Wolf,' who wanted to gain unauthorized access to the houses and their contents. The 'Big Bad Wolf' was known to use the tactics of "huffing and puffing to blow the houses down!"

Consequently, the third little pig designed his house to be more resource intensive, costly, and difficult to construct, but which met the goal of supplying proper shelter. It also mitigated the risks of the home being blown down by the 'Big Bad Wolf.'

- His design was solidly constructed with bricks and mortar on a firm foundation.
- He was the only one that identified that the house needed to both provide shelter from the elements and be resistant to the 'huffs and puffs' of the 'Big Bad Wolf.'

The third little pig's risk scenario revealed the threat and capabilities of the 'Big Bad Wolf' to ensure that the house design did not have any vulnerabilities that could be exploited by the 'Big Bad Wolf.'

6.2 INTRODUCTION TO RISK SCENARIOS

Dependent on what influences your businesses risk management practices, you might use the terms 'threat scenarios' or 'risk (loss) scenarios'; for example, United States Federal Government (NIST SP800-30 Rev 1(Blank and Gallagher, 2012[2]), NIST SP800-161 Rev 1(Boyens et al., 2021[3]), CISA ICT SCRM Task Force Threat Scenarios Report, V3 (CISA n.d.[4]) refer to need to carry out threat scenarios as part of the risk assessment practices. Under this guidance a threat scenario is defined as: "A set of discrete threat events, attributed to a specific threat source or multiple threat sources, ordered in time, that result in adverse effects."

Outside of this guidance, the term that is most often used is 'risk scenario' (Isaca and And[5]), and as highlighted earlier in this book, threat is a subset of risk, so, as you can see from Table 6.1, by carrying out a 'risk scenario' you will incorporate most (if not all) of the elements from the 'threat scenario' practices.

It is important to remember the defined differences between threats and risks. This is best explained by the (Factor Analysis of Information Risk) Approach (Freund and Jones[6]). Risk assessments incorporate the threat analysis.

- To estimate the threats, you need to understand the contact frequency, probability of action, and the capabilities of any threat actor, along with your vulnerabilities.

Table 6.1 Threat and Risk Scenarios

Threat Scenario Component	Description
Threat Source	Threat 'actor' or category of threats
Vulnerability	Threat list working group has generated
Threat event description	Description of the method(s) of exploiting the vulnerability
Outcome	Outline the series of consequences that could occur as a result of each threat event
Organizational units or processes affected	This should reflect how or where in the supply chain the impact occurs

Risk Component	Description
Impact	Description of potential impacts to Supply Chain or consequences of exploiting the vulnerability
Likelihood	
Acceptable level of risk	

Mitigation component	Description
Potential mitigating strategies or SCRM controls	Identify supplier evaluation criteria that would reduce or mitigate the impact of the threat
Estimated cost of mitigating strategies	
Change in likelihood	
Change in impact	
Selected strategies	
Estimated residual risk	

Risk Scenario

Risk Scenario Title:
Risk Scenario Category
High-level description of the scenario category

(Continued)

Table 6.1 (Continued)

Risk Scenario

Describe the risk/opportunity scenario, including a discussion of the negative and positive impact of the scenario. The description clarifies the threat/vulnerability type and includes the actors, events, assets, and time issues.

Risk Scenario Component

Threat Type
The nature of the event

- ☐ **Malicious**
- ☐ **Accidental**
- ☐ **Error**
- ☐ **Failure**
- ☐ **Natural**
- ☐ **External requirement**

Actor
Who or what triggers the threat that exploits a vulnerability.

- ☐ **Internal**
- ☐ **External**
- ☐ **Human**
- ☐ **Non-human**

Event
Something happens that was not supposed to happen, something does not happen that was supposed to happen, or a change in circumstances. Events always have cause and usually have consequences. A consequence is the outcome of an event and has an Impact on objectives.

- ☐ **Disclosure**
- ☐ **Interruption**
- ☐ **Modification**
- ☐ **Theft**
- ☐ **Destruction**
- ☐ **Ineffective design**
- ☐ **Ineffective execution**
- ☐ **Rules and regulations**
- ☐ **Inappropriate use**

Asset
An asset is something of either tangible or intangible value that is worth protecting, including people, systems, infrastructure, finances, and reputation.

- ☐ **Process**
- ☐ **People and Skills**
- ☐ **Organizational Structure**
- ☐ **Physical Infrastructure**
- ☐ **IT Infrastructure**
- ☐ **Information**
- ☐ **Applications**

Resources

A resource is anything that helps to achieve a goal.

- □ **Process**
- □ **People and Skills**
- □ **Organizational Structure**
- □ **Physical Infrastructure**
- □ **IT Infrastructure**
- □ **Information**
- □ **Applications**

Time

Timing	□ Non-Critical	□ Critical		
Duration	□ Short	□ Moderate	□ Extended	
Detection	□ Slow	□ Moderate	□ Instant	
Time Lag	□ Immediate	□ Delayed		

Risk Type

Describe the consequences resulting from the event. Include whether the risk type is primary or secondary.

Risk Type	P/S	Risk Description
IT Benefit/Value Enablement		
IT Program and Project Delivery		
IT Operations and Service Delivery		

Possible Risk Responses

Risk Terminate:

Risk Tolerate:

Risk Transfer:

Risk Treatment:

Risk Take the opportunity

Risk Mitigation

Principles, Policies, and Framework Enabler

(Continued)

Table 6.1 (Continued)

Risk Scenario Title:

Reference	Contribution to Response	Effect on Frequency	Effect on Impact	Essential Control
		Choose and item	Choose and item	Choose and item

Process Enabler

Reference	Title Description	Governance and Management Practices	Effect on Frequency	Effect on Impact	Essential Control
			Choose and item	Choose and item	Choose and item

Organizational Structures Enabler

Reference	Contribution to Response	Effect on Frequency	Effect on Impact	Essential Control
		Choose and item	Choose and item	Choose and item

Culture, Ethics and Behavior Enabler

Reference	Contribution to Response	Effect on Frequency	Effect on Impact	Essential Control
		Choose and item	Choose and item	Choose and item

Information Enabler

Reference	Contribution to Response	Effect on Frequency	Effect on Impact	Essential Control
		Choose and item	Choose and item	Choose and item

Services, Infrastructure and Applications Enabler

Reference	Contribution to Response	Effect on Frequency	Effect on Impact	Essential Control
		Choose and item	Choose and item	Choose and item

People, Skills, and Competencies Enabler

Reference	Contribution to Response	Effect on Frequency	Effect on Impact	Essential Control
		Choose and item	Choose and item	Choose and item

Services, Infrastructure, and Applications Enabler

Reference	Contribution to Response	Effect on Frequency	Effect on Impact	Essential Control
		Choose and item	Choose and item	Choose and item

Key Risk Indicators (KRIs) Related to IT Goals

. . . .

Key Risk Indicators (KRIs) Related to Process Goals

. . .

- To estimate the predicted losses, should the threat actors be successful, you would need to evaluate both the primary and secondary predicted losses.

6.3 THE VALUE OF RISK SCENARIOS

Risk scenarios exist between the risk identification and risk statement steps within the risk assessment process and are designed to help decision-makers understand how adverse events can affect business strategy and goals.

Secondary to this is to set the foundations for the next phase of the risk assessment process: Risk analysis.

Scenarios formalize and clearly define and break down the components that contribute to the frequency and the size of adverse events. This is like meteorology's predictive modeling and computer forecasting, as developed through the work by Norwegian physicist Vilhelm Bjerknes, L. F. Richardson, C. G. Rossby, J. G. Charney, and John Von Neumann ("Meteorology: Modern Meteorological Science and Technology | Infoplease"[7]). Although, unlike meteorology, risk practices are not an exact science, the incorporation of risk scenarios in helping with the prediction of any risks that could affect an organization's essential operations supplies greater credibility to the process and makes it appear to be less of a 'finger in the air'/'guestimation' approach.

Additionally, risk scenarios (as part of the planning phase), require input from an organization's key stakeholders, who will be able to supply critical insights into how different threats might affect their areas of responsibility.

6.4 PRIOR PLANNING WITH RISK SCENARIOS

Looking across the various RMFs and standards (e.g., Gisclard-Biondi[8]; NIST[9]; ISO, "ISO 14971:2019"[10]; ISO, "ISO 31000:2018"[11]; etc.), there are typically seven phases to the risk management lifecycle, as depicted in Figure 6.1.

Risk scenarios span across phases one and two. In phase one, as the result of key stakeholder development, there is a collective development of potential risk scenarios, and in phase two, as a team effort, the initial risk scenarios are discussed, prioritized, and any unrealistic or low-risk scenarios discounted.

During the planning phase, the committee of key stakeholders is presented with several of the latest threat intelligences that are believed to be impactful to the business. These threats are then discussed and evaluated against the business operations and the underlying security posture. Following these discussions, the risk scenarios are then formally documented and agreed upon.

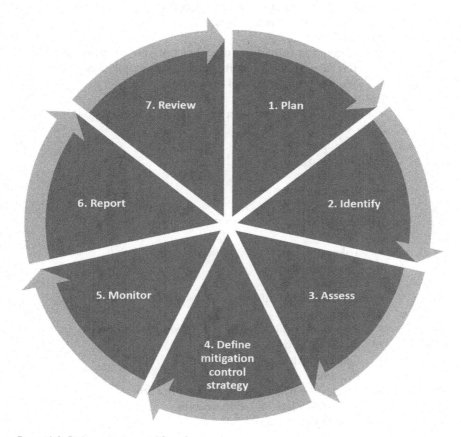

Figure 6.1 Risk management lifecycle.

The formal risk scenarios documentation might articulate such things as:

- A description narrative, to explain each risk scenario.
- Components of the risk scenario:
  - Threat type
    - The nature of the event.
  - Actor(s)
    - Who or what triggers the threat that exploits a vulnerability?
  - Event
    - Something happens that was not supposed to happen, something does not happen that was supposed to happen, or a change in circumstances. Events always have causes and

usually have consequences. A consequence is the outcome of an event and has an impact on goals.

- Asset(s)
  - An asset is something of either tangible or intangible value that is worth protecting, including people, systems, infrastructure, finances, and reputation.
- Resources
  - A resource is anything that helps to achieve a goal.
- Time
  - Timing
  - Duration
  - Detection
  - Time lag
- Risk type
- Risk response(s)
  - Treat
  - Tolerate
  - Terminate
  - Transfer
  - Take the opportunity
- Risk mitigation
  - Principles, policies, procedures, and frameworks
  - Organizational structures
  - Culture, Ethics, and behaviors
  - Information
  - Services, infrastructure, and applications
  - People, skills, and competencies
- Key risk indicator(s) (KRIs)

With this formal documentation in place, prioritized, and approved, you can then use this to help create some risk scenario playbooks.

6.5 CREATING RISK SCENARIO PLAYBOOKS

Many readers of this book may already have heard of the term 'playbook' but, most likely, this will be related to the reactive incident response process. However, even if you have not heard of this term, we shall cover this in the second section of this book.

One meaning ("What Does Playbook Mean?"[12]) of a playbook is: "A scheme or set of strategies for conducting a business campaign or a political campaign." Consequently, to enable a proactive approach, once you have created and prioritized your risk scenarios, you should then consider using this to create your supporting playbooks, to outline your strategies for reducing the risks identified in the various risk scenarios.

These can be used for creating an agreed set of strategies that could be tactically rolled out to reduce the perceived risks to your business. This might include all the recommended risk responses, some of the recommended risk responses, or a phased rollout of the recommended risk responses, as detailed in the risk scenarios.

Additionally, the playbook could supply details of alternative strategies that could be considered ('plays') if the favored approach fails.

6.5.1 Components of a Playbook

What you include in your Playbooks are individual to you and must work for your business. However, as shown in Table 6.2, IBM[13] recommends the following components to be included in any playbook:

However, there is a major difference between a playbook for risk scenarios and those for incident response. Those playbooks that are developed for incident response provide possible 'game plays' that can be implemented in response to an impactful event or incident, whereas risk scenario playbooks should be designed and developed to help implement pre-emptive actions that will help to prevent or reduce the risks of those impactful events or incidents occurring in the first place.

Given that you cannot eliminate all your risks, there is a place for the development of both types of playbook to act as a complement to each other. Consequently, in case of an impactful event or incident occurring, the lessons learned should be used to help update both types of playbook.

6.6 WHEN RISK SCENARIOS BITE BACK

The theme throughout this book is how SRM should be an embedded part of business and how this should be aligned to the business's objectives.

Never has this been so clear than when businesses needed to respond to the challenges that the Covid-19 pandemic presented.

A pandemic would be categorized as being a non-traditional threat; however, few businesses appeared to be suitably prepared for what they were likely to face and, as a result, few organizations had prepared suitable contingency plans for this. In fact, in a survey of global businesses, only 36% of businesses had an emergency response plan for an endemic/pandemic, and 80% of those plans proved to be ineffective for the Covid-19 situation. Companies were forced into making temporary (63%) or permanent (55%) adjustments to the way that they operated, and 43% of companies needed their workforce to work from home, as depicted in Figure 6.2 ("Workplace Commons"[14]).

Additionally, the financial costs on the global economy have been estimated at a 47.9% loss to the global gross domestic product (GDP) (2021–2030), as depicted in Table 6.3 (Yeyati and Filippini[15]), and there was

Table 6.2 IBM Components of a Playbook

Rules	A set of conditional statements that identify relationships and run responses accordingly. Rules define a set of activities that are triggered when conditions are met. Activities include setting incident field values, inserting tasks into the task list, launching workflows, running internal scripts to implement business logic, and placing items on message destinations to be acted upon by remote programs.
Workflow	A graphically designed set of activities that allows you to create a complex set of operations. You can use workflows to implement sophisticated business processes that can be invoked by rules. Workflows can contain various components, such as scripts, functions, and message destinations.
Script	For users familiar with writing Python scripts, you can write scripts to access incident data (same data as accessed by rules) then perform activities more complex than can be handled by rules. Scripts can be triggered by rules or workflows.
Message destination	The location where data is posted and made accessible to remote programs. The message includes details about an object and the activity taken. You can configure rules, workflows, and functions to send messages to one or more message destinations.
Custom field	Design element used in incident layouts to capture specific data. An integrated system can populate a custom field.
Data table	Design element that organizes data in a tabular format. An integrated system can populate the table.
Function	A resilient object that sends data to a remote function processor through a message destination. The function processor is the remote code component that performs an activity and returns the results. The results are acted upon by scripts, rules, and workflow decision points to dynamically orchestrate the security incident response activities. Functions simplify development of apps by wrapping each activity into an individual workflow component. • Inputs Data that is acted on by the function processor. The inputs can be provided by a resilient user or by a pre-process script. • Pre-process script A script that is used to dynamically set the value of one or more of the function's input fields. You can use the script to retrieve the current value of a property then provide that value to the function as an input. A pre-process script cannot perform write activities on objects, such as changing incident values or adding artifacts. • Output Result of the function processor. A post-process script can act upon this result. If saved, objects within the same workflow instanced and executed after the function can also access the data. • Post-process script A script that performs an activity in response to the result provided by the function. The script can change incident values, add artifacts, add data table rows, and more.

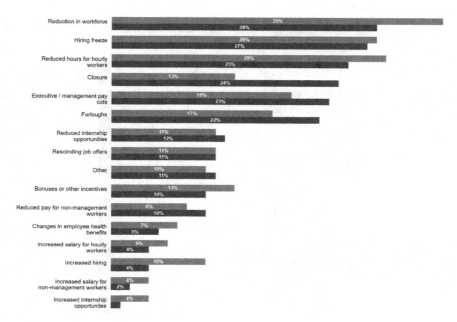

Figure 6.2 Covid-19 actions.

Table 6.3 Economic Costs of the Covid Shock (% of GDP)

	World	AEs	EMEs	LIDCs	LatAm
Lost 2020 global GDP from Covid-19	6.7%	6.5%	7.0%	4.8%	8.5%
Lost 2021–30 global GDP from Covid-19 discounted at 0%	47.9%	13.8%	76.7%	87.6%	84.3%
GDP loss 2020-30 (discounted at 0%)	**54.6%**	**20.3%**	**83.8%**	**92.4%**	**92.8%**
Global fiscal impulse (IMF Fiscal Monitor Apr 2021)					
Above the line	9.2%	16.4%	4.0%	1.6%	5.3%
Below the line	6.1%	11.3%	2.5%	0.2%	4.1%
Fiscal impulse **Output + fiscal**	15.3%	27.7%	6.5%	1.8%	9.4%
	69.9%	**48.1%**	**90.3%**	**94%**	**102.2%**
Statistical value of deaths related to Covid-19					
Total deaths related to Covid-19	2,828,14	1,201,44	1,525,08	65,348	800,100
Deaths per million	6	2	8	41	1,235
Statistical value of a life (lower bound, in USDmm)	363 5.0	1,148	299		
Total value of deaths related to the pandemic	16.2%				
Education and human capital loss					
Average missed days of instruction in	48	15	46	69	174
2020 Lifetime loss in labor earnings for the affected cohort	12%	-	-	-	-
Broader economic cost	**98.1%**				

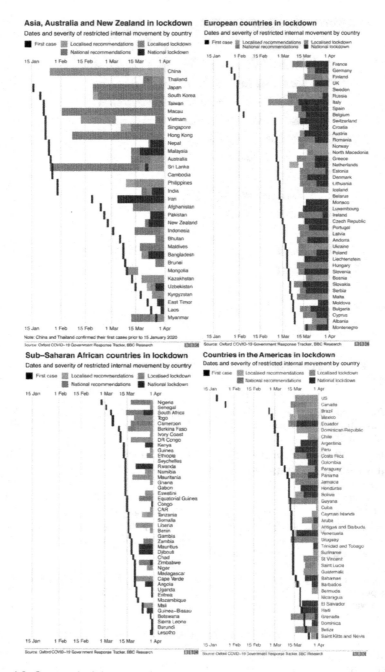

Figure 6.3 Country lockdown timeline.

a reported 74% surge in cybercriminals targeting financial organizations (Haigh[16]), and a 311% increase in ransomware attacks, in comparison to the 2019 statistics (Paul[17]).

Might things have been different if these organizations had started their planning strategy with the use of risk scenarios at the point that they started to see the waves of countries locking down their businesses and communities, as depicted in Figure 6.3 (Yang, "Experience from Other Countries Show Lockdowns Don't Work | AIER"[18])?

Imagine how the development of a Covid-19-specific risk scenario might have helped your business to develop suitable playbooks, which could feed into the prompt development of your business continuity plan (BCP), and to help you understand what contingencies might be needed and what risks each contingency measure might present. For example:

- What would be needed to safely, securely, and rapidly embrace the massive remote-working experiment (Vasel, CNN Business[19]), while avoiding fueling a 'cyberattack pandemic' (Buttice[20])?

6.7 DECODING RISK SCENARIOS

Risk scenarios are often neglected from risk management practices and, as a result, risk can often be regarded as a reactive process (how do we limit the risks after something has happened?). However, the incorporation of risk scenarios into your risk management lifecycles can really help to make this practice more cohesive, proactive, and supportive of the business's goals.

The Covid-19 pandemic was an excellent example of where risk scenarios would have yielded extensive benefits to organizations, helping them to create suitable and specific risk scenario playbooks, which could have helped present several suitable strategies that could have been considered, in advance, of any changing requirements.

Risk scenarios support the continued development of security incident response, business continuity and disaster recovery practices (covered in Section Two of this book), to help ensure that these practices remain current and relevant.

Notes

1 Martin-Vegue, Tony. "How to Write Strong Risk Scenarios and Statements." ISACA, 29 Sept. 2021, www.isaca.org/resources/news-and-trends/newsletters/atisaca/2021/volume-31/how-to-write-strong-risk-scenarios-and-statements. Accessed 3 Sept. 2022.
2 Blank, R. and Gallagher, P. (2012). Guide for Conducting Risk Assessments NIST Special Publication 800-30 Revision 1 JOINT TASK FORCE TRANSFORMATION INITIATIVE. [online] Available at: https://nvlpubs.nist.gov/nistpubs/legacy/sp/nistspecialpublication800-30r1.pdf.

3 Boyens, J., Smith, A., Bartol, N., Winkler, K., Holbrook, A. and Fallon, M. (2021). Cybersecurity Supply Chain Risk Management Practices for Systems and Organizations (2nd Draft). [online] csrc.nist.gov. Available at: https://csrc.nist.gov/publications/detail/sp/800-161/rev-1/draft [Accessed 7 Jan. 2022].

4 CISA. (n.d.). ICT SCRM Task Force Threat Scenarios Report | CISA. [online] Available at: www.cisa.gov/publication/ict-scrm-task-force-threat-scenarios-report ،

5 Isaca and And, A. (2014). Risk Scenarios for COBIT 5 for Risk. Isaca.

6 Freund, J. and Jones, J. (2015). Measuring and Managing Information Risk: A Fair Approach. Oxford: Elsevier, Cop.

7 "Meteorology: Modern Meteorological Science and Technology | Infoplease." www.infoplease.com, 2012, www.infoplease.com/encyclopedia/earth/weather/concepts/meteorology/modern-meteorological-science-and-technology. Accessed 8 Jan. 2022.

8 Gisclard-Biondi, Henri. "Guide to the 5 Steps of the Risk Management Lifecycle." Appvizer.com, 20 May 2021, www.appvizer.com/magazine/operations/project-management/risk-management-lifecycle

9 NIST. "Risk Management." NIST, 30 June 2016, www.nist.gov/risk-management

10 ISO. "ISO 14971:2019." ISO, Dec. 2019, www.iso.org/standard/72704.html

11 ISO. "ISO 31000:2018." ISO, July 2019, www.iso.org/standard/65694.html

12 "What Does Playbook Mean?" www.definitions.net, www.definitions.net/definition/playbook. Accessed 8 Jan. 2022.

13 IBM. "Playbook Components." www.ibm.com, www.ibm.com/docs/en/rsoa-and-rp/38?topic=introduction-playbook-components. Accessed 8 Jan. 2022.

14 "Workplace Commons." ASU College of Health Solutions, 16 July 2020, chs.asu.edu/diagnostics-commons/workplace-commons. Accessed 8 Jan. 2022.

15 Yeyati, Eduardo Levy, and Federico Filippini. "Pandemic Divergence: The Social and Economic Costs of Covid-19." VoxEU.org, 12 May 2021, voxeu.org/article/social-and-economic-costs-covid-19

16 Haigh, Nick. "COVID Cyber Crime: 74% of Financial Institutions Experience Significant Spike in Threats Linked to COVID-19." www.businesswire.com, 28 Apr. 2021, www.businesswire.com/news/home/20210428005365/en/COVID-Cyber-Crime-74-of-Financial-Institutions-Experience-Significant-Spike-in-Threats-Linked-To-COVID-19

17 Paul, Kari. "How Remote Work Opened the Floodgates to Ransomware." The Guardian, 17 June 2021, www.theguardian.com/technology/2021/jun/17/ransomware-working-from-home-russia

18 Yang, Ethan. "Experience from Other Countries Show Lockdowns Don't Work | AIER." www.aier.org, 9 Aug. 2020, www.aier.org/article/experience-from-other-countries-show-lockdowns-dont-work. Accessed 29 Nov. 2022.

19 Vasel, CNN Business, Kathryn. "The Pandemic Forced a Massive Remote-Work Experiment. Now Comes the Hard Part." CNN, 11 Mar. 2021, edition.cnn.com/2021/03/09/success/remote-work-covid-pandemic-one-year-later/index.html

20 Buttice, Claudio. "The Cyberattacks Pandemic: Cybercrime in the COVID-19 Era." Techopedia.com, 11 Nov. 2021, www.techopedia.com/the-cyberattacks-pandemic-a-look-at-cybercrime-in-the-covid-19-era/2/34597. Accessed 8 Jan. 2022.

Chapter 7

Quality Versus Quantity

7.1 THE AGING BRAIN ANALOGY

Our perceptions of risk and how we carry out risk assessments are influenced by the maturity state of our brains (Rudolph et al.[1]). As we get older, we become more cautious about the risks that we decide to take. However, as a child we are less knowledgeable about what could cause us harm and what the potential impact of such a risk-taking activity would be. Consequently, parents and teachers go to great lengths to educate their children and pupils on how to safely navigate their way across a busy road. How do they do this? By teaching them to risk-assess the crossing and how to take appropriate risk responses.

However, as the child grows into an adolescent and their brain starts to develop further, studies show that:

They are increasingly likely to:

- Act on impulse
- Misread or misinterpret social cues and emotions
- Get into accidents of all kinds
- Get involved in fights
- Engage in dangerous or risky behavior

Adolescents are less likely to:

- Think before they act
- Pause to consider the consequences of their actions
- Change their dangerous or inappropriate behaviors.
        (American Academy of Child and Adolescent Psychiatry[2])

All too soon that child has grown into an adolescent who is going through numerous changes and who increasingly seeks independence, which, according to Youell[3], is gained through them "exploring their identity and

DOI: 10.1201/9781003288084-9

develop a stable sense of who they are, becoming more aware of themselves and their thoughts and behaviors, and setting and reaching goals."

Suddenly, instead of carefully crossing a road, they are seeking the excitement and adrenaline rush of those near misses and even start to turn the act of crossing a road into a thrill-seeking game (e.g., chicken (getreading[4])) and this can become increasingly dangerous as they gain in confidence and independence:

- Their impulsive nature increasingly leads them to ignore the risks, in favor of the thrill and the experience of the activities.
- They are risk hungry.

Now, as the adolescent matures, once again they become more cautious and will even start to reduce their levels of risk tolerance (Society for Neuroscience[5]).

Then, as we move through to being a pensioner, our brains change again (Howieson[6]), influencing our risk perceptions and making us even more cautious.

- The elderly become increasingly unwilling to take any risks.
- They become hesitant and risk averse.
- This can often decrease their chances of being involved in an impactful incident or event.

The differences in risk perspectives (Brown[7]), by age demographics, can be seen by the male motor vehicle death rates (Spencer et al.[8]), as depicted in Figure 7.1.

The impact of the aging brain can affect organizations with large age demographics and how they can implement suitable risk assessment practices. As a business owner or as part of the business's leadership team, this can affect the way that risk assessments are carried out and delivered. Such risk assessments may need to be tailored to meet the capabilities of the individuals that are expected to carry out the risk assessments and by those that must review and act on the risk assessments.

7.2 INTRODUCTION TO RISK ASSESSMENTS

Despite some claims that risk assessments are a scientific process (U.S. EPA, ORD, NCEA[9]), unlike meteorology, for me risk assessments have some way to go before they should be classed as a scientific process. However, there are measures that can be taken to help ensure that this process has more formality and credibility, and these start with understanding what is involved in carrying out effective risk assessments.

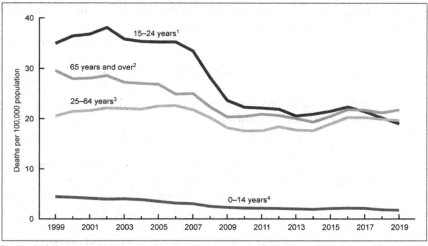

Figure 2. Motor vehicle traffic death rates among males, by age group: United States, 1999–2019

¹Stable trend from 1999 to 2006; significant decreasing trend from 2006 to 2010 (*p* < 0.05); stable trend from 2010 through 2019.
²Stable trend from 1999 to 2005; significant decreasing trend from 2005 to 2010 (*p* < 0.05); stable trend from 2010 through 2019.
³Significant increasing trend from 1999 to 2006; significant decreasing trend from 2006 to 2010; significant increasing trend from 2010 through 2019, *p* < 0.05.
⁴Significant decreasing trend from 1999 to 2010, with varying rates of change (*p* < 0.05); stable trend from 2010 through 2019.
NOTES: Motor vehicle traffic deaths were identified using *International Classification of Diseases, 10th Revision* (ICD–10) codes V02–V04 (.1, .9), V09.2, V12–V14 (.3–.9), V19 (.4–.6), V20–V28 (.3–.9), V29–V79 (.4–.9), V80 (.3–.5), V81.1, V82.1, V83–V86 (.0–.3), V87 (.0–.8), and V89.2. Access data table for Figure 2 at: https://www.cdc.gov/nchs/data/databriefs/db400-tables-508.pdf#2.
SOURCE: National Center for Health Statistics, National Vital Statistics System, Mortality (NVSS–M).

Figure 7.1 Motor vehicle death by age.

At many points in your lifetime, you will have carried out a risk assessment; however, mostly these will have been informal decisions on whether to take an action or not. In the business world, we would be looking for any risk assessments to be formally documented, so that there is a record of the risk decisions and to enable key stakeholders to have an input or to review the risks.

There are numerous definitions of what risk assessments should be:

> The process of identifying risks to organizational operations (including mission, functions, image, reputation), organizational assets, individuals, other organizations, and the Nation, resulting from the operation of an information system. Part of risk management, incorporates threat and vulnerability analyses, and considers mitigations provided by security controls planned or in place.
>
> Process to comprehend the nature of risk and to determine the level of risk.
>
> Overall process of risk identification, risk analysis, and risk evaluation.
> (Source: NIST (NIST Glossary)[10])

A process to identify potential hazards and analyze what could happen if a hazard occurs. A business impact analysis (BIA) is the process for determining the potential impacts resulting from the interruption of time sensitive or critical business processes.

(Source: Ready.Gov (Ready)[11])

The overall process or method where you:

- Identify hazards and risk factors that have the potential to cause harm (hazard identification).
- Analyze and evaluate the risk associated with that hazard (risk analysis, and risk evaluation).
- Determine appropriate ways to eliminate the hazard or control the risk when the hazard cannot be eliminated (risk control).

(Source: Canadian Centre for Occupational Health & Safety (CCOHS)[12])

The practice of reviewing an organization's activities and investments to determine the likelihood of loss. This information is then used to make various operational adjustments in order to reduce those risks that are considered to be excessive.

(Source: Accounting Tools (Bragg)[13])

The process by which the level of risk associated with a particular hazard is identified and categorized.

(Source: (UK Government)[14])

You can see that the requirements for risk assessments, within business, are not exclusive to the security industry. Additionally, common to all these definitions is that risk assessments are part of the risk management (Gartner[15]) process and should include an understanding of the potential threats, the business's exploitable vulnerabilities, the likelihood of a threat actor exploiting any of the business's vulnerabilities, and an estimation of the loss magnitude, should an event or incident occur.

Ultimately, a risk assessment is the forecasting of potential future impactful events, but forecasting is not an exact science and different people will have different interpretations of the probability of an event or incident occurring or the consequences that such an event might bring.

Kenneth Feinberg demonstrated a very good example of this in his role as the Special Master for the 9/11 Compensation Fund (McArdle et al.[16]), which was the subject of a film dramatization (Worth[17]). During this role he had to deal with the very emotive task of trying to calculate the loss magnitude associated with estimating the cost of a life.

In your business, how do you agree on estimating the forecasting of the probability of an event occurring or how impactful such an event or incident might be? How can you increase the confidence with such forecasts?

Typically, there are several types of risk assessment methodologies (jonana et al.[18]), but the main ones that are used are:

Qualitative:
Qualitative risk analysis is the process of rating or scoring risk based on a person's perception of the severity and likelihood of its consequences. The goal of qualitative risk analysis is to come up with a short list of risks which need to be prioritized above others.

Quantitative:
Quantitative risk analysis is the process of calculating risk based on data gathered. The goal of quantitative risk analysis is to further specify how much will the impact of the risk cost the business. This is achieved by using what's already known to predict or estimate an outcome.

(Source: Safety Culture[19])

You may favor one over the other, or (as I do) see the value of developing a hybrid approach, but as long as you develop an approach that works across your business's age demographics and that provides you with the risk intelligence input you need to be able to make informed risk response decisions, you can start to appreciate the value that effective risk assessments can bring to ensuring the safety and security of your business.

An overview of the risk assessment process is shown in Figure 7.2.

7.3 CONDUCTING QUALITATIVE RISK ASSESSMENTS

Qualitative risk assessments are perceived as being the easiest method of delivering risk assessments but equally they are regarded as being less formal and subject to various interpretations on how likely an event or incident might be and how harmful or impactful an event or incident might be on the organization.

Typically, a qualitative risk assessment requires an individual to 'guestimate' the probability/likelihood of an event or incident occurring, and the potential impact should such an event or incident occur.

The individual conducting the qualitative risk assessment is provided with a numerical guide with which they are required to calculate the probability/likelihood and impact scores. These numerical grid guides are often depicted in 4x4, 5x5 or 6x6 formats (as depicted in Table 7.1) and provide a numerical score with a supporting narrative from which the risk assessor will provide a risk score.

To effectively complete this type of risk assessment, it is essential that the business has identified all the assets associated with the risk assessment and

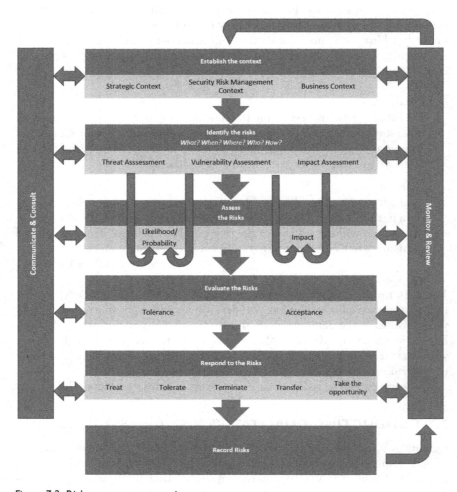

Figure 7.2 Risk assessment overview.

that BIAs or DPIAs have been carried out, together with any relevant threat assessment, and these are made available to the individual responsible for carrying out the risk assessment.

Having completed the risk assessment, the results and any risk responses are typically recorded in a risk register. The entries in your risk register should show a record of the initial risk scores, as well as the details and the residual risk (red, amber, green; or red, amber, yellow, green) scores, after the risk responses have been applied, as depicted in Figure 7.3.

Table 7.1 5x5 Risk Narratives

Likelihood/Probability

Likelihood	Description	Summary
1	Improbable	Has never happened before and there is no reason to think it is any more likely now.
2	Unlikely	There is a possibility that it could happen, but it probably will not.
3	Likely	On balance, the risk is more likely to happen than not.
4	Very Likely	It would be a surprise if the risk did not occur, either based on past frequency or current circumstances.
5	Almost certain	Either already happens regularly or there is some reason to believe it is virtually imminent.

Impact/Consequence

Impact Level		Impact Areas				
Impact Rating	General Description	Effect on Customers	Financial Cost	Health and Safety	Damage to Reputation	Legal, contractual, and organizational Compliance
1	Negligible	No effect	Very little or none (100,000)	Very small additional risk	Negligible	No implications
2	Slight	Some local disturbance to normal business operations	Some (£500,000)	Within acceptable limits	Slight	Small risk of not meeting compliance
3	Moderate	Can still deliver product/service with some difficulty	Unwelcome but could be borne (£1 Million)	Elevated risk requiring immediate attention	Moderate	In definite danger of operating illegally
4	High	Business is crippled in key areas	Severe effect on income and/or profit (£5 Million)	Significant danger to life	High	Operating illegally in some areas
5	Very High	Out of business; no service to customers	Crippling; the organization will go out of business (£10 Million)	Real or strong potential loss of life	Very High	Severe fines and possible imprisonment of staff

Risk Description				
Ref.	Asset	Threat	Vulnerabilities	Risk Owner
1				
2				
3				
4				
5				
6				
7				
8				
9				
10				
11				

Pre-Treatment							
Existing Controls	Likelihood	Rationale	Impact	Rationale	Risk Score	Risk Level	RAG
	1		5		5	MEDIUM	RED
	2		4		8	MEDIUM	AMBER
	3		3		9	MEDIUM	AMBER
	4		2		8	MEDIUM	AMBER
	5		1		5	MEDIUM	AMBER
	3		3		9	MEDIUM	AMBER
	5		5		25	HIGH	RED
	4		2		8	MEDIUM	AMBER
	1		1		1	LOW	GREEN
	2		3		6	MEDIUM	AMBER
	5		4		20	HIGH	RED

Treatment				
Treatment Option	Control	Annex A Reference	Control Requirements	Link to Control Documentation
Mitigate				
Accept				
Avoid				
Transfer				
Transfer				
Accept				
Accept				
Mitigate				
Accept				
Accept				
Transfer				

Post-Treatment					
Impact	Rationale	Risk Score	Risk Level	RAG	Comments
5		5	MEDIUM	AMBER	
Select...		#VALUE!	#VALUE!		
Select...		#VALUE!	#VALUE!		
Select...		#VALUE!	#VALUE!		
Select...		#VALUE!	#VALUE!		
Select...		#VALUE!	#VALUE!		
Select...		#VALUE!	#VALUE!		
Select...		#VALUE!	#VALUE!		
Select...		#VALUE!	#VALUE!		
Select...		#VALUE!	#VALUE!		
Select...		#VALUE!	#VALUE!		

Figure 7.3 ISO/IEC 27001 risk register.

Traditionally, the likelihood/probability score is multiplied by the impact/consequence score to provide the total risk score (e.g., likelihood score = almost certain (5) multiplied by the impact score = very high (5). Total risk score = 25). The total risk scores are then plotted against the risk scoring matrix, as depicted in Table 7.2.

Table 7.2 Risk Scoring Matrix

Risk Rating	Risk Score
VERY HIGH	> 20
HIGH	> 15 <20
MEDIUM	> 5 <15
LOW	< 5

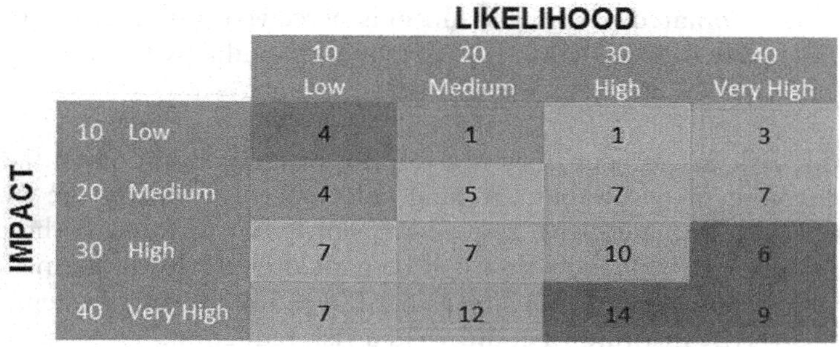

LIKELIHOOD

		10 Low	20 Medium	30 High	40 Very High
IMPACT	10 Low	4	1	1	3
	20 Medium	4	5	7	7
	30 High	7	7	10	6
	40 Very High	7	12	14	9

Figure 7.4 Risk heat map.

Additionally, for ease of communication, the risk assessments are often presented in an easy-to-read risk heat map, as depicted in Figure 7.4 (Caldas[20]). Pros of qualitative risk assessments:

- Easy to understand and complete
- Require less technical or specialist knowledge
- Better for quickly presenting large numbers of perceived risks

Cons of qualitative risk assessments:

- Informal
- Often feel like a 'finger in the air' risk assessment
- Less detailed assessments

7.4 CONDUCTING QUANTITATIVE RISK ASSESSMENTS

Quantitative risk assessments differ, as they go into greater detail when breaking down the components of the threat, vulnerabilities, and loss magnitude (impacts), and they provide a monetary value to your risks. As a result, you are better able to use a qualitative risk assessment to provide a return on investment.

For example, your organization has identified a ransomware threat and that the manual patching process is significantly increasing the risks to the systems supporting a critical business operation of being compromised through a ransomware attack. Consequently, you are wanting to put together a justification for the investment in an automated patching solution (Capterra[21]).

A quantitative risk assessment reveals:

- The risk score 25 (5 [likelihood = almost certain x 5 impact = very high]) is deemed as a HIGH RISK.
- The automated patching solution is perceived to reduce the residual risk score to MEDIUM 10 (2 [likelihood = unlikely x 5 impact = very high]).

What this risk assessment does not tell the business is the potential yield from investing in a suitable patching solution to automate the process. However, with a quantitative risk assessment, you can forecast the potential monetary risk reduction that will be gained from this investment. The risk profiles show that the £100,000/$150,000 investment, as depicted in Figure 7.5 (FAIR Institute[22]), could yield a risk reduction:

- Average: £12,707,900 (94%).
- Maximum: £21,500,000 (55%).

Suddenly, with a risk reduction of between 55% and 94%, the £100,000/ $150,000 investment demonstrates a significant return on investment.

How is this achieved? During a qualitative risk assessment, you will engage with your business's key stakeholders to gain their insights into various aspects of the perceived risks, as depicted in Figure 7.6 (FAIR Institute, "The Importance and Effectiveness of Quantifying Cyber Risk"[23]).

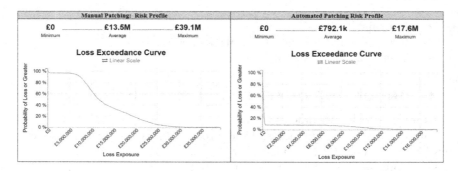

Figure 7.5 Quantitative risk profiles.

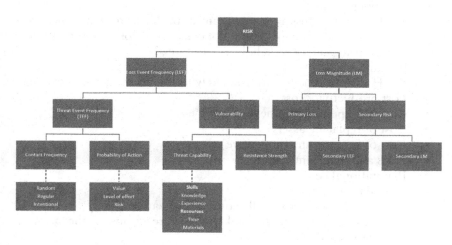

Figure 7.6 FAIR risk model.

For example, this engagement could identify:

- Loss event frequency
  - How many times over the next year is the loss event likely to occur?
- Threat event frequency
  - How many times over the next year is the threat event likely to occur?
  - How many times will the asset face a threat action?
- Contact frequency
  - How many times over the next year is the threat actor/agent likely to reach the asset?
- Probability of action
  - What percentage of threat agent/actor contacts with the asset are likely to result in threat events?
  - How often will the threat decide to act against the asset?

- Vulnerability
  - What percentage of threat events are likely to result in loss events?
- Threat capability
  - How capable is this threat community of successfully carrying out the threat event when compared to the capability continuum?
- Resistance strength
  - Given your controls, what is the highest percentile of the capability continuum you think you will successfully defeat when they take a threat action?

- Loss magnitude
  - How much loss is your organization likely to experience as a direct result of a loss event, not considering losses that may come from secondary stakeholders' reactions?
- Primary loss
  - How much money are you likely to lose from each loss event?
- Lost productivity costs
- Cost of responding to the loss event
- Cost of replacing assets
- Cost of losing your competitive advantage
- Fines and judgment costs
- Reputational costs
- Secondary risk
  - How much loss will your organization likely experience because of secondary stakeholders' reactions to the primary loss event?
- Secondary loss event frequency
  - What percentage of primary loss events are likely to result in losses from secondary stakeholder reactions?
- Secondary loss magnitude
  - How much loss is your organization likely to experience because of secondary stakeholders' reactions to the primary loss event?
- Lost productivity costs
- Cost of responding to the loss event
- Cost of replacing assets
- Cost of losing your competitive advantage
- Fines and judgment costs
- Reputational costs

In a quantitative risk assessment, the risk is calculated using the Monte Carlo Simulation (Kenton[24]) to perform the analysis across several models, where the possible results are substituted with a range of values (a distribution of the probabilities) for any factors that have an inherent uncertainty. This then repeats the results calculations, using a different set of random values from the probability functions. Depending on the number of specified uncertainties and ranges, this could involve thousands or tens of thousands of calculations before the final risk ranges are calculated.

Pros of quantitative risk assessments:

- Provide monetary values
- Provide the ability to show the return on the investments for any risk responses
- Perceived to be more detailed

Cons of quantitative risk assessments:

- Can need more stakeholder engagement and time
- Not always suitable for quick fire-risk assessments
- Can be perceived as being too complicated a process (which is not the case!).

7.5 QUALITY OR QUANTITY?

As you can see, when comparing the components of qualitative with quantitative risk assessments, both bring benefits and are, in fact, complementary to one another. Each has its place within your organization.

However, if you are thinking of employing both approaches within your organization, it is important to ensure that the scoring matrices are aligned. If you have a monetary figure in your qualitative risk scoring matrices, ensure that this is aligned with the output from your qualitative risk assessments.

For example, your qualitative risk scoring matrix has:

Slight risks = anything above £500k (but less than £1 million)
Moderate risks = anything above £1 million (but less than £5 million)
High risks = anything above £5 million (but less than £10 million)
Very high risks = anything exceeding £10 million

In the ransomware example provided, even after the investment in the automated patching solution, the risks against the risk scoring matrix would be:

- Initial risk score:
  - A range of between £13.5 million and £39.1 million
- Residual risk score:
  - A range of between £792,100 and £17.6 million

Consequently, if you were to plot both your qualitative and quantitative risk scores onto a single heat matrix, or risk register, the results could be misrepresented.

Additionally, when carrying out quantitative risk assessments, I would always recommend that you start the engagement with a qualitative risk assessment (gets the stakeholders to start thinking about the risks) and conclude the quantitative risk assessment with a review of these results against the results of the qualitative risk assessment exercise (reaffirms the risk results and provides consistency).

7.6 CHOOSING YOUR RISK ASSESSMENT TYPES

I have focused on two types of risk assessment, but I would encourage you to investigate the use of the myriad of risk assessment methodologies (in addition to these) that are the most appropriate to your business (jonana et al., "The 5 Types of Risk Assessment and When to Use Them"[25]). For example:

Generic Risk Assessment
These assessments are simple enough to be used as templates and adapted for different uses. Assessments of this nature can be useful as a base level for threats throughout your organization. This method is convenient but be careful when implementing a generic assessment because it may not be suited to every situation. Generic assessments are usually most effective in conjunction with other methodologies.

Site-Specific Risk Assessment
As the name implies, this methodology is primarily concerned with how location and environment affect risk. By including these considerations, an assessor can tailor an otherwise generic assessment to a particular department or location. Site-specific assessments are ideal for determining the severity of threats throughout your organization.

Dynamic Risk Assessment
These are specifically designed for environments or situations were risk changes frequently. They are performed in conjunction with traditional risk assessments, usually on the spot when a new risk emerges. These kinds of assessments are particularly useful for more high-risk positions like emergency services or health and safety.

(Source: Reciprocity[26])

Whatever your choice of risk assessment methodology, you should ensure that your risk processes address several goals and practices (as detailed in the CERT Resilience Model and in Table 7.3 (Caralli et al.[27])) to help your organization to be both proactive and reactive in the continued protection of your valued business operations and assets.

Whichever method you decide to use, the output needs to be harmonized and ideally should be managed through a centralized risk platform, enabling ease of management and providing both enterprise-wide and tiered-level (e.g., country, site, department, business operation, etc.) comprehensive views of the risk profiles and workflows, as depicted in Figure 7.7 (Reality Tech[28]).

In today's digital businesses, although it might appear to be the most cost-effective option, the reality is that trying to manage your business's risks is no longer tenable using multiple end-user computer (business) applications (Juergens[29]). If your business is still using such technologies, this may be a sign that your business leaders do not understand or appreciate the value that risk assessments and risk management can bring to the protection of their valuable business operations.

Table 7.3 CERT® Resilience Management Model, Version 1.2 – Risk Management (RISK)

Goals		Practices	
SG1	Prepare for Risk Management	SP1	Determine Risk Sources and Categories
		SP2	Establish an Operational Risk Management Strategy
SG2	Establish Risk Parameters and Focus	SP1	Define Risk Parameters
		SP2	Establish Risk Measurement Criteria
SG3	Identify Risks	SP1	Identify Asset-Level Risks
		SP2	Identify Service-Level Risks
SG4	Analyze Risks	SP1	Evaluate Risks
		SP2	Categorize and Prioritize Risks
		SP3	Assign Risk Disposition
SG5	Address Risks	SP1	Develop Risk Response Plans
		SP2	Implement Risk Strategies and Plans
SG6	Use Risk Information to Manage Resilience	SP1	Review and Adjust Strategies to Protect Assets and Services
		SP2	Review and Adjust Strategies to Sustain Services

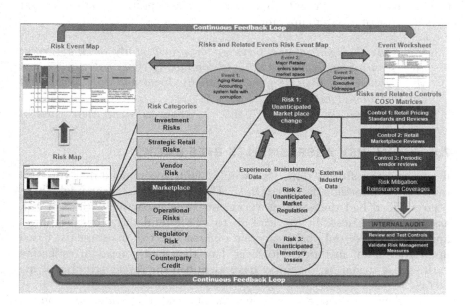

Figure 7.7 Risk management.

7.7 THE VALUE OF RISK ASSESSMENTS

Whether you are a small business or a global enterprise, you all have assets and processes that are valuable to the continued success of your business. Consequently, risk assessments should be at the heart of every decision or action that your teams take. Failure to forecast an event or incident so that you have at hand some pre-designed and developed contingency plans is vital to keeping your business operating efficiently, rather than relying on the reactive (just-in-time) methodology, which (ironically) increases the risks of something going wrong.

Risk assessments should be both proactive and reactive to ensure that your business is forewarned and forearmed. This is the unappreciated value of risk assessments, being able to be pre-emptive of things that could be impactful on your valuable business operations. For example, a 30 to 60-minute discussion to discuss:

- What are we working on?
- What could go wrong?
- What would be the impact if it went wrong?
- What contingency plans are available to us?

Rather than being a waste of time, this is far better than the impact of reacting to an adverse event (e.g., your mainframe going doing for several days because of a system upgrade).

> *Eight in 10 organizations surveyed in a new study on the current cybersecurity landscape see value in conducting cyber risk assessments yet slightly more than 65 percent actually do so and only 39 percent conduct annual audits.*
>
> (Source: MSSP Alert (Kass[30]))

7.8 WHEN RISK ASSESSMENTS BITE BACK

If you have not already done so, I would highly recommend that you read the 9/11 Commission Report (On[31]). This horrendous event might have been avoided had the world governments been proactive with their risk assessment practices. In the lead-up to this fateful day, the authorities appeared to have only been carrying out reactive risk assessments, based upon traditional methods. However, had they had started investigating various risk scenarios, they may have identified the threat actors evolving tactics.

Had they included the evolving threats and the numerous combat indicators into their risk scenarios, they might have identified new attack surfaces (e.g., aircraft-borne attacks). Since, there has been Ramzi Yousef's failed vehicle-borne improvised explosive device attack, on 26th February 1993 (US Department of State[32]), (Federal Bureau of Investigation[33]). Prior to this catastrophic attack, there were several intelligence feeds that could have created differing risk scenarios, for example:

- Boat-borne attack on the U.S.S. *Cole* (Federal Bureau of Investigation, "U.S.S. Cole Bombing | Federal Bureau of Investigation"[34]).
- Flight schools warning (CBS News[35]).
- Federal Bureau of Investigation (FBI) Investigations (Office of the Inspector General[36]).
- FBI, Central Intelligence Agency, and National Security Agency intelligence reports (U.S. Senate Select Committee on Intelligence and U.S. House Permanent Select Committee on Intelligence[37]).

Much like Al Qaeda evolved its tactics, so do today's threat actors, and your business needs to be able to forecast these changes and how vulnerable your organization might be to such evolving threats. For example, look at how ransomware attacks evolved (The 5 et al.[38]) to deal with any organization that sought to mitigate this threat, such as backing up their data assets.

- Data-stealing ransomware, such as Diavol (The DFIR Report[39]).
- Double extortion (Bleeping Computer[40]).
- Triple extortion (Checkpoint[41]).

7.9 DECODING RISK ASSESSMENTS

Rarely do organizations utilize risk assessments to their full potential. Consequently, much like H&S (HASpod[42]), risk assessments are often carried out reactively (e.g., after an impactful event), whereas, when used proactively, risk assessments can really help a business to understand its threats, create realistic risk scenarios, and to reduce a harmful event occurring in the first instance.

Risk assessments need to be an integral part of routine business and considered as the driver for all the other protective strategies, rather than protective strategies driving the risk assessments (i.e., the tail wagging the dog!).

When an organization puts sufficient effort into risk assessments, it will soon see a value in its mitigation efforts, while understanding any 'near misses' (Health & Safety Executive[43]) that have been avoided by the risk assessment work. Additionally, effective risk assessments can provide increased visibility, assurance, and can help to reduce costs.

Notes

1 Rudolph, Marc D., et al. "At Risk of Being Risky: The Relationship Between 'Brain Age' Under Emotional States and Risk Preference." *Developmental Cognitive Neuroscience*, 24, Apr. 2017, pp. 93–106, www.sciencedirect.com/scie nce/article/pii/S1878929316301074, 10.1016/j.dcn.2017.01.010

2 American Academy of Child and Adolescent Psychiatry. "Teen Brain: Behavior, Problem Solving, and Decision Making." Aacap.org, Sept. 2016, www.aacap. org/aacap/families_and_youth/facts_for_families/fff-guide/the-teen-brain-behav ior-problem-solving-and-decision-making-095.aspx

3 Youell, Joy. "Adolescent Psychology: What Makes Teens Different, and How Can Psychology Help? | Betterhelp." Betterhelp.com, BetterHelp, 24 Sept. 2018, www.betterhelp.com/advice/adolescence/adolescent-psychology-what-makes-teens-different-and-how-can-psychology-help/

4 getreading. "Game of 'Chicken' Ends in Serious Injury to Teenager." BerkshireLive, 12 Apr. 2005, www.getreading.co.uk/news/local-news/game-chic ken-ends-serious-injury-4264825. Accessed 10 Jan. 2022.

5 Society for Neuroscience. "Brain Facts: A Primer on the Brain and Nervous System. Washington, DC: Society for Neuroscience, 2018.

6 Howieson, Diane. "Cognitive Skills and the Aging Brain: What To..." Dana Foundation, , Dec. 2015, www.dana.org/article/cognitive-skills-and-the-aging-brain-what-to-expect/

7 Brown, Valerie J. "Risk Perception: It's Personal." *Environmental Health Perspectives*, 122 (10), Oct. 2014, 10.1289/ehp.122-a276

8 Spencer, Merianne Rose, et al. "Products – Data Briefs – Number 400 – March 2021." www.cdc.gov, 17 Mar. 2021, www.cdc.gov/nchs/products/databriefs/db400.htm

9 US EPA,ORD,NCEA. "About Risk Assessment | US EPA." US EPA, 23 Apr. 2018, www.epa.gov/risk/about-risk-assessment

10 NIST Glossary. "Risk Assessment – Glossary | CSRC." Nist.gov, 2015, csrc.nist. gov/glossary/term/risk assessment

11 Ready. "Risk Assessment | Ready.gov." Ready.gov, 2000, www.ready.gov/risk-assessment

12 CCOHS. "Risk Assessment." Ccohs.ca, 2017, www.ccohs.ca/oshanswers/hsp rograms/risk_assessment.html

13 Bragg, Steven. "Risk Assessment Definition." *Accounting Tools*, 7 Aug. 2021, www.accountingtools.com/articles/2017/8/19/risk-assessment. Accessed 11 Jan. 2022.

14 UK Government. "OPSS Risk Lexicon." Gov.UK, 21 May 2021, www.gov.uk/guidance/opss-risk-lexicon. Accessed 11 Jan. 2022.

15 Gartner. "Definition of Risk Management – Gartner Information Technology Glossary." Gartner, www.gartner.com/en/information-technology/glossary/risk-management. Accessed 11 Jan. 2022.

16 McArdle, Elaine, et al. "Kenneth R. Feinberg: 'I'm Very Proud of What We Did.'" *Harvard Law Today*, 9 Sept. 2021, today.law.harvard.edu/kenneth-r-feinberg-im-very-proud-of-what-we-did. Accessed 11 Jan. 2022.

17 *Worth*. Directed by Sara Colangelo, Netflix, 2020.

18 jonana, et al. "The 5 Types of Risk Assessment and When to Use Them." Kavian Scientific Research Association, 1 Dec. 2021, ksra.eu/the-5-types-of-risk-assessment-and-when-to-use-them. Accessed 11 Jan. 2022.

19 Safety Culture. "Qualitative Risk Analysis & Quantitative Risk Analysis." SafetyCulture, 24 Dec. 2021, safetyculture.com/topics/qualitative-and-quantitative-risk-analysis. Accessed 11 Jan. 2022.

20 Caldas, Antonio. "How to Create a Risk Heatmap in Excel – Part 1." *Risk Management Guru*, 17 Nov. 2016, riskmanagementguru.com/create-risk-heatmap-excel-part-1.html. Accessed 11 Jan. 2022.

21 Capterra. "Best Patch Management Software 2022 | Reviews of the Most Popular Tools & Systems." www.capterra.com, 2022, www.capterra.com/patch-management-software. Accessed 11 Jan. 2022.

22 FAIR Institute. "FAIR-U." 2022, app.fairu.net.

23 FAIR Institute. "The Importance and Effectiveness of Quantifying Cyber Risk." Fairinstitute.org, 2019, www.fairinstitute.org/what-is-fair

24 Kenton, Will. "Monte Carlo Simulation." Investopedia, 2019, www.investope dia.com/terms/m/montecarlosimulation.asp

25 jonana, et al. "The 5 Types of Risk Assessment and When to Use Them." Kavian Scientific Research Association, 1 Dec. 2021, ksra.eu/the-5-types-of-risk-assessment-and-when-to-use-them

26 Reciprocity. "The Different Types of Risk Assessment Methodologies." Reciprocity. com, 8 Oct. 2021, reciprocity.com/blog/types-of-risk-assessment-methodologies

27 Caralli, Richard, et al. CERT® Resilience Management Model, Version 1.2 Risk Management (RISK) CERT Program. 2016.

28 Reality Tech. "SharePoint Enterprise Risk Management System | Reality-Tech." Reality Tech, reality-tech.com/solutions/sharepoint-enterprise-risk-management-system. Accessed 12 Jan. 2022.

29 Juergens, Michael. "End User Computing | Deloitte US | Internal Audit Transformation." Deloitte United States, www2.deloitte.com/us/en/pages/audit/articles/end-user-computing-solving-the-problem.html

30 Kass, D. Howard. "What's the Value of Cyber Risk Assessments?" MSSP Alert, 2 Aug. 2021, www.msspalert.com/cybersecurity-research/whats-the-value-of-cyber-risk-assessments. Accessed 12 Jan. 2022.

31 National Commission on Terrorist Attacks upon the United States. "The 9/11 Commission Report: Final Report of the National Commission on Terrorist Attacks upon the United States." New York: Norton, 2004.

32 US Department of State. "1993 World Trade Center Bombing." United States Department of State, 21 Feb. 2019, www.state.gov/1993-world-trade-center-bombing. Accessed 12 Jan. 2022.

33 Federal Bureau of Investigation. "FBI 100 – 1993 Trade Center Bombing." FBI, 2019, archives.fbi.gov/archives/news/stories/2008/february/tradebom_022608.

34 Federal Bureau of Investigation. "USS Cole Bombing | Federal Bureau of Investigation." Federal Bureau of Investigation, 2016, www.fbi.gov/history/fam ous-cases/uss-cole-bombing

35 CBS News. "FBI Was Warned About Flight Schools." www.cbsnews.com, 15 May 2002, www.cbsnews.com/news/fbi-was-warned-about-flight-schools. Accessed 12 Jan. 2022.

36 Office of the Inspector General. "Special Report: A Review of the FBI's Handling of Intelligence Information Related to the September 11 Attacks (Full Report)." Oig.justice.gov, Nov. 2004, oig.justice.gov/sites/default/files/archive/special/s0606/chapter4.htm

37 U.S. Senate Select Committee on Intelligence, and U.S. House Permanent Select Committee on Intelligence. Report of the Joint Inquiry into the Terrorist

Attacks of September 11, 2001 – by the House Permanent Select Committee on Intelligence and the Senate Select Committee on Intelligence. Dec. 2002.

38 The 5, et al. "The Evolution of Ransomware: How Did We Get Here?" TechSpot, 5 July 2021, www.techspot.com/article/2284-ransomware. Accessed 12 Jan. 2022.

39 The DFIR Report. "Diavol Ransomware." The DFIR Report, 13 Dec. 2021, thedfirreport.com/2021/12/13/diavol-ransomware. Accessed 12 Jan. 2022.

40 Bleeping Computer. "PYSA Ransomware Behind Most Double Extortion Attacks in November." BleepingComputer, 21 Dec. 2021, www.bleepingcompu ter.com/news/security/pysa-ransomware-behind-most-double-extortion-attacks-in-november. Accessed 12 Jan. 2022.

41 Checkpoint. "The New Ransomware Threat: Triple Extortion." Check Point Software, 12 May 2021, blog.checkpoint.com/2021/05/12/the-new-ransomware-threat-triple-extortion. Accessed 12 Jan. 2022.

42 HASpod. "Proactive vs Reactive Health and Safety Management." Haspod.com, HASpod, 2 Nov. 2018, www.haspod.com/blog/management/proactive-reactive-health-safety-management

43 Health & Safety Executive. Near-Miss Book: Recording and Reporting near Misses at Work. S.L., Hse Books, 2021.

Chapter 8

Developing a Risk Culture

8.1 THE BRITISH MILITARY DEPLOYMENTS ANALOGY

In preparation for every British military deployment to hostile environments (such as Iraq and Afghanistan, etc.), the British military leadership has recognized the importance of ensuring that every member of an off-base mobile patrol is trained to deputize for other members of the patrol, and embedded in this training is the creation of a risk culture.

During their pre-deployment training, each patrol team member is extensively taught the tactics, techniques, and protocols (TTPs) that are known to be used by their aggressors and are trained to identify and respond to any combat indicators. In addition, they are taught the vulnerabilities associated with their patrol vehicles and how to take preventive as well as reactive measures to help mitigate the associated risks.

As an example, in Afghanistan a river crossing was identified as an environment (pinch point) that was known to significantly increase the risks of an attack (e.g., ambush, placement of clandestine improvised explosive devices (IEDs)). As a result, during their pre-deployment training, each member of a patrol would need to demonstrate their competency in carrying out effective drills to help reduce these risks.

The risk responsibilities are not limited to just a handful of the patrol team (e.g., convoy commander, deputy convoy commander, etc.). The purpose is to ensure that everyone remains vigilant and able to quickly and efficiently respond to the identification of known combat indicators, which if ignored could have severe consequences. As a result, these high-risk and ever-present risks could be partially mitigated through training.

Early patrols utilized lightweight (unarmored), highly mobile, and agile offroad patrol vehicles (e.g., Land Rovers, WIMIK 1, Snatch, Pinzgauer, etc.), which allowed the patrols to vary their patrol patterns.

Table 8.1 British Military Patrol Vehicle Evolution

Earlier Vehicles	Later Vehicles	
2007 British Military Patrol Vehicle	2009 British Military Patrol Vehicle	>2010 British Military Patrol Vehicle

Land Rover (Author).

Mastiff (Jones[3]).

Husky ("SAS to Stop Using Land Rovers" (Elite UK Forces[4])).

WIMIK 1 (Julien[5]).

Jackal ("Supacat Jackal Patrol Vehicle | Military-Today.com"[6]).

Snatch Landrover (Westmacott[7]).

Foxhound (Liam et al.[8]).

Vector/Pinzgauer ("Pinzgauer 2020 – Think Defence"[9]).

Learning the lessons from the earlier deployments, the British military leaders recognized that training (as good as it had been) was not sufficient to bring the risks down to acceptable levels. Consequently, significant investment was made in designing and developing suitable armored patrol vehicles that were able to withstand the direct blast force from an IED (e.g., the Mastiff).

However, with deployed operations such as Afghanistan, which spanned decades, it was inevitable that the threat aggressors would adapt their TTPs so that they would be more effective. Consequently, these new heavily armored patrol vehicles were less mobile and effective across difficult terrains, and this lack of mobility meant that suitable patrol routes were limited. The aggressors used this vulnerability to better place larger, more powerful IEDs that could immobilize these very expensive patrol vehicles.

As a result of these changing TTPs, once again a new risk response needed to be identified and implemented. This came by way of the design and development of yet another bespoke patrol vehicle, which combined some of the capabilities to be both agile and armored (e.g., the Husky, Jackal, Foxhound, etc.).

The evolution of the British military patrol vehicles, otherwise known as utility tactical support vehicles ("The Future of the British Army 12 – Wheels (Options – Part 4 Utility & Tactical Support Vehicles) – Think Defence"[1]), in response to the changing risks is depicted in Table 8.1.

Much like the British military's risk culture, it is equally important that your organization establishes a similar approach to ensure that you are effectively able to identify and respond to any emerging threats.

8.2 AN INTRODUCTION TO RISK CULTURE

When looking at developing a risk culture, you need to design and develop a cohesive approach that will help your business to reduce the risks to its valued business operations. NIST defines a risk as being: "A measure of the extent to which an entity is threatened by a potential circumstance or event" (NIST Special Publication (SP) 800-30, Revision 1, Guide for Conducting Risk Assessments (Blank and Gallagher[2]).

Risks to a business tend to focus on compromised assets that create losses or impacts, as depicted in Figures 8.1 and 8.2, and may be technical, procedural, or managerial, and should be managed at both the organizational (i.e., top-down) and system/operational (i.e., bottom-up) levels.

Loss:

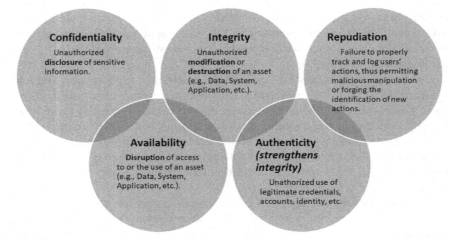

Figure 8.1 CIAAR quintet.

Impacting:

Figure 8.2 Impact elements.

The creation of an effective risk culture should be set up as part of the preparatory stage in any business's creation of a RMF.

8.3 RISK CULTURE VERSUS 'SECURITY' CULTURE

The main differences between a risk culture and a security culture are that a former is proactive, whereas the latter is reactive. Think of a padlock securing a perimeter gate, where a security culture insists that the padlock must always be locked to secure the gate when the gate is not being used. Unfortunately, this approach is not practical in the real world as it is inevitable that the padlock will be left unlocked, so the gate will remain insecure for short periods of time, in breach of the security culture. Additionally, in a security culture, employees would be encouraged to lock the gate or report it as being insecure.

Where a risk culture differs is that employees are granted some flexibility to complete their roles within agreed parameters of risk appetite. Consequently, in the padlock scenario, it would be reasonable and accepted that an employee could leave the gate insecure for a short period of time to fulfill a business task. However, there would be minimum expectations and requirements that would need to be assessed:

- The risk has been assessed.
- The risk is within delegated risk appetites.
- Senior management approval is obtained for risks that exceed the delegated risk appetites.
- Additional mitigation measures may be considered.
- The perceived risks do not present a significant increased risk to the business or its operations.

The UK's 'Orange Book' (HM Treasury[10]) provides a comprehensive overview of risk practices and includes dedicated risk appetite guidance (UK Government Finance Function[11]), which provides numerous descriptions of differing levels of risk tolerance (averse, minimal, cautious, open, eager) and shows how risk appetite levels should be scaled across an organization, as depicted in Figure 8.3.

An effective risk culture enables and rewards individuals and groups for taking the right risks in an informed manner, whereas a security culture is perceived as being a more disciplinary and corrective practice.

The Institute of Risk Management (IRM[12]) define a risk culture as being "a term describing the values, beliefs, knowledge, attitudes and understanding about risk shared by a group of people with a common purpose."

Unless you believe that your organization has numerous employees who are intent on carrying out deliberate actions, you might want to consider the benefits of developing an effective risk culture across your business.

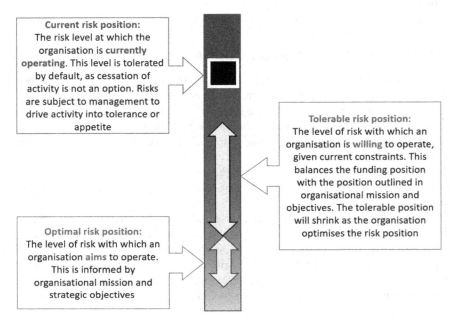

Current risk position:
The risk level at which the organisation is currently operating. This level is tolerated by default, as cessation of activity is not an option. Risks are subject to management to drive activity into tolerance or appetite

Tolerable risk position:
The level of risk with which an organisation is willing to operate, given current constraints. This balances the funding position with the position outlined in organisational mission and objectives. The tolerable position will shrink as the organisation optimises the risk position

Optimal risk position:
The level of risk with which an organisation aims to operate. This is informed by organisational mission and strategic objectives

Figure 8.3 Risk appetite scale.

8.4 DEVELOPING AN EFFECTIVE RISK CULTURE

The IRM has produced a comprehensive guidance document (Institute of Risk Management, The Institute of Risk Management Risk Culture Resources for Practitioners[13]) to help businesses develop their own effective risk culture practices. This model focuses on five components, as shown in Figure 8.4.

An overview of what an effective risk culture might look like and what this would involve is detailed in Figure 8.5 (Kunz and Heitz[14]).

Let's not 'sugar coat' this, the implementation of an effective risk culture is an extremely difficult task and may not be favorable to everyone. The concept requires extensive planning, mentoring, and support, plus a high degree of trust.

This all starts with a very strong leadership team embracing the concept of implementing and supporting a risk culture. Consequently, the qualities of strong leadership (e.g., confidence, assertiveness, motivation, vision, intelligence, etc.) should drive the development of an effective risk culture and inspire others to embrace the concept. Additionally, authority to deal with risks needs to be delegated to within acceptable tolerances, and individuals should be mentored so that they have the confidence in knowing

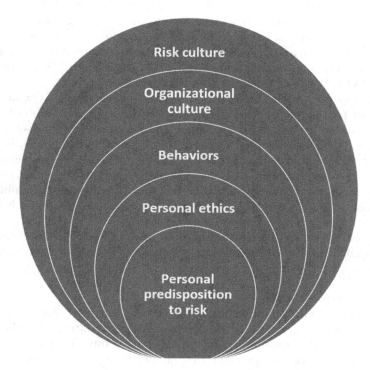

Figure 8.4 IRM Risk culture model.

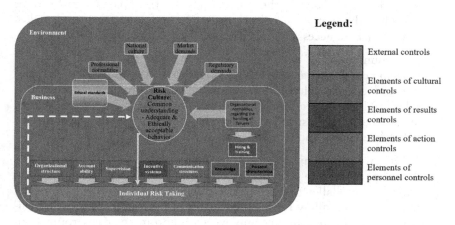

Figure 8.5 Risk culture and management control systems.

that they have delegated responsibilities, along with the knowledge that they can escalate any risks that they are not comfortable dealing with.

As the term implies, risk culture needs to be embraced across all areas of the business, requiring teamwork and a cohesive approach to ensure that everyone understands the business's risk culture (Risk Appetite (RESOLVER[15]) + Risk Tolerance (Bredvick[16]) = Risk Culture).

Risk appetite is "the broad-based amount an enterprise is willing to accept in pursuit of its mission/vision" (The United States White House (United States White House[17])). Risk tolerance, according to ISO Guide 73:2009 (ISO – International Organization for Standardization[18]), is "the organization's or stakeholder's readiness to bear the risk after risk treatment in order to achieve its objectives. Note: Risk tolerance can be influenced by legal or regulatory requirements." The definition of risk culture (Cambridge Dictionary[19]) is "the way of life, especially the general customs and beliefs, of a particular group of people at a particular time."

The concept of a risk culture is nothing new. and in 2014 the Financial Stability Board specified several different indicators of a sound risk culture, including the following:

1. Tone from the top
The board and senior management are the starting point for setting the financial institution's core values and expectations for the risk culture of the institution, and their behavior must reflect the values being espoused. A key value that should be espoused is the expectation that staff act with integrity (doing the right thing) and promptly escalate observed non-compliance within or outside the organization (no surprises approach). The leadership of the institution promotes, monitors, and assesses the risk culture of the financial institution; considers the impact of culture on safety and soundness; and makes changes where necessary.

2. Accountability
Relevant employees at all levels understand the core values of the institution and its approach to risk, are capable of performing their prescribed roles, and are aware that they are held accountable for their actions in relation to the institution's risk-taking behavior. Staff acceptance of risk-related goals and related values is essential.

3. Effective communication and challenge
A sound risk culture promotes an environment of open communication and effective challenge in which decision-making processes encourage a range of views; allow for testing of current practices; stimulate a positive, critical attitude among employees; and promote an environment of open and constructive engagement.

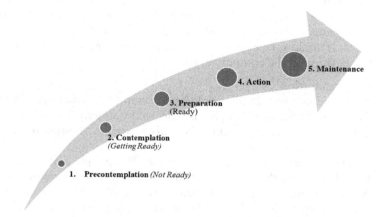

Figure 8.6 Stages of change.

4. Incentives
Performance and talent management encourage and reinforce maintenance of the financial institution's desired risk management behavior. Financial and nonfinancial incentives support the core values and risk culture at all levels of the institution.

(Source: Financial Stability Board[20])

For a successful approach, there is a great deal of psychology involved to aid a smooth transition and to help ensure that the concept is embraced by most of the organization. Two key human factors need to be addressed:

1. The Transtheoretical Model (Raihan and Cogburn[21])
   Human nature and emotional reactions mean that different people will respond differently to changes and with differing timelines. It is important to understand, recognize, and respond to the stages of change, as depicted in Figure 8.6.

   a. Precontemplation
   In the precontemplation stage, individuals are not seriously thinking about changing, and are not interested in any kind of help. In this stage, they tend to defend their current bad habit(s) and do not feel it is a problem. They may be defensive in the face of other people's efforts to pressure them to change.

   b. Contemplation
   In the contemplation stage, individuals are wavering back and forth, weighing up the pros and cons of modifying their behavior. Although

they think about the negative aspects of their bad habit, and the positives associated with changing, they may doubt that the long-term benefits associated with change will outweigh the short-term costs. It might take as little as a couple weeks or as long as a lifetime to get through the contemplation stage.

c.   Preparation

In the preparation stage, people have committed to making a change. Their motivation for changing is reflected by statements such as: "I've got to do something about this—this is serious. Something has to change. What can I do?"

This is sort of an exploratory phase. The people gather information about what they will need to do to change their behavior. Or they will check out websites, organizations, and resources that are available to help them in their attempt. Frequently, they might skip this stage and try to move directly from contemplation into action and fall flat on their faces because they have not adequately researched or accepted what it is going to take to make this major lifestyle change.

d.   Action

This is the stage where individuals are motivated to change their behavior and are actively involved in taking steps to change their bad behavior by using a variety of different techniques. This is the shortest of all the stages. The amount of time they spend in action varies. It generally lasts about six months, but it can be as short as one hour! This is a stage when people most depend on their own willpower. They are making overt efforts to change their behavior and are at greatest risk of relapse.

Mentally, they review their commitment to themselves and develop plans to deal with both personal and external pressures that may lead to slips. They may use short-term rewards to sustain their motivation, and analyze their behavior change efforts in a way that enhances their self-confidence. Individuals in this stage tend to be open to receiving help and are also likely to seek support from others (a very important element).

e.   Maintenance

Maintenance involves being able to successfully avoid any temptations to return to their bad old ways. The goal of the maintenance stage is to retain the new status quo. Individuals in this stage tend to remind themselves of how much progress they have made and constantly reformulate the rules of their lives, and how they are acquiring new skills to deal with life and avoid relapse. They can anticipate the situations in which a relapse could occur, and prepare coping strategies in advance.

They remain aware that what they are striving for is personally worthwhile and meaningful. They are patient with themselves and

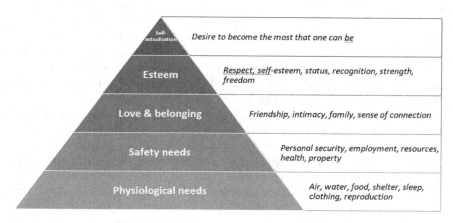

Figure 8.7 Maslow's hierarchy of needs pyramid.

recognize that it often takes a while to let go of old behavior patterns and practice new ones until they are second nature to them. Even though they may have thoughts of returning to their old bad habits, they resist the temptation and stay on track.

2. Maslow's Hierarchy of Needs.
   Unlike a former boss of mine (who wished to own a business that did not need to employ any people) I strongly believe that people can be a great asset to your business and its protection. However, like anything they need investment, mentoring, and management so that they are able (and continue) to perform at their best. Previously, through several deployments (e.g., Afghanistan, Iraq, Cape Verde, etc.) on counterintelligence operations, I have seen the value that people can bring to the effective defense of an organization.

   Much like the creation of an intelligence hub, you need to actively engage with people and ensure that they feel that they are part of the solution and are encouraged to make active contributions. Ultimately, you need to move them up the hierarchy of needs pyramid, as depicted in Figure 8.7 (Kurt[22]).

In an effective risk culture, your employees need to feel like they are just an employee, with their safety needs having been fulfilled. They need to feel like they have a sense of connection with the business and the rest of the team members involved with the risk culture, and they need to receive recognition for their efforts and receive mentoring so that they are encouraged to venture outside of their 'comfort zone' (Page[23]) and to grow into the best that they can be. Suddenly (rather than leaving risk to a handful of senior management staff), when you have nurtured a team of employees, from across the organization, to own any risks that are within their risk appetites and they have the confidence to escalate any risks that exceed their risk tolerances (without any criticism), you start to develop a highly productive and effective risk culture that does not rely upon a handful of risk specialists to try to identify and manage each and every one of the business's risks (which, as you may imagine, can be considerable).

In the financial industry, the development of risk culture appears to have been a popular concept in the mid-2010s but, in recent years, appears to have become a less prevalent concept. In August 2015, the International Finance Corporation produced a comprehensive risk management guide[24], supplying recommendations to emerging market banks to help them strengthen their risk management. This guidance includes a full section on the risk culture in banks. However, in 2021, the MIFIDPRU 7 (governance and risk management) of the FCA's handbook has a single reference to the establishment of a risk culture as being the responsibility of the resident risk committee: "(g) providing advice, oversight and challenge necessary to embed and maintain a supportive risk culture throughout the firm" (Financial Conduct Authority[25]).

Additionally, the implementation of a risk culture is something that appears to be supported by several country governments. In the UK:

> None of this is possible without a supportive risk culture.
> A positive risk culture, one which encourages openness and discusses real business issues in a realistic manner, is absolutely essential to the effective management of risk.
> Everyone, from the board down, has a clear role to play in establishing and maintaining that risk culture.
> (Source: Management of Risk in Government (UK Government[26]))

In the United States, in response to major management challenges to achieving their mission and goals, agencies continue to recognize the utility of enterprise risk management (ERM) as a tool to find, assess, mitigate, manage, and prepare for risk. ERM contributes to risk-informed decision-making, encouraging a proactive rather than reactive approach to risk, and fostering a risk-aware culture (Management's Discussion & Analysis (United States Bureau of the Fiscal Treasury[27])).

Meanwhile, in Canada:

> To that end, effective risk management in the federal government should:
>
> - support government-wide decision-making and priorities as well as the achievement of organizational objectives and outcomes, while maintaining public confidence;

Figure 8.8 Components of a risk culture model.

- be tailored and responsive to the organization's external and internal context including its mandate, priorities, organizational risk culture, risk management capacity, and partner and stakeholder interests;
- add value as a key component of decision-making, business planning, resource allocation and operational management;
- achieve a balance between the level of risk responses and established controls and support for flexibility and innovation to improve performance and outcomes;
- be transparent, inclusive, integrated and systematic; and
- continuously improve the culture, capacity and capability of risk management in federal organizations.

(Source: Framework for the Management of Risk (Treasury Board of Canada[28]))

Australia's risk culture model is depicted in Figure 8.8.

A positive risk culture is one where staff at every level appropriately manage risk as an intrinsic part of their day-to-day work.

Such a culture supports an open discussion about uncertainties and opportunities, encourages staff to express concerns, and maintains processes to elevate concerns to appropriate levels.

(Source: Comcover Information Sheet
(Australian Government Department of Finance[29]))

As the creation of an effective risk culture is very much people-oriented and collaborative, I would highly recommend that you include your human resources people and key stakeholders from across the business in the design and development of a risk culture model that is best suited to your business.

8.5 RISK CULTURE HIERARCHY

If you think of your risk culture as being omnidirectional, it needs to be driven by senior management (top-down), communicated upwards by the team/department managers (bottom-up), and communicated across the peer groups (lateral) to ensure that risk is embedded into every business operation/process and into every new project.

Risk appetite and tolerance levels should be clearly defined, with appropriate levels of delegated responsibilities distributed across the business, so that those personnel have a degree of autonomy to handle those risks that are within parameters that are acceptable for them. Where any risks exceed these parameters, personnel should have the confidence to escalate the risks up the 'chain of command,' to be managed by personnel with greater levels of responsibility. All risks that have been handled by delegated personnel should still be reported up the 'chain of command,' providing insights and reassurances that risks continue to be identified and effectively managed.

As you may imagine, in ensuring that the risk practices remain consistently applied across the organization, it is important to establish a continual risk development program and regular meetings to enable engaging discussions between the business's personnel with delegated risk responsibilities (e.g., risk committee).

8.5.1 Three Lines of Defense Model

Within the financial services industries, they have adopted a 'three lines of defense' (3LOD) model:

First Line – Employees
A firm's employees are the crucial first line of defense against conduct risk and senior managers need to be confident that day-to-day operating

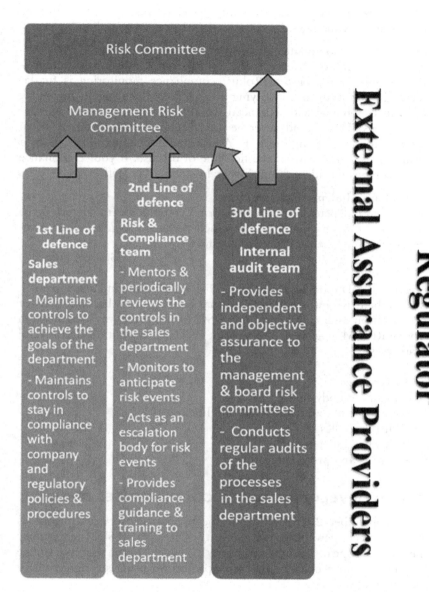

Figure 8.9 3LOD model structure.

procedures deliver regulatory compliance. Front-line teams must be responsible for managing and mitigating their own compliance risks.

Second Line – Compliance monitoring
The second line of defense is the application of a risk-based compliance monitoring program. Robust compliance monitoring is fundamentally important in identifying areas where a firm might be at risk of non-compliance with Financial Conduct Authority (FCA) rules or regulations. This should never be just a quick tick box exercise in an attempt to appease any future FCA visit, but a meaningful review by a firm's compliance team of the first line of defense. If your compliance monitoring is not identifying risks or breaches, it is ineffective.

Third Line – Independent assurance
An annual independent review of a firm's compliance framework is the final line of defense and the one which perhaps provides senior managers with the greatest degree of comfort.

(Source: French[30])

An effective 3LOD model, as depicted in Figure 8.9 (Holland and Floam[31]), seeks to embed risk into the model so that a risk culture becomes part of the organization and, similar to the COSO of the Treadway Commission Enterprise Risk Management Framework (PWC[32]), is built around several key principles:

1. Governance
2. Governing body roles
3. Management and first and second line roles
4. Third line roles
5. Third line independence
6. Creating and protecting value

8.6 WHEN DEVELOPING A RISK CULTURE BITES BACK

On 14th September 2019, many European financial services businesses needed to meet new Payment Security Directive (PSD2) regulatory obligations (European Banking Authority[33]), which meant that any online services had to have enhanced security protection using strong customer authentication (SCA) (Gupta[34]).

Trying to balance the 'customer journey' with their technology and the PSD2 requirements (European Banking Authority[35]) proved to be extremely troublesome for these affected organizations, while the added pressures of a fast-approaching deadline and the potential of substantial fines ("Under PSD2, Member States are free to determine penalties that may be imposed by national authorities following an infringement of the law." (Inside

Privacy[36]) for not having this in place substantially increased the pressure on these businesses to do something.

To ease these pressures, some of the European regulators extended the deadline (Thales Group[37]). However, by the time this deadline extension had been announced most of the affected European financial services businesses had already identified and committed to their approach and solution to meet the PSD2 requirements (PWC[38]).

In their hurry to implement an SCA solution, many financial services organizations failed to identify (during the project phase) the potential implications and risks to their chosen/preferred options. As a result, many organizations chose the more convenient and easier to implement texting of a verification code to the customer's mobile device.

However, what if the customers were doing online banking on the very same mobile device that would receive the texted verification code? What if the receiving mobile device had been compromised?

At the time that many of these financial services were working on their PSD2 projects, there were well-established and well-known criminal tactics that should have been included in their risk assessments; for example, sim swap fraud (Federal Trade Commission[39]). However, without an effective risk culture, the impact of this type of threat (despite being reported by Action Fraud UK as seeing an increase of 400% (Which Magazine[40])) was either not identified, communicated, or considered as being an issue for these organizations.

In January 2022, several leading UK banks suffered significant reputation damage as a report published by *Which?* magazine (*Which?*, "Banking Security Put to the Test: Could Your Bank Be Doing More to Stop Fraud?"[41]), as seen in Figure 8.10, identified these failings and how these organizations were putting their customers at significant risk.

Although an effective risk culture may not have guaranteed that this mistake would not have been made, the opportunity existed for numerous personnel and key stakeholders to discuss the threat that sim swap fraud may have presented to their PSD2 project, to make an informed decision, to document their risk response options, and the preferred choice that was taken.

8.7 DECODING DEVELOPING A RISK CULTURE

People should be an essential part of your organization's risk management practices, so that an efficient risk culture is embedded throughout your business. The greater the number of 'risk-savvy' personnel you have acting as your 'risk radars' to identify, manage (within delegated responsibilities), and communicate risks to your valuable business operations/processes, the greater the chances you have for averting impactful events/incidents from occurring.

Banking security put to the test: could your bank be doing more to stop fraud?

A Which? Money investigation has identified weaknesses in some banks' online and mobile banking security, which could be exploited by criminals

By **Chiara Cavaglieri**   11 Jan 2022

The latest banking security investigation from Which? Money shows that too many banks are neglecting basic housekeeping, potentially leaving their customers at risk of fraud.

With cases of internet banking fraud in the UK up 97% to almost 42,000 in the first half of 2021, and losses hitting a record £108.9m, criminals are still managing to breach banks' defences.

All of the apps and websites we tested are safe enough to use – and banks regularly test their systems for vulnerabilities – but we use our annual banking security investigation to hold the banking industry to the highest standards.

We were concerned to find that some banks aren't using the latest protections for their websites, while others are still allowing customers to set insecure passwords. We also found a gulf between the best and worst mobile banking apps.

Related articles

Inflation rises to 5.4% in December 2021: can any savings rates beat it?
19 Jan 2022
Savings & Isas

Could you cut your 2020-21 self-assessment tax bill?
19 Jan 2022
Tax

One in six shoppers don't know about the cashback without purchase scheme
18 Jan 2022
Banking

Figure 8.10 Which? Article, 11th January 2022.

Effective leadership teams are more likely to embrace the concept of developing and implementing a suitable risk culture, as they will naturally lead by example and have the confidence to delegate some of their risk responsibilities.

An effective risk culture is very much 'people-centric' and needs continual investment of time and effort, so that each participant remains an effective member, and continual communication activities are embedded as part of routine business practice. However, the return on these investments helps to ensure that your organization's risk processes are proactively used in the defense of your business, providing increased longevity and operational resilience.

Notes

1 "The Future of the British Army 12 – Wheels (Options – Part 4 Utility & Tactical Support Vehicles) – Think Defence." www.thinkdefence.co.uk, 30 Sept. 2011, www.thinkdefence.co.uk/2011/09/the-future-of-the-british-army-12-wheels-options-part-3-utility-tactical-support-vehicles. Accessed 14 Jan. 2022.

2 Blank, Rebecca, and Patrick Gallagher. "Guide for Conducting Risk Assessments NIST Special Publication 800-30 Revision 1 JOINT TASK FORCE TRANSFORMATION INITIATIVE". 2012.

3 Jones, Jonathan. "Mastiff 2 (AFV)." Armored Vehicles, 1 Feb. 2012, armour.ws/mastiff-af. Accessed 14 Jan. 2022.

4 Elite UK Forces. "SAS to Stop Using Land Rovers." www.eliteukforces.info, 9 May 2014, www.eliteukforces.info/uk-military-news/09052014-sas-land-rovers.php. Accessed 14 Jan. 2022.

5 Julien. "Land Rover Wolf – Weapons Mount Installation Kit (WMIK)." Britmodeller.com, 28 Oct. 2012, www.britmodeller.com/forums/index.php?/topic/234928621-land-rover-wolf-weapons-mount-installation-kit-wmik. Accessed 14 Jan. 2022.

6 "Supacat Jackal Patrol Vehicle | Military-Today.com." www.military-Today.com, www.military-today.com/trucks/supacat_jackal.htm. Accessed 14 Jan. 2022.

7 Westmacott, Richard. "Bombers Target Our Soldiers on Patrol in Lightly Armoured Land Rovers." www.telegraph.co.uk, 5 Sept. 2006, www.telegraph.co.uk/news/1528107/Bombers-target-our-soldiers-on-patrol-in-lightly-armoured-Land-Rovers.html. Accessed 14 Jan. 2022.

8 Liam, et al. "2 YORKS on Scene at Kabul Hotel Terror Attack." *Warfare Today*, 26 Jan. 2018, www.warfare.today/2018/01/26/2-yorks-on-scene-at-kabul-hotel-terror-attack. Accessed 14 Jan. 2022.

9 "Pinzgauer 2020 – Think Defence." www.thinkdefence.co.uk, 27 Apr. 2013, www.thinkdefence.co.uk/2013/04/pinzgauer-2020. Accessed 14 Jan. 2022.

10 HM Treasury. "Orange Book." Gov.uk, 29 May 2013, www.gov.uk/government/publications/orange-book

11 UK Government Finance Function. "Government Finance Function Risk Appetite Guidance Note." Aug. 2021.

12 Institute of Risk Management. "Risk Culture." www.theirm.org, www.Theirm. org/what-we-say/thought-leadership/risk-culture

13 Institute of Risk Management. "The Institute of Risk Management Risk Culture Resources for Practitioners". 2012.

14 Kunz, Jennifer, and Mathias Heitz. "Banks' Risk Culture and Management Control Systems: A Systematic Literature Review." *Journal of Management Control*, 13 Aug. 2021, 10.1007/s00187-021-00325-4. Accessed 22 Aug. 2021.

15 RESOLVER. "Developing, Defining & Quantifying Risk Appetite." Resolver, 12 Sept. 2021, www.resolver.com/blog/developing-defining-and-quantifying-your-risk-appetite. Accessed 18 Jan. 2022.

16 Bredvick, Dustin. "Cyber Security: What's Your Risk Tolerance? | Huffman Engineering." Huffman Engineering Inc., 29 June 2021, huffmaneng.com/cyber-security-whats-your-risk-tolerance. Accessed 18 Jan. 2022.

17 United States White House. Executive Office of the President Office of Management and Budget F Executive Departments and Agencies from: Subject: OMB Circular No. A-123, Management's Responsibility for Enterprise Risk Management and Internal Control. 15 July 2016.

18 ISO – International Organization for Standardization. "ISO Guide 73:2009." International Standards Organization (ISO), 8 Nov. 2017, www.iso.org/stand ard/44651.html

19 Cambridge Dictionary. "CULTURE | Meaning in the Cambridge English Dictionary." Cambridge.org, 2019, dictionary.cambridge.org/dictionary/eng-lish/culture

20 Financial Stability Board. "Guidance on Supervisory Interaction with Financial Institutions on Risk Culture a Framework for Assessing Risk Culture." 2014.

21 Raihan, Nahrain, and Mark Cogburn. "Stages of Change Theory." *PubMed*, StatPearls Publishing, 2021, www.ncbi.nlm.nih.gov/books/NBK556005

22 Kurt, Dr. Serhat. "Maslow's Hierarchy of Needs in Education." Education Library, 6 Feb. 2020, educationlibrary.org/maslows-hierarchy-of-needs-in-education

23 Page, Oliver. "How to Leave Your Comfort Zone and Enter Your 'Growth Zone.'" PositivePsychology.com, 4 Nov. 2020, positivepsychology.com/comfort-zone. Accessed 18 Jan. 2022.

24 International Finance Corporation. "Recommendations for Strengthening Risk Management in Emerging Market Banks Risk Culture, Risk Governance, and Balanced Incentives." Aug. 2015.

25 Financial Conduct Authority. "FCA Handbook." Financial Conduct Authority, 2022, www.handbook.fca.org.uk/handbook/MIFIDPRU/7/3.html?date= 2022-01-01

26 UK Government. "Management of Risk in Government a Framework for Boards and Examples of What Has Worked in Practice – A Non-Executives' Review Management of Risk in Government." 2017.

27 United States Bureau of the Fiscal Treasury. "Financial Report of the United States Government – Management." www.fiscal.treasury.gov, 23 July 2019, www.fiscal.treasury.gov/reports-statements/financial-report/2018/financial-man agement.html. Accessed 18 Jan. 2022.

28 Treasury Board of Canada. "Framework for the Management of Risk." www. tbs-Sct.gc.ca, 19 Aug. 2010, www.tbs-sct.gc.ca/pol/doc-eng.aspx?id=19422. Accessed 18 Jan. 2022.

29 Australian Government Department of Finance. "COMCOVER INFORMATION SHEET CULTURE Developing a Positive Risk Culture." 2016.

30 French, Joe. "How to Remain Compliant with the Three Lines of Defence Model." Ocorian, 4 Oct. 2021, www.ocorian.com/article/how-remain-compli ant-three-lines-defence-model. Accessed 31 Jan. 2022.

31 Holland, Thomas, and Stacey Floam. "Three Lines of Defense: A New Principles-Based Approach." Guidehouse.com, 10 Feb. 2021, guidehouse.com/insights/ financial-services/2021/public-sector/garp-three-lines-of-defense.

32 PWC. "COSO Enterprise Risk Management Framework – Integrating Strategy and Performance." 2017.

33 European Banking Authority. "Regulatory Technical Standards on Strong Customer Authentication and Secure Communication under PSD2." European Banking Authority, 12 Apr. 2019, www.eba.europa.eu/regulation-and-policy/ payment-services-and-electronic-money/regulatory-technical-standards-on-str ong-customer-authentication-and-secure-communication-under-psd2. Accessed 19 Jan. 2022.

34 Gupta, Neeta. "The September 14th PSD2 Deadline – Are the Banks Ready?" Akeo, 16 Sept. 2019, medium.com/akeo-tech/the-september-14th-psd2-deadline-are-the-banks-ready-5c4c57e39ec5. Accessed 19 Jan. 2022.

35 European Banking Authority. "Payment Services Directive 2 (PSD2)." European Banking Authority, 9 July 2019, www.eba.europa.eu/regulation-and-policy/sin gle-rulebook/interactive-single-rulebook/5402. Accessed 19 Jan. 2022.

36 Inside Privacy. "Overlap between the GDPR and PSD2." Inside Privacy, 16 Mar. 2018, www.insideprivacy.com/financial-institutions/overlap-between-the-gdpr-and-psd2. Accessed 19 Jan. 2022.

37 Thales Group. "PSD2 Regulation – Get Ready with Thales." Thales Group, www.thalesgroup.com/en/markets/digital-identity-and-security/banking-paym ent/digital-banking/psd2

38 Price Waterhouse Coopers. "Roles for Banks and Payment Operators. How the Scenario Might Evolve in the Future. PSD2 in a Nutshell." 2017.

39 Federal Trade Commission. "SIM Swap Scams: How to Protect Yourself." Consumer Information, 23 Oct. 2019, www.consumer.ftc.gov/blog/2019/10/ sim-swap-scams-how-protect-yourself

40 Which Magazine. "Sim-Swap Fraud: How Criminals Hijack Your Number to Get into Your Bank Accounts." Which? News, 5 Apr. 2020, www.which.co.uk/ news/2020/04/sim-swap-fraud-how-criminals-hijack-your-number-to-get-into-your-bank-accounts. Accessed 19 Jan. 2022.

41 Which? "Banking Security Put to the Test: Could Your Bank Be Doing More to Stop Fraud?" Which? News, 11 Jan. 2022, www.which.co.uk/news/2022/01/ banking-security-put-to-the-test-could-your-bank-be-doing-more-to-stop-fraud. Accessed 19 Jan. 2022.

Chapter 9

Risk-Enabling the Human Firewall

9.1 LEARNING HOW TO DRIVE ANALOGY

Continuing the vehicle analogy, think about a department in a business as being like a new driver when it comes to their understanding of risk. Before being allowed to drive, they will have observed the driving practices of their family and friends, or just simply through their observations from being the passenger in a vehicle since they were a baby. They only know what they have observed or what they have overheard. Would you trust this individual to drive a car, motorcycle, or a large truck?

Probably not, which is the same as most governments believe as well. What most countries require if someone wants to drive is typically broken up into two parts:

1. A knowledge-based exam, through the study of the text, and
2. A practical exam where someone must drive a vehicle to show proficiency.

We see a wide range of proficiencies when it comes to people's driving skills, and we see that change when the environments change (e.g., city driving verse rural driving). There are multiple factors to be considered when it comes to someone's driving proficiency:

- Were they allowed to drive small, motorized vehicles (e.g., dirt bikes, tractors, lawnmowers) as a child?
- Were their parents or guardians proficient, risk-averse drivers?
- How much did they study for the written exam?
- How much time did they spend practicing driving an actual vehicle on their learner/driver's permit?
- Who was their teacher? Their parents or a skilled driving instructor?
- Did they practice using a vehicle with multiple driver-assist features?
- Did they learn how to drive a manual transmission vehicle?

DOI: 10.1201/9781003288084-11

When it comes to risk in a business, we see a wide range of different levels in terms of practicing or understanding risk, just like we see a wide range when it comes to people's driving skills. In the previous chapter we provided the tools in developing the culture. Now we will provide you with the tools to operationalize this new culture into risk-enabling your human firewall.

9.2 AN INTRODUCTION TO RISK-ENABLING THE HUMAN FIREWALL

Risk-enabling the human firewall, or educating your workforce, to be risk empowered may seem something of a myth but bringing risk to the departments of an organization through enablement will help facilitate the concepts discussed in the previous chapter. With the increased use of technologies leading to the embracement of new and a wide range of end-user demographics within an organization, it has never been more important to develop a human-centered approach to risk and information security services.

Everyone, including leadership, sees the effect that new technologies are having on people, so it is beneficial to adapt your approach to addressing their difficulties, by making risk services more personalized through strong two-way communication. This can only be achieved through an adaptive and flexible model, where one engages with people/departments and continually identifies risk and opportunities to enhance their processes, and by being an organization's service enabler, through engagement and enabling department-level continuous processes improvement (CPI), facilitating department-level strategic planning and process improvement events so that all areas of risk for a department's processes are identified.

Through this process, you can work with the departments to find solutions that enable them to be more efficient in their job responsibilities, all the while mitigating the risks, and assisting them in implementing solutions from the start. If this is done in a systematic reoccurring method, the departments will be able to map cost, investments, risks, and resources, hopefully five years into the future.

Doing this will also help you better unify with your departments and their risks, across the organization, and ensure that it will not be viewed as a roadblock or prohibitive in them getting their work accomplished.

9.3 SERVICE PROVIDER VERSUS SERVICE ENABLEMENT

Organizations should at least view their security department (or team) as a service provider, much like IT service management (ITSM). As stated by Dr. Boris Piwinger: "The leading companies see information security departments as internal service providers. At its core, information security is an extension of the business – and the information security department should provide security services relevant to the business" (Kearney[1]).

This helps on multiple levels, with the security team having increased awareness of business functions, and departments having increased awareness of risk.

To help visualize security as a service provider, it is probably best to define what ITSM is.

A set of policies, processes, and procedures for managing the implementation, improvement, and support of customer-oriented IT services.

And this term comes contrary to other IT management practices that focus on devices, networks, or systems, the term ITSM aims to continuously improve IT customer service in line with business objectives.

Briefly, ITSM is the craft of implementing, managing, and providing information technology services.

(Source: Ahmad[2])

There are various frameworks, such as ISO/IEC 9000:2015 (International Standards Organization (Brochin[3])) and ITIL (Axelos[4]), which some may see as competing but are, in fact, complementary to each other to help an organization implement ITSM.

As implied by (White and Greiner[5]), the security team could take this approach of leveraging a framework similar to infrastructure library (ITIL) to be a service provider: "ITIL's systematic approach to IT service management (ITSM) can help businesses manage <u>risk, strengthen customer relations</u>, establish cost-effective practices, and build a stable IT environment that allows for growth, scale, and change."

While we have discussed how being a service provider has its advantages in providing IT customer service, in alignment with business goals, it has its limitations when it comes to designing and developing a cohesive approach that will help your business to reduce risk to its valued business operations. This can be seen if you break down and compare the two different terms: Provide versus enable.

The term 'provide' is defined as the following (Merriam-Webster, "Definition of PROVIDE"[6]): "To supply or make available (something wanted or needed). To make something available to." The same source also defines 'enable' (Merriam-Webster, "Definition of ENABLE"[7]): "To provide with the means or opportunity. To make possible, practical, or easy."

You can see from these definitions that service providing is just making the service available, but the person or department must seek out the service or even know that they need the service.

To go back to our analogy, this is much like the written part of getting a driver's license. Materials are provided to a person, but it is on them to seek them out and use them.

This is also the stage we mostly see in businesses when it comes to business-level risk management:

- They have a risk register, and, in some cases, leadership expresses the importance of risk, but it is never brought down to the operational level.
- Businesses may require departments to fill out checklists or submit forms but typically most businesses do not have a hands-on approach to enabling departments to be risk aware in their day-to-day processes.
- They do not have risk SMEs working alongside departments to educate employees on how risk is part of their day-to-day business processes.
- Employees have their 'driving permit' but still rely on someone else to be present when they 'drive' day after day and cannot be left on their own.

By having a service-enabling mindset and leveraging the in-house risk experts, businesses are teaching their employees through hands-on experience how risk is part of their daily processes. By helping them to identify and mitigate risk on their own with minimal direction, the employee is empowered to 'drive' on their own. This helps to propagate the risk culture hierarchy deep into the business.

9.4 ACHIEVING RISK-BASED SERVICE ENABLEMENT

So how do we go from a risk service provider to an enabler? We teach our employees how to 'drive', and we can do this with a slight adjustment to an existing model: Continuous process improvement (CPI). If we add risk as a component of the CPI model and include security or risk employees in this process, we can achieve risk-based service enablement or risk-enabling of the human firewall.

CPI is defined (American Society for Quality[8]) as being "the ongoing improvement of products, services or processes through incremental and breakthrough improvements." This definition is further expanded (SolveXia[9]) to explain that:

CPI is an actual type of work style that is designed to continuously review results and rapidly adopt new measures when deemed necessary. The keyword here is continuous because ultimately broad-scale change and progress stem from small steps along the way that are all geared towards optimisation.

This includes not only when things are not working well but when they are too. Furthermore, as noted by the CIO Wiki, implementing CPI in a business is nothing new, and four main models can be used for CPI (Investors in People[10]):

Six Sigma:
Six Sigma aims to minimize faults, defects, and any variation from the established process to increase the overall quality of outputs. The term denotes the ratio of faulty products expected per million units, which is 3.4 or to put it another way, a 99.99966% success rate.

Kaizen:
A Japanese word meaning 'improvement,' Kaizen's ultimate goal is waste elimination. Its origins are in post-WWII Japanese businesses but it is now used worldwide. It is an inclusive model of continuous improvement in that, opportunities for improvement are expected to be identified by everyone from the CEO downwards – this is unsurprising considering its ubiquity in manufacturing, where front-line workers are often best able to spot inefficiencies in the production cycle. But what this also means is that there's a distinctive cultural element to Kaizen and the implementation of processes and procedures must work along-side cultural re-alignment to the continuous improvement mindset to drive employee suggestions.

"Fail fast, fail forward":
This is about relentlessly moving toward better solutions by making and learning from mistakes quickly, comfortable that as long as you are going in the right direction failures are simple steps on the path to success. It's important to understand what it means: it's not about failing with the big overarching ideas or driving force behind your business, but about tinkering with the small things as you move toward optimal solutions.

Perpetual beta:
Perpetual beta represents a mindset and strategy based on the con-tinuous improvement principle that a product, service, or solution can never be perfect or completed. It has its origins in software develop-ment where the preferred method for delivering software to people has evolved from waiting until it's as good as possible before shipping it out to customers to shipping a product that is as viable as it needs to be and then, on receipt of constructive feedback, improving it continuously to keep up with the evolving demands of customers.

With multiple approaches, a business should choose which one best aligns with its overall culture, but no matter what approach is used, there is a set of foundational principles in all of them that is the core of CPI. KaiNexus (Millard[11]) explains these foundational principles as:

- **Principle 1 – Improvements are based on small changes rather than major paradigm shifts or new inventions**
  This concept is essential because significant changes often feel frightening and destabilizing to organizations. By approaching

change in small, incremental steps, the continuous improvement model reduces the fear factor and increases the speed of improvement. When following this principle, the organization does not need to wait for a strategic shift or a new product release to begin to advance.

- **Principle 2 – Employee ideas are valuable**
  The continuous improvement model relies greatly on employees, not only top management, to identify opportunities for improvement. This bottom-up improvement is effective because employees are closest to the problems and thus better equipped to solve them.

- **Principle 3 – Incremental improvements are typically inexpensive to implement**
  Employees tend to focus on small changes that can be accomplished without a lot of expense. Many ideas from employees involve eliminating process steps rather than adding them, which is an excellent way to ensure that every activity adds some value to the customer and reduces wasted effort.

- **Principle 4 – Employees take ownership and are involved in improvement**
  Getting people to change the way they have always done things is hard. Do you know what makes it easier? Rolling out changes that originated from the front lines. When people come up with ideas to improve their work, they intrinsically see the value of the changes. Knowing that improvements come from their peers inspires faith in the necessity of the changes.

- **Principle 5 – Improvement is reflective**
  Constant feedback is an essential aspect of the continuous improvement model. During every phase of executing an improvement, open communication is critical to both the final results of the improvement and the maintenance of employee engagement.

- **Principle 6 – Improvement is measurable and potentially repeatable**
  It is not enough to simply make a change and call it an improvement. To achieve real success, the impact of change must be measured. This makes it possible to determine whether the change can be applied successfully to other problems. Proving positive return on investment also helps to keep the organization aligned around improvement.

These principles help businesses frame employees' thinking on how to evaluate their processes and think about how to improve them. Because CPI may be a major cultural shift for a business, just like establishing a risk culture, one should remember the CPI's principle: Small incremental change will lead to institutional change.

Using a seven-step approach of continuous improvement of IT services (CSI) from ITIL can help guide a department through improvement processes in these small incremental changes. Additionally, using CSI when performing CPI focuses on service improvement that supports business processes and educates employees. There are seven recommended steps to continual service process improvement, which are as follows:

1. Identify the strategy for improvement
Before an improvement plan is executed it is necessary to understand the need for continuous improvement. The information related to what services or processes need to be addressed and how their performance is to be measured. The information is gathered from a thorough understanding of business objectives and areas are identified that would benefit from continuous improvement. It also focuses on the effectiveness of the continuous improvement plan. This data is then fed into the continuous improvement plan cycle.

2. Define what will be measured
During this process, a gap analysis is done to identify opportunities for continuous improvement. If CSI finds that the available tools and resources are not capable enough or if the cost is non-affordable to deliver the desired data, then the measure identified in the earlier step of the continuous improvement plan needs to be revisited.

3. Gather the data
Data is gathered according to the goals and objectives of service operation. To have raw and quantitative data, monitoring should be in place. The quality of data is critical and it can be gathered through various means – manual or automatic. The data collection method has to be reliable and repeatable to collect quality data for continuous improvement.

4. Process the data
Once the data is collected it is important to provide it to the audience in the required format. The raw data is organized and divided according to its categories and operation which makes it easy to process and transform the data into information.

5. Analyze the information and data
The data which has been converted into information is now carefully analyzed to find gaps and their impact on business. The information is thoroughly evaluated taking into consideration all relevant internal and external factors that can directly or indirectly impact the data. The information is converted into knowledge or facts.

6. Present and use the information
The analyzed data is shared with the business stakeholders in a clear and defined manner, presenting them with an accurate picture of the results

of the improvement plan that is implemented. CSI works closely with senior management and assists them to make strategic decisions and determine the next step to optimize and improve the service through continuous improvement processes.

7. Implement improvement
As CSI has identified the areas that need a change, solutions and remedial plans are communicated to the management to improve the service. A change, thus implemented with continuous improvement sets a new baseline and the seven-step cycle begins again.

(Source: Master of Project Academy[12])

These seven steps of CSI help to establish the baseline of the department's processes, define critical success factors, and identify areas of improvement. But what does this have to do with risk? Risk management and CPI are interrelated. Incorporating risk mitigation methods into CPI can help to improve the process through having less risk from the beginning. On the other side of the coin, having risk as part of the CPI means that CPI can enable the business to identify risks and create unified solutions to mitigate them. CPI helps businesses keep threats in check and helps their risk management capabilities as a whole.

To combine the two, we take the seven steps of CSI and add a risk assessment element into each step. In addition, it is recommended that the following seven steps should be incorporated respectively into the steps of CSI:

1. Assess Documented Risks, Controls, and Processes
Start by collecting information on existing risk management frameworks, current risk controls, previous process improvement documents, and anything else that will help you find ways to improve the current processes. Gather as much information as you can and try to look for the latest details.

2. Define Scope
All stakeholders should understand and have an agreement on what processes need revision, what risks are being evaluated (financial, reputational, compliance, security threats), and what processes could be affected by the risks.

3. Map Processes in Scope
Using information from step one, prepare a draft version of the process flow. Scrutinize the process maps, look for variations, and document potential threats, process improvements, and opportunities for improving performance.

4. Discover and Map Risks and Existing Controls
Look for risks and note down their severity and likelihood. Locate the origin of the risk and all areas it affects inside and outside the process.

Check whether the risk controls are being utilized, and ensure any missing steps are added to the process map and implemented.

5. Determine Gaps in Risk Controls and Process Performance
Check whether any significant risks have not been addressed in the controls and look for any ineffective controls. Also, examine performance indicators to check if there are significant differences between your current and desired business performance. Use this information to make adjustments.

6. Identify, Examine Process Improvement as Well as Risk Elimination Opportunities
This step aims to mitigate risks without adding inefficiencies to the processes and prevent the creation of risks when improving processes.

7. Create and Utilize Integrated Process Improvement and Risks Mitigation Plan
Make sure all process maps are up to date, look for key risk indicators, and establish an action plan to measure, report, and resolve the risks.
(Source Reciprocity Labs[13])

With risk incorporated into the CPI process at the business level, this is the opportunity for security to explain the risk process to the entire group involved in the CPI effort. This opportunity should be used to implement areas that are mentioned in other chapters of this book.

While mapping the current process that is in scope, step 4 from the above is the perfect opportunity to discover all the assets associated with this process and to follow the guidance in Chapter 3 of this book. Additionally, this is another great opportunity to develop risk scenarios, also described in this book. Risk scenarios should be built in conjunction with going through the CPI steps. You should conduct BIAs during the CPI process as well. While scoping the process it will be easy to determine its importance to the business. And finally, bring it all together, creating a detailed inventory of all the assets associated with the process, with documented risk scenarios/playbooks, understanding the impact on the business through BIA to finally incorporate it into the business's BCP.

9.5 WHEN A LACK OF RISK-ENABLING THE HUMAN FIREWALL BITES BACK

There are probably multiple examples in every business when old, outdated, or risky processes have impacted a business. Sometimes it may be small and unnoticeable and other times it could be very impactful. Having a culture of risk and risk-empowered employees can help identify risk behaviors and practices. One of the most difficult threats to identify is an insider threat.

An insider is defined as (NIST[14]): "An entity with authorized access... that has the potential to harm an information system or enterprise through destruction, disclosure, modification of data, and/or denial of service."

In November 2021 an ex-hospital employee of South Georgia Medical Center (Richards[15]) downloaded data to a USB stick the day after they had quit. While security software did alert the medical center of the data download, there were still significant risks in the employee termination process for the hospital:

- Why was the employee's access still in place the day after they had quit?
- Why did they still have access to the sensitive information?

If a risk-focused CPI event had been performed around the medical records systems or human resources practices, this risk of employment termination or out-processing procedures having extended access should have been identified. Even if there was no risk-focused CPI event on these procedures, a risk-enabled human resources employee would have identified the risk and reported it to the proper individuals to mitigate this risk. While it was determined that all the data was recovered and was not used maliciously, the time and response efforts to notify impacted individuals, plus the reputational damages, still bore real cost to the hospital.

9.6 DECODING RISK-ENABLING THE HUMAN FIREWALL

Risk-enabled users are a very rare find in today's working world. Identifying and assessing risk is usually seen as the job of the risk department or the information security team. However, educating users to identify risks in their day-to-day work can greatly increase the resilience of the organization. They can identify bad practices or prevent them from happening. Additionally, having the security team as part of the department CPI event can greatly increase their understanding of users' requirements to get their jobs completed and help them build better risk scenarios and threat profiles. This very cohesive interaction between departments and the security team builds strength across the entire organization.

Notes

1 Kearney. "Read @Kearney: The Golden Rules of Operational Excellence in Information Security Management." Kearney, 30 Dec. 2015, www.kearney.com/digital/article/-/insights/the-golden-rules-of-operational-excellence-in-information-security-management-article. Accessed 22 Aug. 2022.
2 Ahmad, Mohammad. "A Comprehensive Guide – What Is ITIL, and Its Benefits?" RMG, 7 Mar. 2021, www.rmg-sa.com/en/what-is-itil-and-its-benefits. Accessed 22 Aug. 2022.

3 Brochin, Joe. "ITSM and ISO 9000: More Complimentary than Competitors." Www.linkedin.com, 22 May 2022, www.linkedin.com/pulse/itsm-iso-9000-more-complimentary-than-competitors-joe-brochin. Accessed 22 Aug. 2022.

4 Axelos. ITIL® Foundation. Norwich, Tso, 2019.

5 White, Sarah. K., and Lynn Greiner. "What Is ITIL? Your Guide to the IT Infrastructure Library." www.cio.com, 16 May 2022, www.cio.com/article/272 361/infrastructure-it-infrastructure-library-itil-definition-and-solutions.html. Accessed 22 Aug. 2022.

6 Merriam-Webster. "Definition of "PROVIDE."" Merriam-Webster.com, 2021, www.merriam-webster.com/dictionary/provide. Accessed 22 Aug. 2022.

7 Merriam-Webster. "Definition of ENABLE." www.merriam-Webster.com, 2022, www.merriam-webster.com/dictionary/enable. Accessed 22 Aug. 2022.

8 American Society for Quality. "Continuous Improvement Model – Continual Improvement Tools | ASQ." Asq.org, 2019, asq.org/quality-resources/continuous-improvement. Accessed 22 Aug. 2022.

9 SolveXia. "What Is Continuous Process Improvement?" www.solvexia.com, 24 June 2020, www.solvexia.com/blog/what-is-continuous-process-improvement. Accessed 23 Aug. 2022.

10 Investors in People. "Continuous Improvement Models: Four Great Options for You." Investors in People, 28 Jan. 2019, www.investorsinpeople.com/knowle dge/continuous-improvement-models-four-great-options-for-you. Accessed 23 Aug. 2022.

11 Millard, Maggie. "6 Principles of the Continuous Improvement Model." Kainexus.com, 2019, blog.kainexus.com/continuous-improvement/6-principles-of-the-continuous-improvement-model. Accessed 22 Aug. 2022.

12 Master of Project Academy. "7 Steps to Continuous Improvement of IT Services." Master of Project Academy Blog, 2 Jan. 2022, blog.masterofproject. com/continuous-improvement-itil-services. Accessed 22 Aug. 2022.

13 Reciprocity Labs. "The Relationship between Risk Management and Process Improvement." SecuritySenses, 27 Feb. 2020, securitysenses.com/posts/relationship-between-risk-management-and-process-improvement. Accessed 22 Aug. 2022.

14 NIST. "Security and Privacy Controls for Information Systems and Organizations." NIST Special Publication 800-53, Revision 5, 23 Sept. 2020, nvlpubs.nist.gov/nistpubs/SpecialPublications/NIST.SP.800-53r5.pdf, 10.6028/nist.sp.800-53r5. Accessed 22 Aug. 2022.

15 Richards, Terry. "Ex-Hospital Worker Arrested in SGMC Data Breach." *Valdosta Daily Times*, 14 Jan. 2022, www.valdostadailytimes.com/news/local_news/ex-hospital-worker-arrested-in-sgmc-data-breach/article_7ca92b22-a2e5-5541-b3b3-38472d3706b1.html. Accessed 22 Aug. 2022.

Chapter 10

Risk-Based Security Operations

10.1 THE HUMAN SECURITY OPERATIONS CENTER – THE IMMUNE SYSTEM

The immune system is something every human is born with. It is something we need to survive, and it has come into more focus with everyone since the Covid-19 pandemic.

The immune system is summarized as being:

> A network of tissues, cells, and organs first try to keep out germs like bacteria, viruses, fungi, and parasites and then deals with them if they manage to get in. If it senses something in your body that could be bad for you, it triggers the release of special cells. These travel to where the trouble is, attack the intruder, and help gets rid of it.
>
> (Source: WebMD[1])

These measures are much like the security operations process. It needs a layered approach, just like security professionals have been told for years to take when it comes to security defense, and much like the human anatomy's layered defensive structure, it starts with the outer perimeter/boundary skin layer (Jodie[2]).

WebMD goes on to further explains the parts of the immune system as follows:

Skin
It blocks invaders from getting into your body in the first place.

Lymphatic System
A network of fine tubes throughout your body collects fluid to pick up dead cells and germs.

Antigens
These are markers that your immune system can recognize.

Innate vs. Acquired Immunity
Innate immunity comes from those barrier body parts as well as some specialized cells. Acquired immunity comes from antibodies you get

from your mother in the womb or that you make in response to antigens that aren't yours—like from a cold virus or a vaccine.

Phagocytes
They're part of your innate immunity, and they work by eating invaders.

Natural Killer Cells
They recognize and latch onto abnormal cells like cancer, then damage and kill them.

Basophils and Mast Cells
They're also part of your innate immunity, involved with allergic reactions. Basophils are in your blood; mast cells are in tissues. When these cells find certain antigens (typically, harmless things that your body sees as a threat), they release histamine to bring immune cells to the area. Your body sends more blood there, causing inflammation -- redness, warmth, and swelling -- that also helps keeps the invasion from spreading.

Lymphocytes
These infection-fighting white blood cells are the reason you get sick from things like chicken pox only once.

Antibodies
Once your B cells get a read on the antigen of a new invader, they make antibodies to either kill it or flag it as "Trouble here!" These Y-shaped molecules fit into antigens like puzzle pieces, making an immune complex. An antibody can also be called immunoglobulin or Ig.

T Cells
They travel through your blood and lymph systems, waiting to be activated. Killer and helper T cells are part of the search-and-attack team for that antigen. You need suppressor T cells to end the response, and they can sometimes prevent harmful responses from happening.

Memory Cells
Leftover B and T cells called "memory cells" that can recognize that particular germ and respond quickly.

All these systems work together to provide early warnings, through the central nervous system, to the monitoring system (the brain). The same principles should be applied to your security programs and security operations models

10.2 AN INTRODUCTION TO RISK-BASED SECURITY OPERATIONS

For a while now it has been documented that security personnel have been facing the problem of operator burnout. The number of data breaches significantly increases year on year, with some research by Check Point stating: "There was a 50% increase in overall attacks per week on corporate networks compared to 2020" (Greig[3]).

These types of statistics show there is even more pressure on security teams to keep their businesses secure. With ever-increasing threats and demand, we need to look at how security operations have been implemented at most businesses. To start, it is typically known as a security operation center (SOC), which is mainly focused on monitoring/alerting and incident response. These focuses are inherently responsive, and, because of this limited focus, security operations have fallen into a pattern of being ineffective.

A 2020 report (Devo[4]) on the effectiveness of SOCs shows that most businesses rated their SOCs with low effectiveness. This is probably because most SOC models are focused on large ingestions of data sources and logs, causing many alerts to need to be triaged. Operators feel as if they are always reactive and never proactive. Security operations are inherently reactive because actions are not taken until an external force occurs, but there are methods you can implement that can make security operations closer to being proactive.

This can be achieved through adding risk assessment to security operations. This provides the connection and feeds from the business processes into operations, which then enables the loop back into business processes. This creates a continuous cycle, combining all parts of security operations, not just monitoring/alerting and incident response, into a systematic approach on how to best unify and integrate governance areas such as BIAs and business objectives.

Much like the human immune system, security operations starts by preventing a malicious entity from penetrating the system (body), but if it does, to react to contain it, and, finally, proactively take steps to prevent it from occurring again.

10.3 THE GREAT DIVIDE OF SECURITY

Before we can dive deep into risk-based security operations, we must discuss a gap, or in this case a great divide that we see in security programs. Security programs typically are divided up into two main parts:

- TechSec
  This is usually just that, the technical components of security including technological controls, incident response, alerting and monitoring, and threat profiles. This side of the divide gets to use all the tools and has a lot of screens to look at.
- GRC
  This side of the divide has more of the administrative control component of security, including risk assessment, BIA, compliance review and auditing, and policies and procedure development.

The personnel in these areas usually have two different types of skill sets as well. Where the TechSec personnel are strong in technical systems and applications, the GRC personnel are strong in risk analysis and policy development. This can present a problem because, in most businesses, these two sides work almost separately from each other. On one side, GRC work is mostly proactive, whereas TechSec's work is reactive. On rare occasions they do work together on efforts or projects. So, this begs the question: How do security operators truly know what they are trying to protect or understand the value of what they are trying to protect?

10.4 ESTABLISHING A RISK-BASED SECURITY OPERATIONS FRAMEWORK

To push security operations to be more proactive, and to include risk, we must close the great divide. Leveraging your risk assessments of business processes to feed into security operations is a method to achieve this. It makes security operations risk-informed.

In Figure 10.1, we see a visual representation of what a risk-based security operations framework looks like.

In Figure 10.1, the red and blue represent the two sides of the great divide, where red represents a GRC function with a heavy emphasis on risk, and blue represents security operations. The merger of the great divide is in the threat profile area, and it will be explained in greater detail later. From this figure, you can see how each section leads into the next but is cyclic, creating a continuous process, whereas CPI methods mentioned in this book can be incorporated.

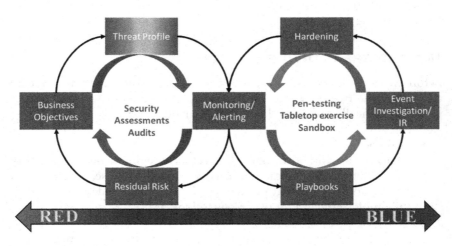

Figure 10.1 Risk-based security operations framework.

10.4.1 Business Objectives

Now that you have seen a visual representation of risk-based security operations, let us break down each section of it. It is possible to start anywhere in the cycle and work through the steps, but for an explanation we will start on the left at business objectives. The connections of risk into security operations and the merger of the great divide start here. Many of the chapters of this book contribute to this step. Ultimately, business processes are what feed this step.

Before moving to the 'Threat Profile' step, you should have fully mapped the business process you wish to monitor from an operational standpoint. Fully mapping the process should include the following:

- Documented risk scenario – see Chapter 6
- BIA – see Chapter 2
- Assets inventory to include – see Chapter 3
  - Hardware
  - Software/applications
  - People
  - Data
  - Infrastructure

Having all this information is critical to ensure you have a complete threat profile of the process or the assets within the process, the most critical information being the risk scenarios. Risk scenarios will help you prioritize which assets or sub-processes to focus on for threat profiling, because risk scenarios could include a lot of assets.

10.4.2 Threat Profile

From the graphic in Figure 10.1, you see threat profiling is colored from red to blue. This is because this step is where we bridge the great divide. Taking the deliverables from the business objective steps, both the GRC side of the house and the operations side should work together to build threat profiles. When building a threat profile, your starting focus should be the business process.

Most of the current documentation you can read starts a threat profile at the asset, with no consideration of the value or the purpose of the identified asset. This approach of a sole focus on an asset limits your ability to see a complete picture of the threat landscape. If you do not know how the asset ties into the business process, then the people charged with monitoring and protecting it do not understand its true value and how it ties into business processes.

Leveraging your risk profile from the previous step that includes the focused asset, you can map the entire threat landscape. When the entire threat landscape is mapped and includes all the different threat vectors plus the value of the asset to the business, you can more effectively monitor and protect it. By understanding how the asset is used in the business, you can establish normal or baseline activity. With the establishment of normal or baseline activities, you can identify threat actors, their attack vectors, and indicators of compromise (IOCs) more effectively because you will know what standard behavior the asset should be performing.

For example, confirming someone's residency is required when they start a new job. Usually, they must provide sensitive information to the new employer, such as valid government identification. The employer scans a copy and stores it in the new employee's personnel record in an employee record database, which contains all the business's employee records. If you were monitoring this database for access activity and had a log of it being accessed in the middle of the night, would you say this is standard activity, or questionable? Should someone be accessing this database at this time or does standard business processes for this database only occur during business hours? If you have documented threat profiles mapped to the risk scenario of the employment verification process, you would know whether this were legitimate activity or not. Once you know baseline activities for the process, you can carry this to the next step of the security operations process.

To continue building on creating a threat profile, you should use the tips and techniques mentioned in Chapter 5 to build your entire threat land-scape. Using both the risk profiles and threat modeling will give you a strong understanding of what is normal behavior of a process and the associated assets, and how a threat actor might try to exploit a weakness in the process.

10.4.3 Monitoring and Alerting

There is an ongoing problem with the monitoring and alerting practice in security operations that is heavily contributing to operator burnout mentioned previously. Monitoring and alerting has a heavy reliance on tools such as a security information and event management (SIEM) system.

A SIEM is defined as: "The real-time monitoring and analysis of events as well as tracking and logging of security data for compliance or auditing purposes" (IBM[5]). While this sounds exactly what you need (as it performs all these actions), it is not as simple as acquiring and turning it on. It involves a lot of preliminary work and planning.

IBM continues by recommending the following SIEM implementation best practices:

Begin by fully understanding the scope of your implementation.
1. Define how your business will best benefit from deployment and set up the appropriate security use cases.

2. Design and apply your predefined data correlation rules across all systems and networks, including any cloud deployments.

3. Identify all of your business compliance requirements and ensure your SIEM solution is configured to audit and report on these standards in real-time so you can better understand your risk posture.

4. Catalog and classify all digital assets across your organization's IT infrastructure. This will be essential when managing collecting log data, detecting access abuses, and monitoring network activity.

5. Establish BYOD (Bring Your Own Device) policies, IT configurations, and restrictions that can be monitored when integrating your SIEM solution.

6. Regularly tune your SIEM configurations, ensuring you're reducing false positives in your security alerts.

7. Document and practice all incident response plan and workflows to ensure teams can respond quickly to any security incidents that require intervention.

8. Automate where possible using artificial intelligence (AI) and Security Orchestration, Automation, and Response (SOAR) capabilities.

9. Evaluate the possibility of investing in an MSSP (Managed Security Service Provider) to manage your SIEM deployments. Depending on the unique needs of your business, MSSPs may be better equipped to handle the complexities of your SIEM implementation as well as regularly manage and maintain its continuous functionality.

(Source: IBM[5])

While this is a very good list, it is very extensive and possibly requires other advanced technologies and/or services. Additionally, there is a lot of preliminary work that is recommended as well, such as in step 2.

As a result of this complex system with extensive pre-work that needs to be accomplished to be successful, standard practice for SIEM has been to send everything and anything, log or data-wise, to the system. For a standard medium-size business, security operators could see over a million events and thousands of alerts a week. We also see that businesses will use 'out-of-the-box' alerts and notifications, with no consideration of how it relates to business processes or threats. Furthermore, the standard practice also dictates that every alert should be reviewed and addressed if required. This is probably why IBM recommends businesses evaluate investing in a managed security service provider, (Fortinet, "What Is a Managed Security Service Provider (MSSP)?"[6]). Most operators are overwhelmed by the sheer number of alerts.

Now that I have described this never-winning battle, let me explain how alerting and monitoring can have a risk focus and be a major asset to a business. Armed with the deliverables from strong threat profiles, which are normal behaviors of the processes, potential attack vectors, a list of attack techniques, and IOCs, you can start to build business-focused monitoring efforts and actionable alerting. Using the deliverables from the threat profile, team members who are responsible for monitoring understand what is being monitored and why an alert is being triggered. Monitoring and alerting is a critical stage in this entire framework, and therefore it is the central step in the process. From this step, you can continue to the more operational side of the framework, or perhaps in this step you can identify a gap or blind spot for monitoring, which can go to the GRC side and be documented as a residual risk.

By having a list of attack vectors, techniques, and IOCs, you can set up monitoring controls to identify when the attack is occurring and from where. An attack vector is defined as: "A pathway or method used by a hacker to illegally access a network or computer in an attempt to exploit system vulnerabilities" (Fortinet[7]).

Fortinet continues to define IOCs as: "Data that indicates a system may have been infiltrated by a cyber threat" (Fortinet, "Indicators of Compromise (IOCs)"[8]).

Much like memory cells from the human immune system, having monitoring and alerting controls or parameters in place can quickly identify a threat so action can be taken to prevent or eliminate the threat. If this occurs, you would continue to the next step in the framework cycle on the operational side, playbooks, or incident response. If you did not have controls (log source or tool) in place to identify the threat, you have identified a gap and would move to the residual risk step. Having this detailed understanding of the alert and exactly what it tells you, operators can quickly respond when it is triggered. It also generates the deliverable to the next step in the operational cycle: Playbooks.

10.4.4 Incident Response Playbooks

Much like T cells that travel through your blood and lymph systems, waiting to be activated at the sign of a foreign entity, incident response playbooks are detailed guidance for handling malicious attacks or when you receive an alert in the previous step.

Incident playbooks are defined as: "A standard procedures and steps for responding and resolving incidents in real-time" (Atlassian[9]).

Having all the information from the three previous steps, you can develop targeted effective playbooks for when an alert is triggered that align back to the business process. Playbooks like those described in Chapter 12 of this book should have detailed procedures that follow the steps of incident response:

- Detection
- Identification

- Analysis
- Containment
- Eradication
- Recovery
- Post-incident

Each step should be descriptive, with flowcharts and checklists to provide responders with a simple step-by-step process to guide them through the incident. This helps to ensure that important information or actions are not missed. The playbooks should be repeatable as well. Not all alerts or incidents are going to be proactively identified before they occur, therefore you should also develop a generic playbook that will cover the unknowns. This will also cover zero-day incidents that are impossible to specifically plan for.

10.4.5 Event Investigation/Incident Response

Having risk-based threat profiles, monitoring, alerting, and playbooks prepared, you should be ready to tackle event investigation and incident response. You should leverage the teaching from Chapter 12 of this book and standards or guides from the NIST or ISO to fully develop these processes. But, as a reminder, if you do not have a developed playbook for the event or incident and you use the generic plan, you should thoroughly document the new or unknown events so that you can develop a new playbook to cover that event or incident. You should also ensure that your post-incident, after-action review, and/or lessons learned process is well-defined so that any gaps or shortfalls in the previous steps are identified. If gaps or shortfalls are identified, those will be the deliverables for the next step of the framework. More than likely there is something to be learned or that could have been done differently after an event investigation or incident response has been completed.

10.4.6 Hardening

This step is much like antibodies, where you take your gaps or lessons learned from incident response to apply changes to systems or processes, so in the future you are better prepared for attacks. Doing this is to re-establish the normal behavior of a process and/or minimum-security configuration standards. You should leverage process improvement events that are mentioned in Chapter 9 for modifying a risk process. For systems that need to be hardened, you should use hardening baseline recommendations that organizations such as the Center of Internet Security has published. While taking these actions you should revisit the appropriate risk assessments and threat profiles. These will more than likely have changed and need to be adjusted to reflect the hardening efforts you have taken. Taking these actions should help you close any identified gaps or risky processes.

10.4.7 Monitoring and Alerting Revisited

Once you take these corrective actions, you are not done. After making these changes to the processes and systems, plus the associated risk assessments and threat profiles, you will need to adjust your monitoring and alerting. The updated threat profiles should have the deliverables discussed earlier. With those, you adjust your monitoring and alerting parameters to incorporate those changes.

10.4.8 Residual Risk

Once you have completed the monitoring and alerting step, either from an original step-up of a threat profile or from actions after an incident, you will probably have identified additional gaps or lack of visibility (blind spots) when it comes to identifying a threat. None of us have unlimited resources, time, or money to establish perfect security operations, and some of us are very far from having that.

Therefore, this step is important to make sure it gets completed. Anything that is a gap or a blind spot should be documented as residual risk, which is defined as: "The risk that remains after efforts to identify and eliminate some or all types of risk have been made" (Shackleford and Sales [10]).

This 'leftover risk' should be added to the company's risk register or risk monitoring efforts. It should also be reviewed for its criticality and determined whether it should be mitigated. To continue the cycle and make the entire process cyclic, these risks should be added to the department's BIA for visibility, which then means it would be part of the regularly reviewed risk assessments discussed in the first step of the framework.

10.4.9 Auditing and Testing

The framework has a lot of components, so it must be reviewed so that the components are completed effectively. Both sides of the loop have processes that can be implemented to ensure the components are completed. The audit function would be done for the GRC side of the framework, and testing would be performed for the operational side of the framework. When auditing the GRC functions you should make sure that the documentation is completed for the risk profiles and the threat profiles, along with updating risk registers and BIAs for any residual risk. Internal and external audits can include this type of activity, or they can be performed by the leadership. As for the testing of the operational portion, internally the business can perform tabletop incident response exercises of the playbooks, sandbox testing, and/or blue-team exercises. External testing can be performed as well. For example, the business could conduct penetration testing. This will provide a lot of valuable information because it would be the more realistic type of testing.

10.5 WHEN RISK-BASED SECURITY OPERATIONS BITE BACK

Security operations are a critical part of protecting a business. When you read in the headlines of a new data breach or an organization falling victim to a cyberattack, there is usually a security gap or a missed vulnerability that, if properly reviewed and if there was an understanding of business processes, may have been prevented the data breach or it would have had a low impact to the organization. The T-Mobile breach of 2021 is a good example of when security operations missed an attack vector and areas of risk:

> The breach involved the theft of personal information for more than 54 million people, including social security numbers, names, phone numbers, and addresses for some, but not financial info. Device identifiers and PINs were obtained for certain accounts. Current, former, and prospective T-Mobile customers were among those with personal data stolen. Business customers also had information taken.
>
> (Source: Fletcher[11])

The CEO of T-Mobile is reported to have stated that:

> The bad actor leveraged their knowledge of technical systems, along with specialized tools and capabilities, to gain access to our testing environments and then used brute force attacks and other methods to make their way into other IT servers that included customer data...
>
> (Source: Fletcher[12])

This was not T-Mobile's first significant data breach. When this breach occurred, it was the third major one that it disclosed in the past two years. This would be an indication of risky operational practices. The hacker responsible for this breach was able to gain access to T-Mobile's network through an unsecured router that was exposed to the internet. From there they were able to move from system to system because of store credentials on the systems. If proper risk assessments and threat profiles had been completed, the exposed router should have been identified. Even if it was not, properly documented normal behavior activities or IOC should have alerted T-Mobile that systems were being accessed that should not have been and data could have been prevented from being exfiltrated.

10.6 DECODING RISK-BASED SECURITY OPERATIONS

Security operations are an important part of protecting an organization from malicious entities but have fallen into a pattern of focusing on assets and not including risk and business processes. This limited scope has caused operations to become ineffective and overwhelming to the organization. This has led to operator burnout, employee turnover, and, ultimately, data breaches. T-Mobile was a good example of where, if risk-based security operations had been used, maybe they could have prevented one of their three data breaches or significantly limited their impact.

Notes

1 WebMD. "Slideshow: Guide to Your Immune System." WebMD, 2019, www.webmd.com/cold-and-flu/ss/slideshow-immune-system. Accessed 27 Aug. 2022.
2 Jodie. "How the Immune System Protects Us." In Fitness and in Health, 18 Sept. 2020, medium.com/in-fitness-and-in-health/how-the-immune-system-protects-us-59e6a0553baf. Accessed 27 Aug. 2022.
3 Greig, Jonathan. "Cybersecurity: Last Year Was a Record Year for Attacks, and Log4j Made It Worse." ZDNET, 11 Jan. 2022, www.zdnet.com/article/report-increased-log4j-exploit-attempts-leads-to-all-time-peak-in-weekly-cyberattacks-per-org. Accessed 27 Aug. 2022.
4 Devo. "2020 Devo SOC Performance ReportTM: A Tale of Two SOCs." 2020.
5 IBM. "What Is Security Information and Event Management (SIEM)?" www.ibm.com, 2022, www.ibm.com/topics/siem. Accessed 27 Aug. 2022.
6 Fortinet. "What Is a Managed Security Service Provider (MSSP)?" Fortinet, 2022, www.fortinet.com/resources/cyberglossary/what-is-mssp. Accessed 27 Aug. 2022.
7 Fortinet. "What Is a Cyber Attack Vector? Types & How to Avoid Them." Fortinet, 2022, www.fortinet.com/resources/cyberglossary/attack-vector#:~:text=Attack%20Vector%20Definition. Accessed 27 Aug. 2022.
8 Fortinet. "Indicators of Compromise (IOCs)." Fortinet, 2022, www.fortinet.com/resources/cyberglossary/indicators-of-compromise#:~:text=Indicators%20of%20compromise%20(IOCs)%20refer. Accessed 27 Aug. 2022.
9 Atlassian. "How to Create an Incident Response Playbook." Atlassian, 2022, www.atlassian.com/incident-management/incident-response/how-to-create-an-incident-response-playbook#:~:text=An%20incident%20response%20playbook%20empowers. Accessed 27 Aug. 2022.
10 Shackleford, Dave, and Francesca Sales. "What Is Residual Risk? How Is it Different from Inherent Risk?" SearchSecurity, 2022, www.techtarget.com/searchsecurity/definition/residual-risk. Accessed 27 Aug. 2022.
11 Fletcher, Bevin. "T-Mobile CEO Says Hacker Used 'Brute Force' Attacks to Breach IT Servers." Fierce Wireless, 27 Aug. 2021, www.fiercewireless.com/operators/t-mobile-ceo-says-hacker-used-brute-force-attacks-to-breach-it-servers. Accessed 27 Aug. 2022.
12 Fletcher, Bevin. "T-Mobile CEO Says Hacker Used "Brute Force" Attacks to Breach IT Servers." Fierce Wireless, 27 Aug. 2021, www.fiercewireless.com/operators/t-mobile-ceo-says-hacker-used-brute-force-attacks-to-breach-it-servers. Accessed 27 Aug. 2022.

Chapter 11

Creating Visibility and Insights Through Effective Security Risk Metrics

11.1 A VEHICLE WARNING LIGHT ANALOGY

Imagine the value you gain from the warning lights that you have in your vehicle dashboard, as shown in Figure 11.1 (Aksoy[1]).

Your vehicle's dashboard warning lights supply clear and concise indications of anything that could affect the vehicle's operations. These warning lights are color-coded (e.g., red, amber, yellow, green or blue) to clearly show their degree of importance and to show the urgency of any follow-up actions.

- If you see a red warning light, showing that there might be an issue with the braking system, you intuitively know this presents a potential critical risk and needs to be prioritized for remediation.
- If you see an amber warning light, showing that the fuel filter is defective, you will know that this is a potential considerable risk and needs to be scheduled to be looked at by a mechanic.
- If you see a yellow warning light, showing that there might be an issue with the tire pressures being low, you will know that is a potential moderate risk and you need to check the tire pressures.
- If see a green warning light, showing that your vehicle's dipped/low beam headlights (Wilson[2]) are on. This is an important thing to be aware of when driving during periods of darkness or fog, while enabling you to switch these off during daylight periods.
- Whereas, if you were to see a blue warning light, showing that your vehicle's main/long beam headlights are on, this warns you that your headlights might affect other road users and allows you to return them to the dipped beam, to avoiding blinding the drivers of any oncoming vehicles.

As you can see, effective vehicle warning lights supply extremely essential functions and are essential to safe driving and the operational resilience of the vehicle.

DOI: 10.1201/9781003288084-13

Red Warning Lights
- High Risk/Urgent

Yellow/Amber Warning Lights
- Caution/Investigate

Green Lights (Signal Is Green (SIG))
- All is operational

Figure 11.1 Ford F150 vehicle warning lights.

11.2 INTRODUCTION TO SECURITY RISK METRICS

The focus of this chapter is to investigate key risk indicator (KRI) metrics, but it is important to remember that your key performance indicator (KPI) metrics could also be an indicator of underlying issues that could increase the risks to your business. Imagine the risks that may be associated with a failure to meet your defined RTOs, (Banik, "What Is Recovery Time Objective (RTO), Why Is It Important?"[3]), or RPOs, (Banik, "What Is Recovery Point Objective (RPO), Why Is It Important?"[4]). These defined aims should be based upon your organization's risk appetite, so not meeting these goals would show that you are exceeding your risk tolerances. In support of this, you should be risk-assessing and documenting the identified risks that are associated with exceeding the defined RTOs and RPOs.

The term 'metrics' is about providing measurements:

> "science of versification," 1760, from Latinized form of Greek he *metrikē* "prosody," plural of *metron* "meter, a verse; that by which anything is measured; measure, length, size, limit, proportion" (from PIE

root *me- (2) "to measure"). Middle English had *metrik* "the branch of music which deals with measure or time" (late 15c.), from Medieval Latin *metricus*.

(Source: Online Etymology Dictionary[5])

Much like the vehicle warning lights, your security risk metrics need to supply a sign of the measurements of risks, but it is particularly important to understand what measurements need to be taken and checked. Consequently, it is important to ensure that your metrics are relevant to what is important to the business and should supply a risk measurement against those valued business operations (found through the BIA exercise).

An abstract from a chapter on metrics in the Wiley Handbook of Science and Technology for Homeland Security (Voeller[6]), (Black et al.[7]), states that:

Metrics are tools to facilitate decision making and improve performance and accountability.

Measures are quantifiable, observable, and objective data supporting metrics. Operators can use metrics to apply corrective actions and improve performance.

Regulatory, financial, and organizational factors drive the requirement to measure IT security performance.

Potential security metrics cover a broad range of measurable features, from security audit logs of individual systems to the number of systems within an organization that were tested over the course of a year.

Effective security metrics should be used to identify weaknesses, determine trends to better utilize security resources, and judge the success or failure of implemented security solutions.

When creating suitable metrics for your organization, it is essential to reach out to your key stakeholders to show what information resources are available to you and what the decision-makers are interested in having metrics raised against. Once you have this information at hand, you can then start to design a suitable way to present this. Remember that a picture paints a thousand words, so consider whether numerous words can be replaced with a more effective chart or image, which is supported by a short narrative to supply some added context.

TechTarget (Wheatman[8]) summarizes this using the following five steps:

1. Clearly connect to business outcomes
A common metric in many security programs is the number of missing patches across the enterprise. While it's important that systems are patched, such a metric is essentially meaningless because it comes with zero business context or alignment with organizational goals. What kind of patches are missing? What kinds of systems need to be patched?

How old are the missing patches? Each security metric must clearly align with a business goal.

2. Provide appropriate context

When presenting data to an executive audience, the numbers aren't as important as the why. Context is the bridge between action and value. Providing context helps connect data with business needs. When security leaders ask for more budget or suggest a process change, business decision-makers have a clearer picture of why that request is important. There are different types of context, including technical, time, location, risk and business context.

3. Match the message to the audience

Every business audience has a different goal and, therefore, cares about different metrics and messages. When speaking to the CFO, metrics should be presented in the context of the business's financials and bottom line. When presenting to sales leadership, the message should look at the impact for customers and prospects. Also, consider the audience's familiarity with the data and issues at hand. While the CIO may understand security acronyms and jargon, the board of directors may need those terms spelled out. Evaluate what your audience cares about most and what decisions they are making every day to select and frame metrics accordingly.

4. Report on alignment with targets

Metrics can be improved by reporting on alignment with targets. This context tells business leadership that more security resources are needed to help the European team meet its goals and reduce the organization's risk posture.

5. Build strong narratives and tell stories

Using a narrative can help security leaders tie the above steps to together and develop a story that matters to business leadership. Think about telling your metrics story using the following framework:

We did/should do <action> in this <time frame> to address <technical issue> in order to <limit/prevent/slow down> this <risk>, which would impact this <business goal>.

Additionally, it is worth noting that, at the time of drafting this book, NIST is in the process of updating its Special Publication (SP) 800-55 Revision 1, Performance Measurement Guide for Information Security (NIST[9]), which could prove to be a useful reference in the future.

11.3 CREATING VISIBILITY AND SHOWING A RETURN ON INVESTMENTS

A common mistake that companies may make is generating metrics that supply little or no value or context to the business leadership teams. Imagine creating metrics that state:

1. 1,000 systems need critical patches to be applied.
2. 1,000 systems had critical systems applied.
3. The network systems have 20,000 CRITICAL vulnerabilities.
4. The network systems have 200,000 HIGH vulnerabilities.
5. The network systems have 500,000 MEDIUM vulnerabilities.
6. The network systems have 1,000,000 LOW vulnerabilities.

In a visualization of this metric, you might decide to create a chart, as depicted in Figures 11.2 and 11.3.

Is this of value to the business? Does it answer the 'so what?' question or supply the context needed for the decision-owners to act?

Instead, what if these metrics were more targeted and what if you started to add some added context to these metrics as depicted in Figure 11.4?

1. 100 of the most critical business systems require critical patches to be applied to help prevent these assets from being compromised, by remote access or ransomware attacks.
2. 100 of the business's most critical systems have had the latest critical patches applied, significantly reducing the risks of compromise.
3. Of the network systems that are found to have 20,000 CRITICAL vulnerabilities:
    *   100 of these are associated with the business's most critical systems.
    *   50 are associated to systems involved in the processing, storage, or transmission of personal data.
    *   10 are associated with internet-facing systems.

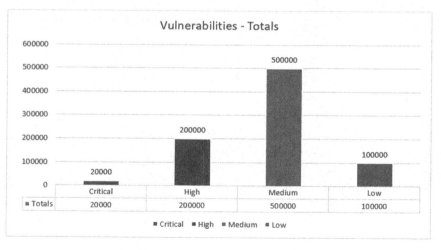

Figure 11.2 Total monthly vulnerabilities metrics graph.

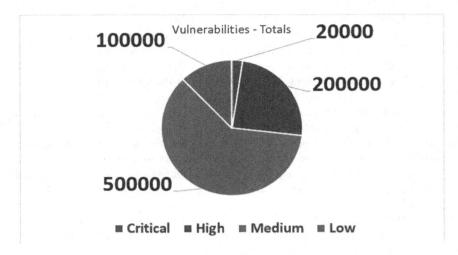

Figure 11.3 Total monthly vulnerabilities pie chart.

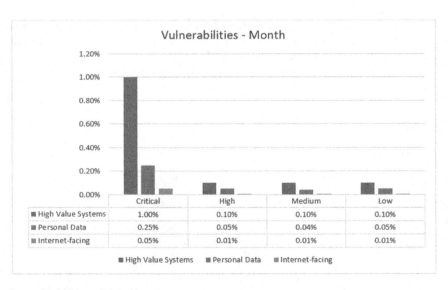

Figure 11.4 Vulnerabilities by system type.

4. Of the network systems having 200,000 HIGH vulnerabilities:
   - 200 of these are associated with the business's most critical systems.
   - 100 are associated to systems involved in the processing, storage, or transmission of personal data.
   - 20 are associated with internet-facing systems.
5. Of the network systems having 500,000 MEDIUM vulnerabilities:
   - 500 of these are associated with the business's most critical systems.
   - 200 are associated to systems involved in the processing, storage, or transmission of personal data.
   - 50 are associated with internet-facing systems.
6. Of the network systems having 1,000,000 LOW vulnerabilities:
   - 1,000 of these are associated with the business's most critical systems.
   - 500 are associated to systems involved in the processing, storage, or transmission of personal data.
   - 100 are associated with internet-facing systems.

Suddenly, the context of the identified vulnerabilities starts to increase and both risk assessments and prioritization becomes an easier task.

Next, what if you were to start adding some trend analysis to these metrics, so that the recipient can see how well the systems are being supported? Depicted in Table 11.1. (Security Scorecard[10]), is a comparison between the ABC Company and the ABC Company.

In these metrics, you can clearly see that the ABC Company's IT team may be struggling to patch its internet-facing IT systems, which may be above the risk tolerances of the organization, whereas for the ABC Bank, the leadership teams expects the patching cadence to be closer to the A grade rating.

If your business has invested in expensive security tools, why not use the security metrics to show all the challenging work that is going on in the background? For example, if the support teams have worked extremely hard to find any systems affected by any new and concerning vulnerabilities (e.g., Log4j (Federal Trade Commission (FTC)[11]) and supply a metric of how many systems were affected, how many have been remediated and how many are still to be remediated? For example, if the business has paid out hundreds of thousands of pounds, dollars, or Euros on security tools, why not show the value that these security tools are providing (e.g., the monitoring tool identified ## unsuccessful login attempts by ## accounts, resulting in coaching sessions for users who appear to be struggling with the management of their account credentials, network configuration audits revealed three out of the 15 network security controls, (Panhalkar[12]), were

Table 11.1 Patching Cadence Metrics

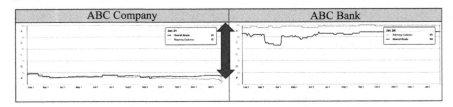

vulnerable to compromise – potentially allowing clandestine unauthorized access between internal network segmentations, the quarterly internal vulnerability scanning identified 30 valuable business systems that had critical patches missing – 25 of the 30 missing patches have been remediated to significantly reduce the ransomware threats, etc.).

Suddenly, the business leadership team starts to gain a better appreciation of all the work that is being done to keep the business operationally resilient.

11.4 CONVERTING INFORMATION INTO ACTIONABLE INTELLIGENCE

Strangely I am not going to tell which type of metrics you should implement, as every business is different and employs different security tools and methods that can be used to create useful information data sets, which can then be refined into actionable intelligence. However, not all the information might be relevant to your valued business operations.

Look at the things that are important to your business leadership teams and then investigate what information outputs are available to you to help articulate both the things that are of concern (and that could affect the valued business operations) and those things that have improved or are working well (supply reassurance).

11.5 DELIVERING THE 'ELEVATOR (LIFT) PITCH'

Previously, I had been really frustrated with an organization that had insisted on my delivering monthly security risk metrics. I spent days trying to enhance what they had previously produced, only to be told (by the only person requesting them and who was the only person that looked at them) that they wanted them to be returned to the old format.

What was the old format? Pages, upon pages, of generic content output from their various security tools (e.g., vulnerability totals, internet alerts, antivirus risk reports, etc.), of little or no interest or use to anyone.

With my enthusiasm to make these reports better squarely curtailed, I spent one day every month for the next 12 months replicating metrics that did not have any context, relevance, or usefulness. However, it 'ticked a box' for their ISO/IEC 27001 compliance (Clause 9.3):

Management review
Top management shall review the organization's information security management system at planned intervals to ensure its continuing suitability, adequacy and effectiveness. The management review shall include consideration of:

    a) the status of actions from previous management reviews;
    b) changes in external and internal issues that are relevant to the information security management system;
    c) feedback on the information security performance, including trends in:
       1) nonconformities and corrective actions;
       2) monitoring and measurement results;
       3) audit results; and
       4) fulfillment of information security objectives;
    d) feedback from interested parties;
    e) results of risk assessment and status of risk treatment plan; and
    f) opportunities for continual improvement.

The outputs of the management review shall include decisions related to continual improvement opportunities and any needs for changes to the information security management system. The organization shall retain documented information as evidence of the results of management reviews.

I am not sure that the intention of this clause was for organizations to waste time producing trends and metrics that did not bring any benefit or value to the business. However, once you start looking, you will be amazed at the amount of information that is available to you, but remember, you do not have to use it all at once, and some will not be relevant or of interest to your target audience.

Easily the most difficult part of designing effective metrics is being able to suitably tailor your reports for your target audience. Traditional wordy reports are often not suitable for the modern digital business, with both the influence of technology shortening the attention span of your audience (Floyd[13]), and your audience being extremely busy people.

Do your reports address the differing attention types (Ocasio[14])? For example:

- Selective attention (Cherry[15])
- Executive attention (Blatchley[16])

- Vigilance attention (Psynso Inc.[17])
- Sustained attention (Mir et al.[18])

Understanding the attention types of your audience can help you to create improved reports that may hook your audience to be engaged with the content. Do you focus on a goal-driven, top-down (Dean[19]) or stimulus-driven, bottom-up approach, or a hybrid of these two?

Additionally, if the audience is your C-Suite personnel, remember that, despite being good at running a business, they may not understand technical or cyber/information security specific terminology.

Make sure that the reports clearly and concisely deliver the 'so what?' message and let them know why this is being reported. For example, what is the value of telling them that the antivirus software detected ## instances of potentially malicious malware?

Remember, these reports are not to show the audience how much experience and knowledge the report author has but to provide the relevant information they need to know on what is working well and what areas may need some attention (so that they are able to make an informed decision as to whether they need to press the button, or not).

11.6 WHEN SECURITY RISK METRICS BITE BACK

With the increased number of businesses (Sharm[20]) that are transferring the responsibility for managing their more and more complex IT systems and networks, be that moving to a cloud service provider (GeeksforGeeks[21]), managed service provider (IONOS[22]), or shared hosting provider (Gran[23]), and the increased targeting by cybercriminals (Raj[24]), (Acronis[25]), it has never been more important to create and regularly review metrics to monitor the performance and risks associated with any high-value outsourced services.

It is very unlikely that you will be your third-party service providers' only client, and the more plates that they need to keep spinning, the greater the risks. Consequently, it is essential that they provide you with periodic metrics to review, you conduct due diligence, and, where possible, you obtain independent metrics.

For instance, if we take a look at the trend metrics for the internet-facing digital footprint of a handful of businesses that were victims of a ransomware attack in 2021 (Touro College Illinois[26]), as depicted in Figure 11.5 (Security Scorecard, "Security Ratings | SecurityScorecard"[27]), we can see that many of these had low scoring profiles (or had a dip in their profile scores) before they fell victim to the ransomware attack.

Had these been one (or all) of your third-party service providers, you might have seen this, conducted a prompt risk assessment and engaged with the third-party to help avert these incidents from happening.

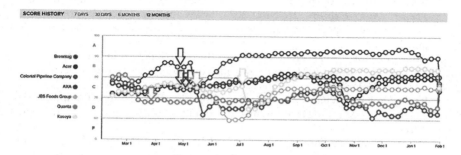

Figure 11.5 Metrics for businesses victim of cyberattacks.

11.7 DECODING SECURITY RISK METRICS

Effective security risk metrics are extremely difficult to design and implement, and when correctly created they can supply considerable value to an organization. However, most security risk metrics fall short of where they should be and they end up being lengthy, regurgitations of security tools data, not relevant, too technical, and/or without the context needed to engage the intended audience to allow them to quickly understand what is performing well, improving or which need a decision making to invoke remediation actions.

Consequently, what happens is that the intended audience rarely read the content (especially if they are busy doing their 'day jobs') or do not understand the implications of the content, so they then just go through the motions (tick the box).

Your metrics should be like your CV/resumé: Concise and direct to quickly explain the situation, task, action, and result for each risk (remember that a 'picture paints a thousand words') and be aligned to those valued business operations/assets.

You will soon know when you are heading in the right direction, when you start to get questions on the content and when the target audience start making the reviews a priority. Suddenly, (that world that was once invisible to the key business stakeholders) the security risk metrics start to show the key stakeholders the cost-benefits for their investments in security tools.

Notes

1 Aksoy, Hüseyin. "Ford F-150 Warning Lights | Ford F-150 Dashboard Symbols and Meaning." Car Warning Lights, 12 Aug. 2021, carwarninglights.net/warning-light/ford/ford-f150-warning-lights. Accessed 24 Jan. 2022.

2 Wilson, James. "What Are Dipped Headlights and When Should You Use Them?" *Auto Express*, 26 Nov. 2021, www.autoexpress.co.uk/car-news/100 723/what-are-dipped-headlights-and-when-should-you-use-them. Accessed 24 Jan. 2022.

3 Banik, Shibani. "What Is Recovery Time Objective (RTO), Why Is it Important?" Zmanda, 17 May 2021, www.zmanda.com/blog/recovery-time-objective-rto. Accessed 26 Jan. 2022.

4 Banik, Shibani. "What Is Recovery Point Objective (RPO), Why Is It Important?" Zmanda, 11 May 2021, www.zmanda.com/blog/recovery-point-objective-rpo. Accessed 26 Jan. 2022.

5 Online Etymology Dictionary. "Metrics | Etymology, Origin and Meaning of Metrics by Etymonline." www.etymonline.com, www.etymonline.com/word/metrics#etymonline_v_44676. Accessed 26 Jan. 2022.

6 Voeller, John G. "Wiley Handbook of Science and Technology for Homeland Security." Hoboken, N.J.: Wiley, 2010.

7 Black, Paul, et al. "Cyber Security Metrics and Measures." Apr. 2010.

8 Wheatman, Jeffrey. "How to Create Security Metrics Business Leaders Care About." SearchSecurity, 16 Nov. 2021, www.techtarget.com/searchsecurity/post/How-to-create-security-metrics-business-leaders-care-about. Accessed 26 Jan. 2022.

9 NIST. "PRE-DRAFT Call for Comments: Performance Measurement Guide for Information Security." Csrc.nist.gov, 24 Sept. 2020, csrc.nist.gov/publications/detail/sp/800-55/rev-2/draft. Accessed 26 Jan. 2022.

10 Security Scorecard. "Security Ratings | SecurityScorecard." Securityscorecard.com, securityscorecard.com/product/security-ratings

11 Federal Trade Commission. "FTC Warns Companies to Remediate Log4j Security Vulnerability." Federal Trade Commission, 4 Jan. 2022, www.ftc.gov/news-events/blogs/techftc/2022/01/ftc-warns-companies-remediate-log4j-security-vulnerability

12 Panhalkar, Tushar. "Network Security Controls." Infosavvy Security and IT Management Training, 18 Nov. 2019, info-savvy.com/network-security-controls

13 Floyd, Courtney. "Technology and Attention (1/3/22)." Texts.mandala.library.virginia.edu, 23 Oct. 2020, texts.mandala.library.virginia.edu/book_pubreader/67228. Accessed 2 Feb. 2022.

14 Ocasio, William. "Attention to Attention." *Organization Science*, 22(5), Oct. 2011, pp. 1286–1296, 10.1287/orsc.1100.0602

15 Cherry, Kendra. "What Is Selective Attention?" *Explore Psychology*, 16 Jan. 2022, www.explorepsychology.com/selective-attention. Accessed 2 Feb. 2022.

16 Blatchley, Barbara. "Meditation and Executive Attention | Psychology Today." www.psychologytoday.com, 2 Dec. 2021, www.psychologytoday.com/us/blog/what-are-the-chances/202112/meditation-and-executive-attention. Accessed 2 Feb. 2022.

17 Psynso Inc. "Vigilance." Psynso, 2018, psynso.com/vigilance. Accessed 2 Feb. 2022.

18 Mir, SuhailRafiq, et al. "An Evaluation of Sustained Attention with Frontal Electroencephalogram." *Advances in Human Biology*, 11(1), 2021, p. 56, 10.4103/aihb.aihb_5_20. Accessed 27 Aug. 2021.

19 Dean, Mary Elizabeth. "What Is a Schema? Psychology, Definition, and Examples | BetterHelp." www.betterhelp.com, 11 Feb. 2021, www.betterhelp.com/advice/psychologists/what-is-a-schema-psychology-definition-and-examples. Accessed 2 Feb. 2022.

20 Sharm, Swati. "How Outsourcing Practices Are Changing in 2021: An Industry Insight." InfoQ, 2 July 2021, www.infoq.com/articles/outsource-practices-change-2021. Accessed 2 Feb. 2022.

21 GeeksforGeeks. "Cloud Based Services." GeeksforGeeks, 26 Jan. 2018, www.geeksforgeeks.org/cloud-based-services. Accessed 2 Feb. 2022.

22 IONOS. "Managed Service Provider: What Is an MSP?" IONOS Digitalguide, 27 July 2021, www.ionos.com/digitalguide/server/know-how/managed-service-provider-msp. Accessed 2 Feb. 2022.

23 Gran, Ben. "Shared Hosting vs. Cloud Hosting." Business.org, 11 Jan. 2022, www.business.org/services/website/shared-hosting-vs-cloud-hosting. Accessed 2 Feb. 2022.

24 Raj, Aaron. "Cybercriminals Targeting MSPs as More Attacks on Supply Chain Expected in 2022." TechHQ, 20 Dec. 2021, techhq.com/2021/12/cybercriminals-targeting-msps-as-more-attacks-on-supply-chain-expected-in-2022. Accessed 2 Feb. 2022.

25 Acronis. Acronis Cyberthreats Report 2022: At War with Ransomware Gangs: A Year in Review Introduction and Summary. 2022.

26 Touro College Illinois. "The 10 Biggest Ransomware Attacks of 2021." Illinois. touro.edu, 10 June 2021, illinois.touro.edu/news/the-10-biggest-ransomware-attacks-of-2021.php

27 SecurityScorecard "Security Ratings | SecurityScorecard." Securityscorecard.com, 2022, securityscorecard.com/product/security-ratings

Survive to Operate

Reducing the Impacts/Consequences

Chapter 12

Security Incident Management

Having a plan enabled us to keep our hope alive. Perhaps similarly, people who are in their own personal crises—a pink slip, a foreclosure—can be reminded that no matter how dire the circumstance, or how little time you have to deal with it, further action is always possible.

There's always a way out of even the tightest spot.

(Source: Newsweek Staff[1])

12.1 AN EMERGENCY AND MILITARY SERVICES ANALOGY

You would expect your local emergency and military services to have been trained, suitably resourced, able to respond, and deal with all manner of different incident scenarios. The number of incident scenarios that they need to be able to effectively respond to and deal with is constantly evolving and changing. To match their capabilities with the potential scenarios (no matter how unlikely), these teams need to be constantly evaluating themselves against any existing or emerging threats.

The scenarios can range from the mundane (e.g., a cat stuck up a tree) to what might appear to be the far-fetched (e.g., a zombie apocalypse; yes, you read that correctly!). Both the United States and the UK are known to have incident plans for responding to and dealing with a zombie apocalypse (Department of Defense[2]), (Redd[3]), (Elhassan[4]), (Griffin[5]).

As well as being prepared for the far-fetched, they also need to be suitably prepared for those more commonly occurring incidents and to enhance their capabilities to meet any evolving threats.

For example, during the recent UK heat wave, the London Fire Brigade had its busiest day since the Second World War (Rhoden-Paul and Faulkner[6]). Now imagine how it managed to deal with the events of that day:

1. Incident room receive multiple reports of 'urgent' incidents.
2. Incidents are recorded.

DOI: 10.1201/9781003288084-15

3. Incident room triages and prioritizes the incident reports, based on the perceived impacts.

4. Fire teams are tasked to respond to fulfill the following objectives:
   a. Quickly re-establish normal operations.
   b. Minimize losses (e.g., life, property, etc.).
   c. Quickly and thoroughly extinguish fires or stop fires from spreading.
   d. Strengthen response capabilities to avoid future incidents (apply lessons learned).

Unlike hotter climates, the expectation of 'wildfires' (Merriam-Webster Dictionary[7]) having such an impact, as was observed in July 2022, were unlikely. However, the London Fire Brigade was seen to be suitably trained and prepared, and, as a result, although it was extremely stretched, it was able to quickly respond and contain these wildfires, limiting the losses from over 1,000 fire incidents and 2,670 calls. Thankfully, these losses were limited to property (circa 40 houses and shops) and there was not a single loss of life (BBC News[8]).

Prior to this fateful day, extensive 'wildfires' affecting London were forecasted to be extremely unlikely. However, the London Fire Brigade showed a return on investments for its planning, training, and firefighting equipment. Imagine if the firefighters had been sent to respond to a fire for which they had not been issued equipment, or had failed to ensure that their response vehicles had been loaded up with the required equipment.

This should be the same for your business. We hope that we do not have an impactful incident, but we need to be suitably prepared for a wide range of potential incidents. Imagine suffering an outage as the result of a cyberattack and not having the resources, capabilities, or tools needed to identify, respond, contain, and recover from such an impactful event quickly and efficiently.

Would you rather discover any failings during the actual incident or during the planning and testing phases?

12.2 INTRODUCTION TO SECURITY INCIDENT MANAGEMENT

Imagine your security incident management practices as being your emergency services. Do you have the required assurances for these emergency services being effective across a variety of different, but plausible, scenarios, or are you one of those organizations that have merely 'ticked that box' for compliance by having a documented incident response plan but have never (or rarely) tested it for effectiveness?

Accidents and errors happen, and while every human participates in supporting your operational resilience program, it is likely that you will need to invoke your incident response plan to help reduce the impact and risks associated with these incidents.

12.3 WHAT IS A SECURITY INCIDENT?

It is important to understand the differences between a security event, a security incident, and a breach, as there is often a fine line between an event becoming an incident, leading to a security breach.

The NIST SP800-161, Volume 1 (Systems Security Engineering Considerations for a Multidisciplinary Approach in the Engineering of Trustworthy Secure Systems) (Ross et al.[9]) defines an event as being: "Occurrence or change of a particular set of circumstances."

The FIPS 200 (Minimum Security Requirements for Federal Information and Information Systems), (Gutierrez and Jeffrey[10]), defines a security incident as being:

> An occurrence that actually or potentially jeopardizes the confidentiality, integrity, or availability of an information system or the information the system processes, stores, or transmits or that constitutes a violation or imminent threat of violation of security policies, security procedures, or acceptable use policies.

Techopedia defines a Security Breach (Techopedia[11]) as being:

> A security breach is any incident that results in unauthorized access of data, applications, services, networks and/or devices by bypassing their underlying security mechanisms. A security breach occurs when an individual or an application illegitimately enters a private, confidential, or unauthorized logical IT perimeter.
>
> A security breach is also known as a security violation.

I have a good example to help you distinguish between these terms. One Christmas holiday period, the armory of a military establishment was found to be insecure. During the out-of-hours checks, an external door to the building was found to be closed but not locked. The insecure external door allowed unauthorized access to assets that were categorized as being secret.

- Was this a security event, a security incident, or a security breach?

On the face of it, most people would automatically lend themselves toward this being either a security incident or a security breach and would, most definitely, warrant a further investigation. Consequently, the event of the failed locking mechanism resulted in a security incident, whereby the physical security policy, requiring the unoccupied station armory to be secured, had not been adhered to.

Upon further investigation, it was discovered that the armory staff had followed their lockup procedures to the letter and this insecurity had occurred because of Mother Nature's influence. Due to the cold weather, the locking mechanism to the electronic automated access control systems (EAACS) had become frozen in the open position, so when the armory staff conducted their lockdown procedures, they set the alarm and pushed the door closed. In normal conditions, the locking mechanism would have engaged and the door would have been secure. However, despite all the alarm contacts still being active, on this occasion the door lock had not maintained the integrity of the building.

Consequently, this event/occurrence presented the potential to jeopardize the confidentiality, integrity, or availability of the secret assets stored within the armory. The follow-up checks from this security incident confirmed that this had not escalated into a security breach, as the alarm system had not registered any activation of tampering, motion, and contact alarms, and the EAACS had not recorded any opening or closing of any access or egress points.

This was treated as a security incident and the lessons learned from it resulted in an extra step being applied to the lockup procedures (the doors and windows to be pulled, to ensure the locking mechanism had engaged) and an additional insulation layer was fitted around the locking mechanism to help prevent further chances of freezing.

A significant part of a successful security incident management practice is reliant on knowing what NORMAL looks like, being able to identify the presence of the ABNORMAL, and being able to identify the presence of an attacker's known TTPs.

For many businesses, it becomes difficult to effectively achieve NORMAL, as business operations can create so much noise that it makes it easier for an attacker to have their actions remain unnoticed. Therefore, it has been reported that the dwell time averages at 287 days. The term dwell time is defined as:

> Dwell time represents the length of time a cyberattacker has free rein in an environment, from the time they get in until they are eradicated.
> Dwell time is determined by adding mean time to detect (MTTD) and mean time to repair/remediate (MTTR) and is usually measured in days.
> It's sometimes referred to as the "breach detection gap."
>
> (Source: Raja[12])

Imagine how successful an attacker's plans could be with almost four-fifths of a year at their disposal to conduct extensive recognizance, identify potential targets, and safe escape routes.

When things go wrong (which they inevitably will) or an opportunist attacker seizes their opportunity to compromise your business's infrastructure, it is important that you are able to quickly identify and respond to such activities. The prompt detection of potentially harmful activities is often discovered through an effective monitoring practice (Carnegie Mellon University: Software Engineering Institute[13]); for example, use of a SIEM of the network, systems, and user activities, or through the development of business-wide risk culture, such as identifying and reporting potential breaches of policy or harmful activities.

12.4 THE IMPORTANCE OF AN EFFECTIVE SECURITY INCIDENT MANAGEMENT PRACTICE

Up to this point, you should have gained an appreciation of the importance of being suitably prepared to respond to and handle any incidents that may come your way. This is especially important for operational resilience, where the effectiveness of your security incident management practice can help determine how quickly you are able to recover (bounce back) and how well you are able to limit the potential impact (damage limitation) of an adverse incident.

Although you might expect that most of the security industry frameworks (e.g., Center for Internet Security (CIS[14]), ISO/IEC 27001:2013 (ISMS Online[15]), NIST (NIST CSF Tools[16]), Req 12.10 PCI DSS v4.0 (PCI SSC[17])) would include the requirement to have an effective incident management program, it is important to remember that operational resilience is more than just protecting your critical systems from internal and external threats; it involves responding and dealing with outage incidents. Consequently, as depicted in Figure 12.1 (Slide Model[18]), as part of service operations, incident management is an inclusion in the ITIL v4.0 framework (Bigelow and Montgomery[19]), (Axelos[20]).

ITIL (Information Technology Infrastructure Library)

What is ITIL (Information Technology Infrastructure Library)?

ITIL (Information Technology Infrastructure Library) is a framework designed to standardize the selection, planning, delivery, maintenance, and overall lifecycle of IT services within a business. The goal is to improve efficiency and achieve predictable service delivery. The ITIL framework enables IT administrators to be business service partners, rather than just back-end support. ITIL guidelines and best practices align IT department actions and expenses to business needs and change them as the business grows or shifts direction.

(Source: Bigelow and Montgomery[20])

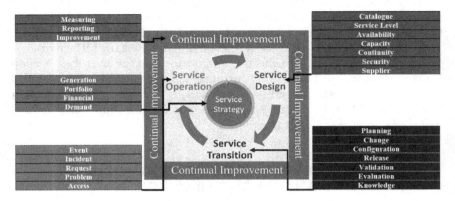

Figure 12.1 ITIL v4.0 framework.

12.5 COMPONENTS OF AN EFFECTIVE SECURITY INCIDENT MANAGEMENT PROGRAM (SIMP)

As someone that has been directly involved in far too many incidents to count, I can personally affirm the importance that a well-drilled, planned, and documented SIMP plays in limiting the delays in responding to, containing, and recovering from an unexpected impactful occurrence.

Take it from me, with a documented and tested SIMP you will be faced with a variety of natural but different responses. Much like the human responses to trauma, your employees will respond differently to a security incident; for example, the 'Six Fs,' as detailed in Table 12.1 (Munier[21]).

Having a defined, tested, and effective SIMP helps to mitigate the way your employees might respond, giving additional confidence to those employees that might otherwise lend themselves toward the 'Fawn' end of the Six Fs.

Such responses can be increased through uncertainty or remote working conditions, so it is important to ensure that the SIMP remains effective during different working conditions (e.g., change to increased remote working conditions in response to a pandemic).

How often do you assess your incident response?

- Once a year?
- After a change of the business operating model?
- Periodically, based on the risk profile?
- In response to the changing threat landscapes?

Now that you have an appreciation of the importance that the SIMP provides to your organization's SRM and operational resilience, next it is important to know who you are going to include in the SIMP.

Table 12.1 Six Fs of Response

Response Type	Definition	May present as...	Mislabeled as...
Fight	Posturing against or confronting the perceived threat.	Explosive outbursts, anger, defiance, or demanding.	Narcissistic
Freeze or Find a Friend	Dissociating in response to the perceived threat.	Spacing out, losing time, feeling unreal, brain fog, or feeling numb.	Dissociative Disorder
Fawn	Placating the perceived threat to forestall imminent danger.	People-pleasing, fear to express self, flattery, "yes" person, exploitable, fear of not fitting in.	Co-dependent Disorder
Flood	Being flooded with emotions in response to a perceived threat.	Emotional flooding, emotional dysregulation.	
Fatigue/Flop	Feeling tired or sleepy in response to a perceived threat.	Disassociating, numbing.	
Flight	Fleeing or symbolically fleeing the perceived threat by way of a "hyperactive" response.	Anxiety, fidgeting, over-worrying, workaholic tendencies, or fidgeting.	OCD

- SIMP team?
- Leadership teams?
- Senior management?
- Data protection officer?
- Public relations officer?
- Forensics team?
- Key stakeholders?
- All employees?

The correct answer is that all these representatives should be involved (in some way or another) in the SIMP. The more people that understand and are confident in their roles and responsibilities in support of the SIMP, the greater the chance of the SIMP being successful.

Imagine the scenario where an employee receives a malicious email, which has a piece of clandestine malware embedded into an attached document. The individual recognizes this as being potentially malicious, avoids clicking

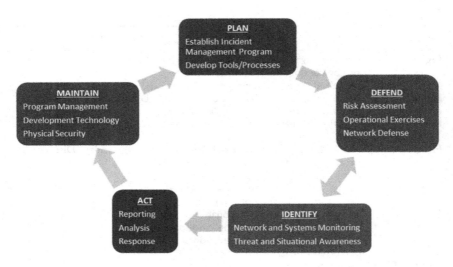

Figure 12.2 Security incident management cycle.

on the email or downloading the attachment, and simply deletes the dangerous email. However, they fail to report this as being an incident, as they have no knowledge of the reporting process, and this lack of knowledge lends them to the 'Flight' response.

This malicious email has managed to get through your business's defensive layers but was stopped in its tracks by the initiative-taking actions of this individual. However, they were not the only recipient of this malicious email, and the failure of this employee to initiate the 'Identify' step of the security incident management process, as depicted in Figures 12.2 (Fritz[22]), 12.3 (NERC[23]), 12.4 (Cichonski et al.[24]), and 12.5 (CREST[25]), resulted in one, or more, of the recipients clicking, downloading, and infecting theirs and all the connected IT systems, leading to a catastrophic incident.

- **PLAN** focuses on implementing an operational and successful incident management program.
- **DEFEND** relates to actions taken to prevent attacks from occurring and mitigate the impact of attacks that do occur as well as fixing actual and potentially malicious activity.
- **IDENTIFY** includes proactively collecting information about current events, potential incidents, vulnerabilities, or other incident management functions.

- **ACT** includes the steps taken to analyze, resolve, or mitigate an event or incident.
- **MAINTAIN** focuses on preserving and improving the computer security incident response team (CSIRT) or incident management function itself.

Given that this book has been designed to address SRM, in support of operational resilience, I am going to avoid your typical security incident management practices and embrace more generic incident management practices, as depicted in Table 12.2 (Lucid Content Team[26]).

12.6 IT IS ALL IN THE PLAY

Think like a sports coach; in preparation for each match, the coach will study the plays of the opposition and create step-by-step guides on the measures to be taken to defend against such plays.

The same approach should be applied in the defense of your critical business operations and to help ensure that your teams are prepared for most thinkable scenarios. In response to cybersecurity incidents, the CISA[27] and Microsoft (Davies[28]) have created some useful cybersecurity playbook resources, but it is important that for operational resilience you consider scenarios that could impact your critical business operations.

While writing your playbook, remember to include the initial risk and/or security assessments that should yield the type of incidents you might expect to see with the particular systems and configurations in place. Once you have determined potential scenarios, you need to think about how to outline the specific questions that may arise from the incident, then try to pinpoint the right places to search for answers.

In addition, you should consider the following, when drafting incident response playbooks:

- Consider the first-timer – the employee who has recently been hired or the new member of the project team.
  - The plan should be easily understandable and implementable, with careful instructions that anyone could follow.
- Remember the human should always be at the center of the investigation – one of your employees will discover the incident, another will execute the remediation plan, another will answer questions.
  - Placing the human at the center of the questioning and executing process will remind you of their purpose.

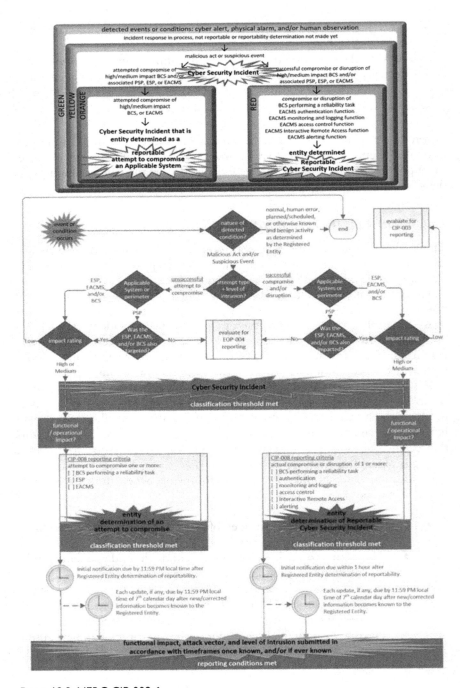

Figure 12.3 NERC CIP-008-6.

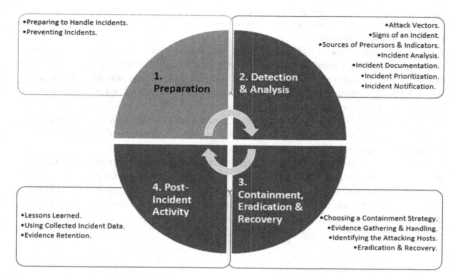

Figure 12.4 NIST SP800-61, Rev 2.

Figure 12.5 CREST cyber incident model.

Table 12.2 ITIL Incident Management Process Flows

1. Incident identification

Your incident management process all starts with a timely identification and notification of a suspicious or potentially impactful occurrence. Consequently, it is very important that you have an effective mix of people and technologies that can identify any potential **ABNORMAL** activities, that could potentially harm, or impact, your business' critical operations *(as per the business mission statement).*

To improve your understanding of the type of incidents that might be appropriate to your business operations, it is important that you align the creation of your incident management playbooks with your risk scenarios.

To enable this, it is important that you create a holistic approach, aligning SRM practices to your incident management practices and ensure that the risk-based incident scenarios are communicated out to your network of eyes and ears – Be that your general end users or those individuals that have been assigned roles and responsibilities that support the operational resilience.

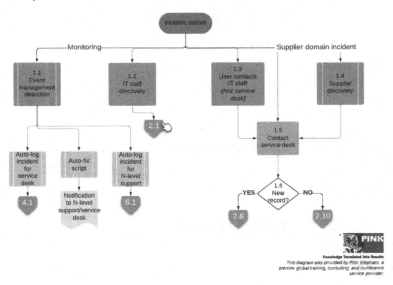

This diagram was provided by Pink Elephant, a premier global training, consulting, and conference service provider.

2. Incident logging

This next stage is very important in support of both the initial analysis, for post-incident investigations and to feed into the ongoing risk assessment process. The greater the detail, the more effective the data will prove to be.

Table 12.2 (Continued)

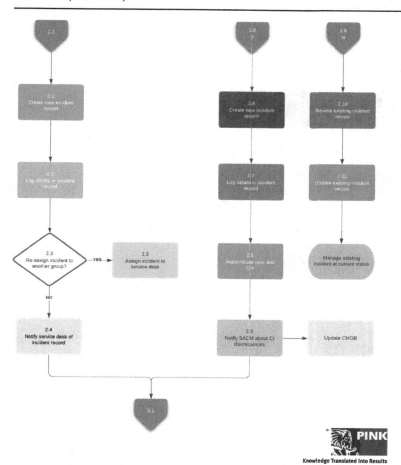

This diagram was provided by Pink Elephant, a premier global
training, consulting, and conference service provider.

3. Incident categorization and prioritization

This is where your incident management practices link into your asset management and risk management practices, without the knowledge of the importance of the affected assets/business processes it will prove to be extremely difficult to categorize and prioritize your incident response activities.

It is not unusual for an organization to receive multiple, simultaneous, incident notifications or be busy delivering important business operations. Consequently, without the ability to quickly categorize and prioritize your responses, effective incident management becomes almost impossible to achieve and maintain.

(Continued)

Table 12.2 (Continued)

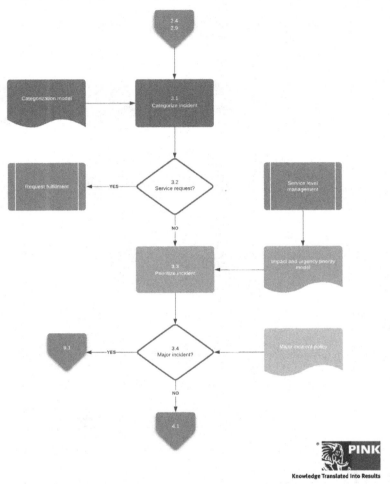

This diagram was provided by Pink Elephant, a premier global training, consulting, and conference service provider.

4. Initial diagnosis
The initial time taken to carry out the initial diagnosis can prove to be invaluable and can help to reduce the likelihood for unnecessary escalation for an incident that could be easily rectified through troubleshooting activities.

Table 12.2 (Continued)

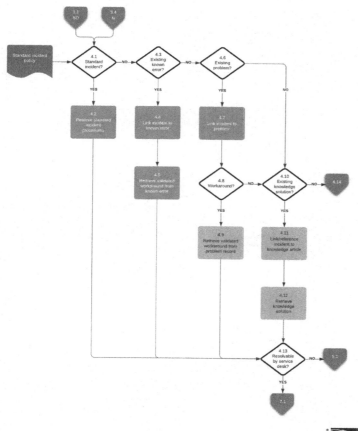

Knowledge Translated into Results

This diagram was provided by Pink Elephant, a premier global training, consulting and conference service provider.

5. Functional and hierarchic escalation

In the instances where the the 1st level support team is unable to resolve the situation, through the initial analysis, there may be a need to escalate this further, through the means of functional and/or hierarchic escalation.

• **Functional escalation:** The process escalating the ticket/incident to a higher level or more specialized team, who can deliver the proper appropriate in order to resolve the incident.

• **Hierarchic escalation:** Passing the incident further up the 'Chain of Command' so that they can determine if additional, or more skilled, resources should be assigned to resolve an incident.

(Continued)

Table 12.2 (Continued)

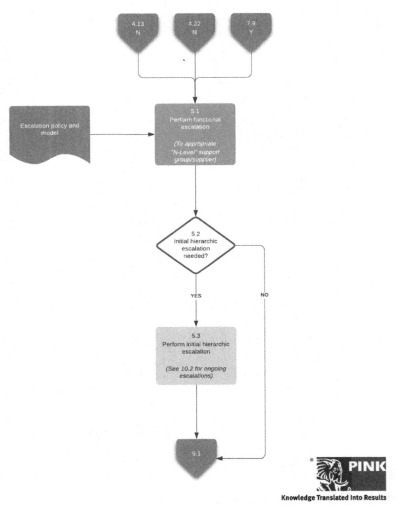

Knowledge Translated into Results

This diagram was provided by Pink Elephant, a premier global training, consulting, and conference service provider.

6. Investigation and diagnoses

Following on from the initial resolution hypothesis, this is tested for viability (based upon the most likely cause) before being implemented.

Table 12.2 (Continued)

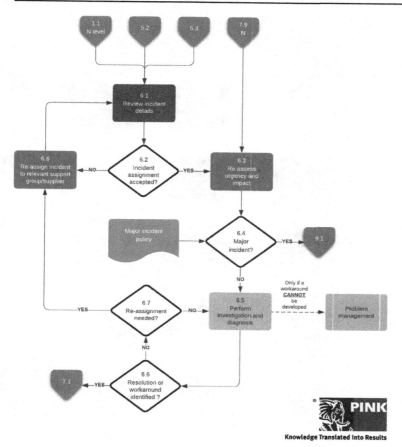

This diagram was provided by Pink Elephant, a premier global
training, consulting, and conference service provider.

7. Resolution and recovery

Having confirmed the correct, or most appropriate, cause of action, the next stage is
the application of these actions so as to contain, minimize the impact or establish the
recovery of the affected business operations.

(Continued)

Table 12.2 (Continued)

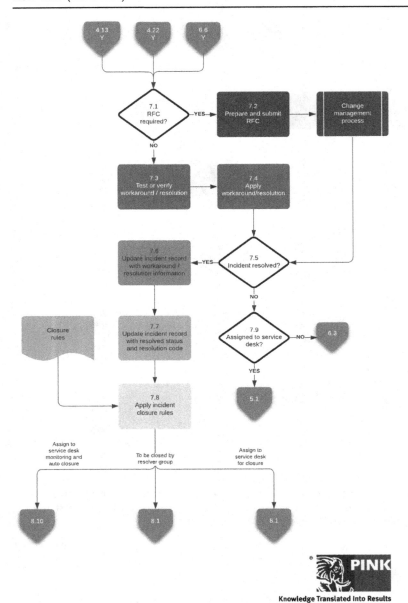

Knowledge Translated Into Results

This diagram was provided by Pink Elephant, a premier global training, consulting, and conference service provider.

8. Incident closure

Having rectified or recovered from the impactful situation, it is important to close the loop and to ensure that the root cause is fully understood, so that measures can be implemented to prevent the reoccurrence.

The incident ticket should be closed down and formally recorded.

Table 12.2 (Continued)

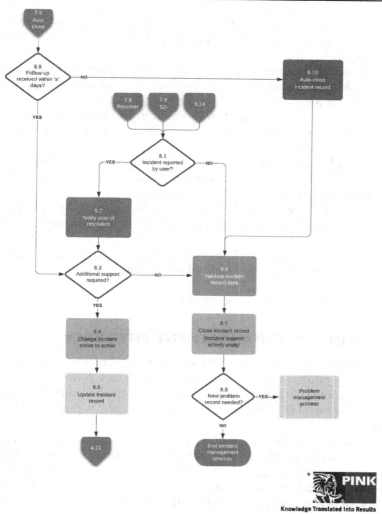

This diagram was provided by Pink Elephant, a premier global training, consulting, and conference service provider.

- All employees and the affiliates of your business should be made aware of the incident response plan and be given training on how it should be properly executed.
  - Suspicious activity should be noticed by any of your employees, at any given time, so this becomes especially important to reduce response time.
- Reconsider your document access protocols when it comes to sharing playbooks – the best place to store them might be the company social interface for accessibility.
  - Remember that this needs to be instantly and readily available to all your response teams, so it needs to work across multiple working environments.
  - Consider the storage locations of the playbooks. Have you created a backup storage location to mitigate against your primary storage location being compromised?
- Incidents are extremely high-stress situations, and it is unlikely that your responders will be operating at their peak performance during an incident.
  - Playbooks should be developed to help ensure that nothing is overlooked during the height of the action.

Example playbooks are shown at Figures 12.6 and 12.7.

12.7 WHEN INCIDENT MANAGEMENT BITES BACK

On 28th October 2020, St. John's City network was breached following the receipt of a phishing email (Donkin[29]), which was followed a few days later by a virus attack, plus a ransomware attack (believed to be through a malicious MS Excel attachment), at around 9 p.m. on 13th November 2020.

Soon after discovering the cyberattack, part of the incident response was for the city to disconnect all the information technology infrastructure and devices, in a bid to try to contain the attack and limit the damage. However, this action was not taken soon enough to prevent thousands of hours of lost work, with many services remaining offline for two weeks and costing nearly $3 million to recover from the attack.

12.8 DECODING INCIDENT MANAGEMENT

Incident management is an essential part of operational resilience and is actively supported by your SRM practices. You need to be prepared for all potential impactful occurrences, from the obvious to the not so obvious, ensuring that your employees and everyone involved in supporting incident

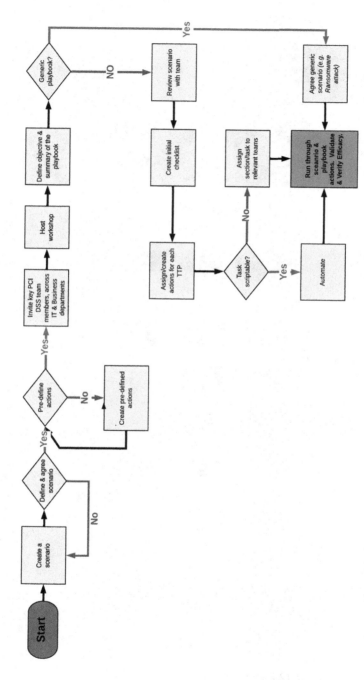

Figure 12.6 Example playbook-1.

Figure 12.7 Phishing playbook.

management are fully aware and competent to deal with any incidents that may occur.

The quicker the incidents can be identified and responded to, the greater the chance of reducing the potential impact and damage from the incidents.

Following every incident, whether impactful or not, it is important to ensure that you engage in post-incident reviews to identify the root cause (preventing reoccurrence), what went well, and what areas can be improved upon.

Notes

1 Newsweek Staff. "My Turn: The US Airways Pilot on Life as a Hero." Newsweek, 12 Feb. 2009, www.newsweek.com/my-turn-us-airways-pilot-life-hero-82161. Accessed 3 Sept. 2022.

2 Department of Defense. "CONPLAN 8888-11." I2.Cdn.turner.com, 30 Apr. 2011, i2.cdn.turner.com/cnn/2014/images/05/16/dod.zombie.apocalypse.plan. pdf. Accessed 23 July 2022.

3 Redd, Wyatt. "The U.S. Military Has an Actual Zombie Defense Plan—Here's What It Says." All That's Interesting, 18 July 2018, allthatsinteresting.com/ conop-8888. Accessed 23 July 2022.

4 Elhassan, Khalid. "The Pentagon's Plan to Fight Zombies and Other Unusual Military Schemes." History Collection, 7 Aug. 2021, historycollection.com/the-pentagons-plan-to-fight-zombies-and-other-unusual-military-schemes. Accessed 23 July 2022.

5 Griffin, Andrew. "The Country's Plans for a Zombie Outbreak Have Finally Been Revealed." *The Independent*, 8 Sept. 2017, www.independent.co.uk/tech/ zombie-plan-uk-apocalypse-us-america-attack-what-to-do-yougov-hole-up-hide-away-a7935951.html. Accessed 23 July 2022.

6 Rhoden-Paul, Andre, and Doug Faulkner. "London Fire Brigade Had Busiest Day Since World War Two, Says London Mayor." BBC News, 20 July 2022, www.bbc.co.uk/news/uk-62232654. Accessed 23 July 2022.

7 Merriam-Webster Dictionary. "Definition of WILDFIRE." Merriam-Webster. com, 2019, www.merriam-webster.com/dictionary/wildfire. Accessed 23 July 2022.

8 BBC News. "London Wildfires: Crews Say They Experienced Absolute Hell." BBC News, 20 July 2022, www.bbc.co.uk/news/uk-england-london-62236 018?at_medium=RSS&at_campaign=KARANGA. Accessed 23 July 2022.

9 Ross, Ron, et al. "Systems Security Engineering: Considerations for a Multidisciplinary Approach in the Engineering of Trustworthy Secure Systems, Volume 1."Mar. 2018, nvlpubs.nist.gov/nistpubs/SpecialPublications/NIST. SP.800-160v1.pdf, 10.6028/nist.sp.800-160v1. Accessed 23 July 2022.

10 Gutierrez, Carlos, and William Jeffrey. "FIPS PUB 200 Minimum Security Requirements for Federal Information and Information Systems." 2006.

11 Techopedia. "What Is a Security Breach? – Definition from Techopedia." Techopedia.com, 2019, www.techopedia.com/definition/29060/security-breach. Accessed 23 July 2022.

12 Raja, Sanjay. "The Number 1 Enemy of XDR and SIEM: Dwell Time." Gurucul, 10 Jan. 2022, gurucul.com/blog/the-number-1-enemy-of-xdr-and-siem-is-dwell-time. Accessed 23 July 2022.

13 Carnegie Mellon University: Software Engineering Institute. "Monitoring (MON) CERT-RMM Process Area." Resources.our sei.cmu.edu, Feb. 2016, resources.sei.cmu.edu/library/asset-view.cfm?assetid=514850. Accessed 23 July 2022.

14 Center for Internet Security. "CIS Control 17: Incident Response and Management." CIS, 2022, www.cisecurity.org/controls/incident-response-man agement. Accessed 23 July 2022.

15 ISMS Online. "ISO 27001 – Annex A.16: Information Security Incident Management." ISMS.online, 2020, www.isms.online/iso-27001/annex-a-16-information-security-incident-management. Accessed 23 July 2022.

16 NIST CSF Tools. "IR: Incident Response – CSF Tools." Csf.tools, 5 Mar. 2021, csf.tools/reference/nist-sp-800-53/r5/ir. Accessed 23 July 2022.

17 PCI SSC. "PCI DSS V4.0." Pcisecuritystandards.org, Mar. 2022, docs-prv. pcisecuritystandards.org/PCI%20DSS/Standard/PCI-DSS-v4_0.pdf. Accessed 23 July 2022.

18 Slide Model. "ITIL Framework Diagram in PowerPoint." SlideModel, 2022, slidemodel.com/templates/itil-framework-powerpoint-diagram/itil-framework-diagram-in-powerpoint. Accessed 23 July 2022.

19 Bigelow, Stephen J., and James Montgomery. "What Is ITIL (Information Technology Infrastructure Library)?" SearchDataCenter, 2022, www.techtarget. com/searchdatacenter/definition/ITIL. Accessed 23 July 2022.

20 Axelos. "What Is ITIL®? | Axelos." www.axelos.com, 2022, www.axelos.com/certifications/itil-service-management/what-is-itil. Accessed 23 July 2022.

21 Munier, Donna "Ara". "The 6Fs of Trauma Responses." NeuroClastic, 28 Sept. 2021, neuroclastic.com/the-6fs-of-trauma-responses. Accessed 23 July 2022.

22 Fritz, Mike. "Top 5 Incident Management Issues." SEI Blog, 13 Feb. 2019, insights.sei.cmu.edu/blog/top-5-incident-management-issues. Accessed 23 July 2022.

23 NERC. "Cyber Security – Incident Reporting and Response Planning Implementation Guidance for CIP-008-6 NERC | Report Title | Report Date I NERC | DRAFT CIP-008-6 Implementation Guidance |." 2019.

24 Cichonski, Paul, et al. "Computer Security Incident Handling Guide: Recommendations of the National Institute of Standards and Technology." NIST Special Publication 800-61, Revision 2, Aug. 2012, nvlpubs.nist.gov/nistpubs/SpecialPublications/NIST.SP.800-61r2.pdf, 10.6028/nist.sp.800-61r2. Accessed 24 July 2022.

25 CREST. "Cyber Security Incident Response Maturity Assessment." Crest, 2022, www.crest-approved.org/approved-services/cyber-security-incident-response-maturity-assessment. Accessed 24 July 2022.

26 Lucid Content Team. "How to Implement an ITIL Incident Management Process | Lucidchart Blog." www.lucidchart.com, 9 Aug. 2018, www.lucidchart.com/blog/incident-management-process. Accessed 24 July 2022.

27 Cybersecurity & Infrastructure Agency. "Cybersecurity Incident & Vulnerability Response Playbooks Operational Procedures for Planning and Conducting

Cybersecurity Incident and Vulnerability Response Activities in FCEB Information Systems." Nov. 2021.

28 Davies, Joe. "Incident Response Playbooks." Docs.microsoft.com, 8 June 2022, docs.microsoft.com/en-us/security/compass/incident-response-playbooks. Accessed 24 July 2022.

29 Donkin, Karissa. "Inside Saint John's Response to a "Devastating" Cyberattack." Cbc.ca, 11 Nov. 2021, www.cbc.ca/news/canada/new-brunswick/saint-john-cyberattack-records-1.6252873. Accessed 24 July 2022.

Chapter 13

Business Continuity Management

13.1 ROADSIDE ASSISTANCE ANALOGY

It is time for you to go on a road trip for a well-deserved vacation. Before going, you do all the necessary checks to make sure your vehicle is ready for the trip:

- Windshield washer fluid is topped off
- A full tank of gas or petrol
- Tires are inflated to the proper pressure

A little time or distance into your trip, your vehicle suddenly starts pulling to one side, it seems to be dragging, or some force is dragging it backward. You begin to panic a little because you know something is wrong and you need to pull to the side of the road. You think to yourself, *Do I have a flat tire?* Your brain then begins to think about all the things you did not check. *Do I have a spare tire, and if I do, is there a jack in the vehicle?*

You pull over and look around the vehicle for the issue. All the tires seem to still be inflated. You notice smoke coming from one of the rims of the vehicle and then you notice the smell of a hot brake. *The brake is dragging on the rotor!* A dangerous failure of a vehicle component and something you know means you cannot continue your journey. More panic begins to set in that you are stranded on the side of this road. This was something you had not planned for before you set out on your road trip… or did you?

You remember that you have emergency roadside assistance. Something you made sure to have not long after buying the vehicle. You look in the glovebox, find the number, and give them a call. You made sure when you got the assistance that it included towing of the vehicle. Sure enough, after some time, a service vehicle meets you on the side of the road and determines what you suspected to be a dragging brake. They load the vehicle on a tow truck and take it to a service center to be repaired. While this was a definite interruption to your trip, within a few hours your vehicle is repaired and you are back on your way, grateful you purchased this service long ago.

DOI: 10.1201/9781003288084-16

To take a journey it is not mandatory to have roadside assistance cover, and you may never need to call upon this service during any of your journeys (especially if you have a well-maintained vehicle to reduce your risks of having a vehicle malfunction), but knowing that you have someone to come to your assistance, should an unfortunate event occur, provides you with that added level of assurance and peace of mind.

Much like the scenario just described here, for operational resilience it is equally important that organizations be prepared or have a plan in place for the possible and the unexpected.

13.2 INTRODUCTION TO BUSINESS CONTINUITY MANAGEMENT

Business continuity management is typically thought of as something that only large businesses need to be concerned about because they have a lot to lose if their operations are completely stopped or heavily impacted. Additionally, it is perceived as a large effort to undertake and is very complicated.

This is far from the truth. Everyone does business continuity in their day-to-day life. Even the human body performs it without your knowledge. Our scenario described above is business continuity management.

13.3 UNDERSTANDING BUSINESS CONTINUITY

As the name suggests, this is the ability of an organization to continue running its essential business operations when faced with adverse or impactful events or occurrences. However, this does not just happen, and you need to plan and prepare for any predicted impactful events or occurrences.

The effectiveness of your business continuity capabilities is dependent on your threat intelligence, BIA, risk scenarios, and incident management playbooks, and acts to complement these practices. You can even start to think about applying case studies for other incidents that have impacted other businesses (Rock[1]), to try to appreciate how this type of occurrence might impact your type of business and what capabilities you have in place to make a difference.

TechTarget defines business continuity as: "An organization's ability to maintain essential functions during and after a disaster has occurred" (Sullivan and Crocetti[2]). Mainly it is about an organization being able to do what it needs to do to survive during significant interruptions to its mission when a major threat is experienced. Much like incident response, business continuity should establish a plan that identifies all your threats and disasters and understands their impact on the organization so that it can react quickly and methodically to limit loss.

While all organizations have industry-specific threats, they all have a set of threats they all face and should plan for. These industry-specific threats are described as:

Global Pandemics

A worldwide pandemic can lead to big disruptions in the economy and the market, and it can also be the cause of big problems for companies. The organization's employees will not be able to come into the office to work and they will be forced to work from home. This creates a situation where the company's workforce needs to be adaptable to successfully go remote quickly and continue to do so for an indefinite period.

Natural Disasters

Any natural disaster is a force of nature that can act as a significant threat to the human condition and health and safety. It also includes threats to property and critical infrastructure. Natural disasters can be any of the follow such as:

- Wildfires
- Tornadoes
- Hurricanes
- Winter storms
- Floods
- Earthquakes
- Man-made Disasters

A man-made disaster can be considered to be any catastrophe that takes place because of human negligence, any mistakes, or even large-scale accidents.

These man-made disasters can be any of the following:

- Chemical explosions
- Gas leaks
- Oil spills
- Factory fires
- Hazardous material spills
- Improper disposal of waste

Utility Failures

Utility failures take place when utility providers do not follow through when it comes to providing service for some reason. Utility failures can include instances such as:

- Electricity or power failure
- Loss of communication lines
- Disruption of water service

Intentional Sabotage

This threat to business continuity includes various acts that people can commit with the sole intention of putting an organization's business at risk, Sabotage can come in many forms such as:

- A bomb threat
- A financial information leak
- Arson

Cybersecurity Attacks

Any attack on an organization's technical assets by someone is a cybersecurity attack. These threats can be, but are not limited to:

- Information leaks
- Ransomware
- SQL injection attacks
- Distributed Denial of Service (DDoS) attacks

A cybersecurity attack can lead to causing a lot of harm to the business as well as its customers. The implications of attacks like these can be felt way past the Information Technology (IT) department.

(Source: Horvath[3])

With this list of threats and potentially others based on your organization's industry, it should show the need to have effective business continuity management, which is the combination of the following.

13.3.1 Risk Assessments

This is the initial and critical component of business continuity management. The risk assessment's purpose is to identify potential hazards or threats to an organization, such as the threats listed above. Assessments should be conducted organization-wide to help the organization have a complete understanding of its risks and where they are. This book is all about risk and conducting risk assessments. You should leverage multiple chapters in the book to have robust risk assessments to help build your business continuity. The two key chapters are Chapter 6 on risk scenarios, because this will help identify all the threats to the organization, and Chapter 9 on risk-enabling the human firewall, because this helps to explain the importance of educating all employees on how to identify and assess risk. Risk assessments are much like the scenario mentioned above when you checked certain components of the vehicle to make sure they were in working order.

13.3.2 Business Impact Analysis

The next critical component of business continuity management is BIAs, because they help you identify critical processes of your organization and establish RPOs and RTOs. As a reminder, BIAs reveal possible weaknesses, as well as the impact of threats on various areas of the organization. Again, this book has a whole chapter (Chapter 2) dedicated to BIA to help guide you through this critical process. By having robust BIA, you should have identified all interdependencies and researched them.

Jumping back to our earlier scenario with the dragging break, a BIA was used when assessing whether you should continue your journey or call to have the vehicle towed by emergency services. You quickly determined that it was better to get it fixed than to continue.

13.3.3 Business Continuity Plan Development

The actual plan is the most critical piece of business continuity management and a resilient organization. A BCP features a clear process for the steps an organization should take to maintain operations. If the plan must be activated there should be no questions about what or how to continue operations. Not having a BCP can lead to financial loss, lower confidence, and a negative impact on reputation. The plan can be broken down into seven steps:

1. Identify Objectives and Goals of the Plan
    While I have not explicitly said it to this point, and much like what has been discussed in the other chapters of the book about risk, business continuity management includes the entire organization and beyond, not just information technology or information security. It applies to all critical organizational functions. This may be planning for services outside of your organization that you depend upon. This could include software-as-a-service (SaaS) providers and other supply chain services. Every organization is different, so you need to identify the goals and objectives that are most important to the way your organization functions.
2. Establish a Business Continuity Preparedness Team
    Much like with your incident response plan, you should have a cross-functional team comprised of leadership and key individuals who can make organizational-level decisions. In the middle of a disaster this team needs to be able to make decisions to restore the organization and in what order to implement recovery. Sometimes the decision will be difficult, whereas one operation may be restored before another, and the immediate impact may cause a loss, but in the long term it will be less than if the restoration of the operation

was delayed. Leadership, not lower-level individuals, must take these types of organizational-wide decisions.

3. Identify Essential Organizational Functions

The team will have to determine how the organization will maintain essential services in the event of a disaster or emergency. Leveraging their goals and objectives they should identify what processes are critical or would have the most impact on the organization if they were no longer able to be performed.

4. Prioritize Processes

This step in your plan combines your risk assessments, BIAs, and goals and objectives. Leveraging your goals and objectives, use the identified risk and RTOs to establish a prioritization recovery list of your processes and systems. The BIAs should show the interdependencies of your processes and systems. This will be critical in understanding that a system or process in one department may depend on other processes or systems in other departments. This could cause those other processes or systems to have a higher priority for recovery. You could create a business continuity recovery register that lists recovery priority from high to low. This would give the business continuity preparedness team a very clear picture of what needs to be recovered and in what order.

5. Prepare a Plan for Every Essential Function

After essential functions have been identified and prioritized, a plan, or 'playbook', should be developed for each of your essential functions. The whole purpose of the BCP is to have a step-by-step plan of how to recover from a disaster. These playbooks will help guide the team and organization in the event of a crisis when things are typically chaotic and unorganized. These playbooks should have plans for every level of the organization that make use of or have a dependency on an essential function. They should include the following:

- Level of risk they have to the organization
- Impact on employees and customers
- Communication plans, both internal and external
- Emergency policies – predeveloped
- Financial resources that can be leveraged if a disaster were to occur
- Establish contacts with external organizations or partners that can assist during a disaster

6. Ensure Every Business Function has Been Reviewed

All business functions should be in the BCP. While this sounds like a large task, remember that they all should have been captured in your BIAs for each department. They all should be reviewed and include the following things listed in step five:

- Level of risk they have to the organization
- Impact on employees and customers
- Communication plans, both internal and external
- Emergency policies – predeveloped
- Financial resources that can be leveraged if a disaster were to occur
- Establish contacts with external organizations or partners that can assist during a disaster

7. Train, Test, Revise, and Update the Plan

The BCP should be presented to all stakeholders, so they understand their responsibilities for business continuity and what is expected of them during a disaster. It is highly recommended that testing through trial runs or tabletop exercises be conducted. During these tests, all recovery times should be validated according to the BCP to ensure they are aligned with the BIA, and adjusted or updated if your tests produce different results than expected. Recovery times that are part of the planned tests should be validated regularly to ensure they still meet the needs of the organization. Employees or anyone that would be involved in the BCP if a disaster were to strike need to be trained on the BCP. These tests are a good way to train employees with real-world simulations. It will give them experience in what to expect and to understand how they might react during a real disaster.

Additionally, to ensure that you avoid single point of failure scenarios, consider training members of the team to carry out the roles and responsibilities of other members of the business continuity team. The benefits of such an approach were well demonstrated in the film adaption of the retraining of the United States Army 7th Cavalry to deploy from helicopters, during the Vietnam War film (*We Were Soldiers*[4]). In one scene, Mel Gibson is training the platoon using real-life scenarios and after one team's leader has prepared his team for the helicopter's landing, so that they were to be the best.

Figure 13.1 We were soldiers helicopter training scene.

As depicted in Figure 13.1, as the helicopter lands and the squad are making ready to rapidly disembark, Mel Gibson reaches into the helicopter, grabs the jacket of the leader, and yells: "Bang, your dead!" He then looks to the rest of the squad and shouts: "Your commander's dead, what yer going do? ... Alright, he hesitated, he's dead. What yer going do?"

The rest of the team had not been expecting this and, out of the shock of losing their leader, had stopped doing anything. In a real-life situation this would have led to all their deaths, so proved to be an excellent training scenario.

Once the BCP has been refined and tested it should get leadership approval. Furthermore, approved plans need to be made accessible to all staff in various ways so they can be used during a business disruption that may impact the primary method of storing the plans. For example, if you store the plans on a file share, what would you do if the network or access to the file share was unavailable? Do you have a method to get another copy of the plans? What good is a plan if you cannot use it when it is needed?

13.4 CONSTRUCTS OF A BUSINESS CONTINUITY PLAN

There are no set rules for what must be included in (and in what format) your organization's BCP, as long as it works for your business continuity response. After all, that is the only thing we are bothered about, right? Work with your key stakeholders and business continuity to develop a BCP that is appropriate to your BCP.

However, to get started with the development of your BCP, do not hesitate to use whatever resources you can find as a starting point. For example, if you are looking at what type of content you might want to include in your BCP, the following provides extensive useful information, including the following list of suggested sections:

Section 1 – the document control (it is about updating the documents)

Section 2 – general information (emergency contact information, threat types, business functions, timeframes for recovery, and recovery strategy)

Section 3 – the activation process for plans (contact information of continuity team, personal and contact information about stakeholders, implementation process for plans, procedures, and policies about information utilization)

Section 4 – restoration & recovery process (processes for securing the assets, recovery tasks and activities, restoration operations, and relocation of working processes if needed)

Section 5 – contact lists (it includes the information about every stakeholder involved in the continuity plan and processes, along with contact number, physical address, and email address)

Section 6 – testing the BCP is important and it must be tested as soon as it's ready. This testing phase will check if the plan is viable or not

Section 7 – education and training (teach the expected results, different training, and education methods, evaluation of success, and determine who will receive the information)

Section 8 – additional information in form of the appendix (it includes supplier and partner plans, disaster recovery plans, communication, and expense tracking, and references)

(Source: Saud[5])

13.5 WHEN BUSINESS CONTINUITY MANAGEMENT BITES BACK

A lot of organizations' BCPs would have been tested if the following event unfolded. In April 2021, a man was arrested by the FBI for trying to purchase explosives from an undercover agent. The individual "hatched a plan to use C-4 explosives to blow up an AWS data center in Ashburn, Virginia, with the intent to 'kill off about 70% of the internet'." (ITSecurity.Org[6]

For an organization that is using the cloud in its environment, would you be prepared if that part of your operations was unavailable? Even if you do not use Amazon Web Services, do you have SaaS solutions you rely on that do use it?

- Do you have a plan to operate if they were unavailable?
- Do you know whether Amazon Web Services or your cloud provider can quickly transfer your services to a backup site, or will that transfer meet your documented RTOs?

While this event never occurred, it should hopefully generate the type of questions you should be asking while developing your BCP. Although this example impacts the cloud, if you look at a more local approach, what disasters or interruptions would affect your on-premises data center(s)?

- Do you have backup power to the data center, such as a generator?
- Do you have a backup data center far enough away that in the event of an explosion it would not also be destroyed? Is that one on backup power?

Something as extreme as an explosion will impact the power across the whole organization. So, your backup data center also needs backup power and cooling. While this seems extreme, extreme disaster events are becoming more of a reality.

- Has your organization thought about how climate change may impact them?
- Are you in the path of extreme weather such as hurricanes or heat waves?

These are scenarios in business continuity management and planning that will help prepare your organization.

13.6 DECODING BUSINESS CONTINUITY MANAGEMENT

The ability to survive is a fundamental need, as stated as part of Maslow's Hierarchy of Needs in Chapter 8. For an organization to survive a disaster or major interruption, it must have effective business continuity management. The only certainty in this world is uncertainty. Business continuity management is a way to bring some order and certainty to our uncertain world. Maybe a disaster will never strike your organization but, much like when taking a road trip, would it not be better to be prepared? Being fully aware of your risks and knowing what needs to be in place to keep an organization moving forward is a good first step to being more resilient. Then, creating a full BCP incorporating your risk assessment and BIAs will give you peace of mind that your organization can recover from a major interruption and survive long into the future to come.

Notes

1 Rock, Tracy. "7 Real-Life Business Continuity Examples You'll Want to Read." Invenio IT, 14 Mar. 2022, invenioit.com/continuity/4-real-life-business-continuity-examples. Accessed 28 Aug. 2022.
2 Sullivan, Erin, and Paul Crocetti. "What Is Business Continuity and Why Is it Important?" SearchDisasterRecovery, Jan. 2020, www.techtarget.com/searchd isasterrecovery/definition/business-continuity. Accessed 28 Aug. 2022.
3 Horvath, Ingrid. "Key Strategies to Implement Business Continuity Management." Invensis Learning Blog, 11 July 2020, www.invensislearning.com/blog/business-continuity-management-key-strategies. Accessed 28 Aug. 2022.
4 We Were Soldiers. Directed by Randall Wallace, Icon Entertainment International, 1 Mar. 2002.
5 Saud, Danish. "What Is the Primary Goal of Business Continuity Planning?" Folio3 Dynamics Blog, 29 Aug. 2021, dynamics.folio3.com/blog/business-continuity. Accessed 28 Aug. 2022.
6 ITSecurity.org. "This Man Was Planning to Kill 70% of Internet in a Bomb Attack against AWS on April 12, 2021 at 4:57 Pm Feedzy." Itsecurity.org, 12 Apr. 2021, itsecurity.org/this-man-was-planning-to-kill-70-of-internet-in-a-bomb-attack-against-awson-april-12-2021-at-457-pm-feedzy. Accessed 28 Aug. 2022.

Chapter 14

Disaster Recovery Management

14.1 A DISASTER RECOVERY ANALOGY

You might think that the California wildfires are starting to become an annually expected event and that the fire service has increased its capabilities to respond to and contain such events, and to help businesses and lifestyles continue with minimal disruption quickly and effectively. However, each year, nature evolves, and businesses and families' homes are completely destroyed (as seen in the 2022 wildfires, as depicted in Figure 14.1 (Lloyd and Associated Press[1]).

Despite having a highly effective fire service (incident response and business continuity), these wildfires are still proving to be highly destructive, so any business or people intending to continue operating and living in these areas need to develop appropriate disaster recovery plans (DRPs) to help manage the impact of these ever-present natural threats.

With the increasing impact of global warming and the increased risk of these devastating wildfires, you might think that the affected towns or cities would not look to rebuild in the same locations; however, you would be wrong. The local governments are implementing DRPs for any such towns or cities affected by past and future devastating wildfires (Truong[2]). With awareness of the wildfire critical risks, the local governments, businesses, and residents need to ensure that they can effectively plan for such catastrophic events. For example:

- Emergency food/water supplies (CalFresh[3])
- Emergency housing (California Department of Housing and Community Development[4])
- Government agency support (FEMA.gov[5])
- Emergency supplies distribution (Legion[6])
- Restrictions of future property developments (ABC News[7])
- Wildfire resilience program (CA.Gov[8])
- Wildfire recovery strategies (Sierra Nevada Conservancy[9])

DOI: 10.1201/9781003288084-17

Figure 14.1 California wildfires.

The California governments, businesses, and residents may hope that next year they will have done enough to prevent the reoccurrence of their annual wildfires so that they are not adversely affected. However, the reality is that they cannot afford to rely on 'hope' and they need to adequately plan and prepare for the worst-case scenarios, so that if their protective measures, incident response, and business continuity measures fail they are appropriately prepared to quickly recover from any disastrous wildfire events.

The same approach should be applied to your business to ensure minimal impact on your organization's operational resilience.

14.2 INTRODUCTION TO DISASTER RECOVERY

TechTarget (Sullivan et al.[10]) explain Disaster Recovery (DR) as being:

> An organization's ability to respond to and recover from an event that negatively affects business operations. The goal of DR methods is to enable the organization to regain use of critical systems and IT infrastructure as soon as possible after a disaster occurs.
>
> To prepare for this, organizations often perform an in-depth analysis of their systems and create a formal document to follow in times of crisis. This document is known as a disaster recovery plan.

In essence, this is making plans to recover against the worst-case scenarios that could befall your business's essential operations and assets. Ultimately, you should be looking to link together the output from your BIAs with your risk scenarios and incident playbooks to identify the disaster recovery requirements that would be needed to minimize the impact on your essential business operations.

Disaster recovery should not be confused with crisis management. A disaster is a sudden event, whereas a crisis is a situation that develops over time, as explained by their very definitions:

- **Disaster** (Merriam-Webster[11]):
  "A sudden calamitous event bringing great damage, loss, or destruction."
- **Crisis** (Cambridge Dictionary[12])
  "A time of great disagreement, confusion, or suffering."

As you can see, a crisis may develop over a period of time, allowing you more time to prepare for the evolving situations, whereas a disaster is a sudden occurrence, allowing you extremely limited time to prepare for when your incident management and business continuity management operations fail to prevent a sudden cessation of essential business operations.

Consequently, it is vital that you prepare and plan for such occurrences. However, once again, this is dependent on your business's (and your clients'/customers') risk appetite and tolerances to absorb any unexpected outages.

To understand what is acceptable, you need to start by using the key performance metrics from your incident management (e.g., MTTR/Repair/Recover, MTBF, MTTF, Mean Time to Acknowledge (MTTA), Mean Time to Know (MTTK), etc.), as depicted in Figure 14.2 (ScienceLogic[13]), to help calculate the potential associated costs.

The longer the estimated recovery times, the higher the potential costs, and where these estimated costs exceed your business's (or customers'/clients') tolerance levels, it is important to ensure that you have alternative arrangements in place to get your valuable business operations back up and running promptly.

The Mean Time To Recovery (MTTR) Stages

Figure 14.2 Recovery metrics.

Such decisions must be risk-based to ensure that the potential costs of these disaster recovery risk responses do not exceed the potential cost of your disaster scenarios. Consequently, this may lead you to the decision to use a third-party service, a 'hot site,' a 'warm site,' or a 'cold site.'

14.3 CONSTRUCTING YOUR DISASTER RECOVERY PLAN/PROGRAM

As previously mentioned, your disaster recovery is a subset of your BIA, incident management, and business continuity management functions and is enforced after important business operations fail, despite the incident response and business continuity management practices being initiated.

Your DRP should be developed in alignment with the estimated costs and forecasted risks, following the BIA and risk assessments of the valued business operations. Based on the input, it is important to understand the business's risk appetite levels so that you can balance the risk with the predicted costs of the DRP.

Your DRP needs to define the data and assets required, as well as the steps to restore the business's most critical processes. This should be developed with consideration and input from your business continuity management operations, such as the details of the backup plans and alternative operations sites (hot site, warm site, cold site) that will be used to quickly get these important business operations back up and running once again.

> A Hot Site is a fully configured environment, similar to the normal operating environment, that can be operational immediately or within a few hours, depending on it configuration and the needs of the organization.
>
> A Warm Site is partially configured, usually having the peripherals and software but perhaps not the more expensive main processing computer. It is designed to be operational within a few days.
>
> A Cold Site will have the basic environmental controls necessary to operate but few of the computing components necessary for processing. Getting a cold site operational make take weeks.
>
> (Source: Wm Arthur Conklin et al.[14])

When creating your DRP, you need to understand the business's key stakeholders' aspirations for the RTOs and RPOs, so that the plan can fulfill these defined goals.

14.4 CREATING A DISASTER RECOVERY PLAN

Okay, so your security program and measures have failed or proved to be ineffective, and you have invoked your incident response and BCPs, but still your business's vital operations or systems are not available to support those services that are essential to the business's mission statement. Each second, minute, hour, day, and month that these services are not operational is creating a significant impact on the business.

It is time to invoke your DRP to minimize this downtime and impact. However, what should you include in your plans to get these operations back up and running promptly?

Firstly, you need to identify which of your business's critical functions need to be protected by the invoking of a DRP and then compile the answers to the following questions:

- Who is responsible for each of these critical business operations?
- What actions do these individuals need to perform for these operations?
- How are these operations relative to another and when must they be conducted?
- Where are these operations performed?
- What are the supporting processes?
- Why are these operations so critical to the continuance of the business mission statement?

Armed with this information, you can then start to prioritize the disaster recovery considerations against the business operations and their supporting processes. For example:

1. Critical
   Absolutely essential to the operations. Without these operations, the business mission statement will fail.
2. Necessary
   Required for normal processing but the business can survive for short periods of unavailability.
3. Desirable
   Not required for normal processing but this enhances the business's ability to conduct its mission efficiently.
4. Optional
   A nice to have but has little, or no, impact on the business's operational effectiveness.
5. Consider eliminating
   Loss of such operations would not impact the business's operational effectiveness.

14.4.1 Components of an Effective Disaster Recovery Plan

NIST (Swanson et al.[15]) defines a DRP as being: "A written plan for recovering one or more information systems at an alternate facility in response to a major hardware or software failure or destruction of facilities."

Additionally, this overlaps with NIST's final stage of the incidence response lifecycle (Salfati and Pease[16]) and, as mentioned, overlaps with business continuity management (CSF Tools[17]). Consequently, if you are not careful, there is likely to be some duplication between these subject areas. However, it is better to have some duplication rather than having omitted an important consideration. For example, does it matter whether backups are covered within the BCP or the DRP? No, as long as the backups are invoked promptly, either to keep the valued business operations functional or to promptly get those valued business operations back up and running, minimizing the impact on the operability of the business's mission statement.

You are looking for contingency planning that harmonizes your incident response, business continuity, and disaster recovery so that you can minimize any unwanted outages/downtime. Consequently, the design and development should incorporate all the perceived scenarios that could impact the continued operations of your valued business functions (i.e., operational resilience (NIST[18])), to help you design and develop appropriate contingency plans.

Unfortunately, I cannot provide you with a definitive guide for a DRP that would be effective for your business, as each business is unique. However, there are various DRP templates (TemplateLab[19]) that are available to you to use as a reference for creating your own unique and bespoke plan to help your valued business operations recover from disasters.

What I can do is provide you with an insight into what your DRP (as part of your contingency planning) should cover:

1. Start by using the output from your risk assessment and BIA exercises. Use this information to start formulating what is important for the continued support of the business mission statement.
2. Determine your recovery objective.
    Engage with the business's key stakeholders to determine the time thresholds (e.g., RTOs & RPOs) over which these identified valued business operations should be brought back to full (or near) operability. Your DRP should be designed to ensure that these thresholds for recovery are not exceeded, ensuring that minimal impact to the business operations is felt.
3. Define and document all the required roles and responsibilities.
    Make sure that everyone is fully aware of their roles and responsibilities if the DRP is invoked. This should never be regarded as just putting names/job positions into the DRP. Each role and responsibility should serve an important function, at a specific time, within the recovery cycle.
4. Identify the type of disaster recovery locations you need.
    Not all your valued operations will need the same contingency site where alternative business operations can divert to run from. Where

the defined recovery time thresholds are extremely short, you may need to set up fully operational redundancy (e.g., hot site) at an alternative location, which will not be impacted by the same event.

5. Where required, establish a suitable fallback site.

Based on your various playbooks, what type of fallback sites will you need and what are the best places to establish these? Think of a natural disaster such as an earthquake:

- Have you considered whether your disaster recovery site might be on the same fault line?
  Or a wildfire:

- Is the disaster recovery site near enough to quickly relocate to but not so near that a quickly spreading wildfire could also engulf the site soon after you have relocated the valued business operations?

Such things need to have been considered so that they can be included in the formally documented DRP. In times of crisis or contingency, the responders will need to know where to recover, to as the result of a particular type of incident or event. In some situations, businesses may establish different fallback sites for several types of incident or event occurrences.

6. Remote critical data backups.

Should your primary and essential data resources become compromised (integrity and availability), there may be a need to recover operations using secondary remote critical data backups. If your primary critical data becomes worthless, you need to ensure that you have an alternative source of good data that is sufficiently distanced from the primary critical data so that you are not trying to recover your critical data using duplicate corrupted data sources.

7. Understand and appreciate your equipment needs.

The last thing you want to be dealing with during a time of crisis is not to have the right equipment to relocate quickly or to get the critical business operations back up and running promptly. Think about the various scenarios and the plans that you have in place. What ancillary equipment, logistics, and other resources will be needed for each different scenario if, for example, you need to quickly relocate lots of office equipment to one of your disaster recovery sites (to get these operations back up and running)?

- Do you have the right vehicles available to move this type of equipment?

- Do you have the personnel needed to move this type of equipment?

- If not, what contingency arrangements can you implement at short notice, and what prior arrangements do you need to establish?

8. Establish suitable communication channels.
   Based on the various scenarios from your playbooks, have you considered all the communication channels that you are likely to need?
   • Do you have these contact details readily available?
   • Is your communication equipment suitable for all these scenarios?
   • What alternative communication channels might you need?
9. Detail the disaster recovery steps.
   In times of crisis, people react differently and having an easy-to-follow reference or reminder of the steps that an individual is expected to follow can really help to mitigate the natural behavioral responses to crisis events (e.g., fight, flight, freeze, friend, faint, flop, etc.).
10. Know the stakeholder escalation prioritization.
    Understand and document to whom and in which order of priority the reporting to the stakeholders should be conducted. At times of crisis, every person in a position of power is likely to want to be informed straight away. However, if the order is agreed upon and documented beforehand, the 'pecking order' is already established and the stakeholders will be aware that there is a defined reporting order and that, as part of the DRP, they will be notified in the agreed priorities.
11. Periodically test and update the DRP.
    There is little or no point in creating a DRP and never testing and refining it. Consequently, you should schedule periodic evaluations of the DRP against different scenarios from your playbooks. Your DRP should detail how often it should be evaluated and how this should be used to enhance the effectiveness of the DRP.
12. Align the DRP to your intended recovery strategies.
    If you decide to use a DRP template, ensure that the content aligns with your business strategies and objectives. You should be continually seeking opportunities to enhance the supporting processes so that they effectively meet your organization's recovery strategies and time objectives.

14.5 VALIDATING THE EFFECTIVENESS OF YOUR DISASTER RECOVERY PLAN/PROGRAM

All too often an effective 'on paper' DRP is undermined by the lack of competencies and teamwork of those people entrusted to recover the valued business operations within the expected recovery time thresholds. However, this does not tend to be down to the capabilities of an individual, but is caused by the inability of those capable individuals to work as a team, against specific scenarios, or to face scenarios they have never had to face before. Consequently, they might waste precious time familiarizing themselves with the specific nuances of a specific scenario.

In times of crisis or desperation, there is a need to adapt very quickly to different daily tasks, such as seen in the roles and responsibilities of some of the women pilots of the Air Transport Auxiliary (Poad[20]) during the Second World War. A good example of the Women's RAF Volunteer Reserve's adaptability and resilience was a recollection from Jackie (Retter[21]):

> Jackie told one other notorious story of her ATA service. It involved giving a male RAF officer a lift.
>
> The weather was terrible, but Jackie landed safely. Met by a commanding officer, her passenger complained: "Not only did you send me a mere schoolgirl, but she was reading a novel!"

Fortunately, in your business, this should not be the chosen approach and you should be thoroughly planning and assessing the effectiveness of your teams to conduct their roles in support of the steps within the DRP, against a variety of different scenarios.

Each time the DRP is evaluated against the applicable scenarios, the results should be documented and analyzed, and the lessons learned incorporated into the evolving DRP. Your DRP should never, ever, be treated as a 'tick box' or something that is not important or a priority for your business, because when 'it hits the fan" you will be extremely grateful that you had an effective and tested one.

14.6 WHEN DISASTER RECOVERY BITES BACK

I can think of few examples of real-life incidents that demonstrate the importance of having efficient 'survive to operate' capabilities than the one that affected an undisclosed company within the automotive industry (Smith et al.[22]). This was despite earlier warnings from the FBI that the automotive industry was being actively targeted by criminals using ransomware (NARFA[23]).

Had the automotive industry paid heed to this warning, it could have fed this threat report into its incident scenarios, created playbooks (FRSecure[24]), and risk-assessed against this ransomware threat. Additionally, it could have identified its risk mitigation security controls (Barker et al.[25]) and carried out a security controls review, to help ensure that it was adequately mitigating against this ever-present and evolving threat.

In doing so, the industry might have identified which of its important business operations and or suppliers had supporting assets that were vulnerable to not just one but all three of the ransomware attacks. For example:

- Firewall misconfiguration/vulnerabilities (as demonstrated in Figure 14.3 (CVE Details, "Cisco: Products and Vulnerabilities"[26]) and Figure 14.4 (CVE Details, "F5: Products and Vulnerabilities"[27]),

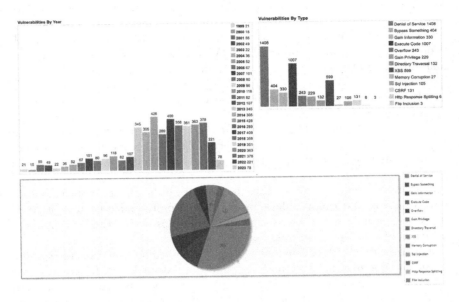

Figure 14.3 Cisco vulnerabilities.

presenting RDP vulnerability (Bisson[28]). This resulted in three ransomware attacks (by three different criminal groups (LockBit (Electronic Transactions Development Agency (ETDA)[29]), Hive (MITRE ATT&CK® [30]) & BlackCat/ALPHV (Hinchliffe[31])) being carried out within the space of just two weeks (ThreatAdvice[32]).
*   The ability to detect and respond to the use of Mimikatz (Smith[33]).
*   The use of weak passwords, enabling successful brute force attacks (Konetschni[34]).

Note:
Risk = Threat x Vulnerability *(Probability)* **x Impact**

*   **Threat =**
    *   Ransomware gangs
*   **Vulnerability =**
    *   Firewall misconfiguration (RDP)
    *   Ineffective monitoring
    *   Weak access credentials
*   **Impact =**

    *   Loss of availability of essential supplier services

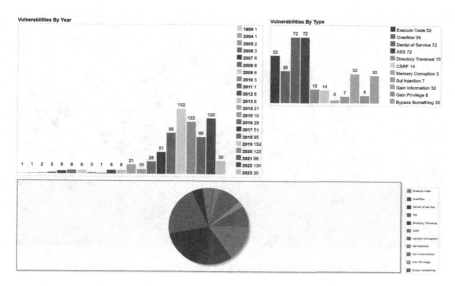

Figure 14.4 F5 vulnerabilities.

As you can clearly see, SRM and the ability to 'survive to operate' go hand in hand, and the proactive use of SRM can really assist your business to prevent such tragic events from impacting your valued business operations and their supporting assets.

14.7 DECODING DISASTER RECOVERY

The difficulty or problem with disaster recovery is that it tends to get blended in with the recovery phase of the incident response cycle or that it is not given the respect that it deserves. At the end of the day, when everything else has failed and all is lost, your disaster recovery is your business's cavalry and is the part of your defense program that can come riding in to save the day.

- Why would you not want a well-drilled and proficient calvary on standby, so that you can call on them in times of emergency?

It is important to know what part of your business needs the cavalry support and what resources they need to be given.

- Do you need your cavalry to be waiting on horseback, wearing full armor?
    - Hot site.
- Can you cope with the calvary being at stand-to (First World War. com[35] and Collins Dictionary[36]) in their barracks, available to be called upon when needed?

Figure 14.5 GoT 'Knights of the vale' coming to the rescue.

- Warm site.
- Are you able to cope with cavalry that can be developed from scratch (e.g., cavalry members recruited, trained, equipment purchased, etc.)?
  - Cold site.

It is much like the fictional scene (Season 6, Episode 9) from *Game of Thrones*[37], when the battle was just about lost and almost all the fighting forces had been nearly defeated, until the 'Knights of the Vale' arrived to provide re-enforcements, as depicted in Figure 14.5 (Evil[38]).

Next, if your primary and valued resources become corrupted, or unavailable, how long can you afford to be without them and how long will it take for you to get them replaced? What will be the impact of the prolonged unavailability of these resources?

The objective of disaster recovery is to plan for any forecasted impactful scenarios and to engage with the business stakeholders to identify the measures that are needed to ensure that the potential impact is aligned with the business's levels of risk appetite and tolerance.

Careful disaster recovery planning can help to show the business's key stakeholders that you are investing in the correct level of contingencies for the perceived risks, which have been documented, approved, and tested to ensure that they remain effective to respond to any ever-present or emerging threat landscapes.

No business wishes that their systems and data will become unavailable or compromised, but every business should be adequately prepared for such an eventuality (aka the Five Ps): **Prior Planning Prevents Poor Performance.**

Notes

1 Lloyd, Jonathan, and Associated Press. "Firefighters Gain Ground on California's Largest Wildfire of 2022." NBC Los Angeles, 4 Aug. 2022, www.nbclosange les.com/news/california-news/wildfires-mckinney-fire-siskiyou-county/2957067. Accessed 6 Aug. 2022.

2 Truong, Hanh. "Rebuilding After Devastating California Wildfires." GovTech, 3 Aug. 2022, www.govtech.com/em/safety/rebuilding-after-devastating-california-wildfires. Accessed 6 Aug. 2022.

3 CalFresh. "Disaster Response." www.cdss.ca.gov, 2022, www.cdss.ca.gov/infore sources/calfresh/disaster-calfresh. Accessed 6 Aug. 2022.

4 California Department of Housing and Community Development. "DR Multifamily Housing Program | California Department of Housing and Community Development." www.hcd.ca.gov, 2022, www.hcd.ca.gov/dr-mult ifamily-housing-program. Accessed 6 Aug. 2022.

5 FEMA.gov. "California | FEMA.gov." www.fema.gov, 2022, www.fema.gov/ locations/california#declared-disasters. Accessed 6 Aug. 2022.

6 Legion, The American. "Department of California Collecting, Distributing Supplies to Wildfire Victims." The American Legion, 18 Aug. 2021, www.leg ion.org/emergency/253429/department-california-collecting-distributing-suppl ies-wildfire-victims. Accessed 6 Aug. 2022.

7 ABC News. "Judge Blocks Big California Development over Wildfire Danger." ABC News, 8 Oct. 2021, abcnews.go.com/Business/wireStory/judge-blocks-big-california-development-wildfire-danger-80470079. Accessed 6 Aug. 2022.

8 CA.Gov. "Wildfire Resilience." California Grants Portal, 8 June 2022, www.gra nts.ca.gov/grants/wildfire-resilience. Accessed 6 Aug. 2022.

9 Sierra Nevada Conservancy. "Five Wildfire Recovery Strategies for the Sierra Nevada." Sierra Nevada Conservancy, 12 Jan. 2022, sierranevada.ca.gov/five-wildfire-recovery-strategies-for-the-sierra-nevada. Accessed 6 Aug. 2022.

10 Sullivan, Erin, et al. "What Is Disaster Recovery (DR)?" SearchDisasterRecovery, 2022, www.techtarget.com/searchdisasterrecovery/definition/disaster-recov ery#:~:text=Disaster%20recovery%20%28DR%29%20is%20an%20organ ization%27s%20ability%20to. Accessed 13 Aug. 2022.

11 Merriam-Webster. "Definition of DISASTER." Merriam-Webster.com, 2019, www.merriam-webster.com/dictionary/disaster. Accessed 13 Aug. 2022.

12 Cambridge Dictionary. "CRISIS | Meaning in the Cambridge English Dictionary." Cambridge.org, 13 Nov. 2019, dictionary.cambridge.org/dictionary/english/ crisis. Accessed 13 Aug. 2022.

13 ScienceLogic. "MTTR, MTTA & MTTD Incident Management Metrics." ScienceLogic, 18 July 2022, sciencelogic.com/blog/mttr-vs-mttr-vs-mttr-incident-management-metrics. Accessed 13 Aug. 2022.

14 Wm Arthur Conklin, et al. Principles of Computer Security. New York: Mcgraw-Hill Education, 2021.

15 Swanson, Marianne, et al. Contingency Planning Guide for Federal Information Systems. May 2010.

16 Salfati, Eran, and Michael Pease. "Digital Forensics and Incident Response (DFIR) Framework for Operational Technology (OT)." Digital Forensics and Incident Response (DFIR) Framework for Operational Technology (OT), 22 June

2022, https://nvlpubs.nist.gov/nistpubs/ir/2022/NIST.IR.8428.pdf,   10.6028/nist.ir.8428. Accessed 21 Aug. 2022.

17 CSF Tools. "BCR-01: Business Continuity Planning – CSF Tools." Csf.tools, 30 Jan. 2021, csf.tools/reference/cloud-controls-matrix/version-3-0-1/bcr/bcr-01. Accessed 21 Aug. 2022.

18 National Institute of Standards and Technology (NIST). "Community Resilience Planning Guide Playbook Templates & Additional Resources." NIST, 1 Aug. 2020,   www.nist.gov/topics/community-resilience/planning-guide/planning-guide-playbook-templates-additional-resources. Accessed 21 Aug. 2022.

19 TemplateLab. "52 Effective Disaster Recovery Plan Templates [DRP] – TemplateLab." TemplateLab, 20 Aug. 2017, templatelab.com/disaster-recovery-plan. Accessed 21 Aug. 2022.

20 Poad, Richard. "ATA's First 8 Women Pilots." Air Transport Auxiliary, 14 Jan. 2020, atamuseum.org/atas-first-8-women-pilots. Accessed 21 Aug. 2022.

21 Retter, Emily. "Inside the Inspiring Life of Women Pilots Who Flew in Face of Dangers during WW2." Mirror, 17 Aug. 2022, www.mirror.co.uk/news/uk-news/inside-inspiring-life-women-pilots-27765091. Accessed 21 Aug. 2022.

22 Smith, Linda, et al. "Lockbit, Hive, and BlackCat Attack Automotive Supplier in Triple Ransomware Attack." Sophos News, 10 Aug. 2022, news.sophos.com/en-us/2022/08/10/lockbit-hive-and-blackcat-attack-automotive-supplier-in-triple-ransomware-attack. Accessed 24 Aug. 2022.

23 NARFA. "FBI Cybersecurity Alert to the Automotive Industry." NARFA, 21 Nov. 2019, www.narfa.com/fbi-cybersecurity-alert-to-the-automotive-industry. Accessed 24 Aug. 2022.

24 FRSecure. "Ransomware Response Playbook | FRSecure." Frsecure.com, 24 Aug. 2021, frsecure.com/ransomware-response-playbook. Accessed 24 Aug. 2022.

25 Barker, William, et al. "Ransomware Risk Management: A Cybersecurity Framework Profile." NISTIR 8374 Ransomware Risk Management: A Cybersecurity Framework Profile, Feb. 2022, nvlpubs.nist.gov/nistpubs/ir/2022/NIST.IR.8374.pdf, 10.6028/NIST.IR.8374. Accessed 6 Apr. 2022.

26 CVE Details. "Cisco: Products and Vulnerabilities." www.cvedetails.com, 2012, www.cvedetails.com/vendor/16/Cisco.html. Accessed 24 Aug. 2022.

27 CVE Details. "F5: Products and Vulnerabilities." www.cvedetails.com, 2020, www.cvedetails.com/vendor/315/F5.html. Accessed 24 Aug. 2022.

28 Bisson, David. "What You Need to Know about RDP Security Going into 2022." Security Intelligence, 20 Dec. 2021, securityintelligence.com/articles/remote-desktop-protocol-rdp-security-2022. Accessed 24 Aug. 2022.

29 Electronic Transactions Development Agency. "LockBit Gang – Threat Group Cards: A Threat Actor Encyclopedia." Apt.etda.or.th, 20 July 2022, apt.etda.or.th/cgi-bin/showcard.cgi?g=LockBit%20Gang. Accessed 24 Aug. 2022.

30 MITRE ATT&CK®. "TA505, Hive0065, Group G0092 | MITRE ATT&CK®." Attack.mitre.org, 1 Dec. 2021, attack.mitre.org/groups/G0092. Accessed 24 Aug. 2022.

31 Hinchliffe, Alex. "Threat Assessment: BlackCat Ransomware." Unit 42, 27 Jan. 2022, unit42.paloaltonetworks.com/blackcat-ransomware. Accessed 24 Aug. 2022.

32 ThreatAdvice. "Automotive Supplier Breached by 3 Ransomware Gangs in 2 Weeks." www.threatadvice.com, 15 Aug. 2022, www.threatadvice.com/blog/automotive-supplier-breached-by-3-ransomware-gangs-in-2-weeks. Accessed 24 Aug. 2022.

33 Smith, Brendan. "Mimikatz HackTool, or about Windows Passwords Vulnerability." How to Fix Guide, 3 Dec. 2020, howtofix.guide/mimikatz-hacktool/#:~:text=About%20Mimikatz%20and%20ransomware%20joint%20action%20Infecting%20the. Accessed 24 Aug. 2022.

34 Konetschni, Janos. "Mimikatz: How to Stop Ransomware from Spreading." BeforeCrypt, 2 Feb. 2021, www.beforecrypt.com/en/mimikatz-stop-ransomware-spread/#:~:text=Ransomware%20gangs%20use%20Mimikatz%20in%20conjunction%20with%20brute. Accessed 24 Aug. 2022.

35 First World War.com. "First World War.com – Encyclopedia – Stand-To." www.firstworldwar.com, 22 Aug. 2009, www.firstworldwar.com/atoz/standto.htm. Accessed 29 Aug. 2022.

36 Collins Dictionary. "Definition of 'Stand To'." Collins Dictionary, 2022, www.collinsdictionary.com/dictionary/english/stand-to. Accessed 29 Aug. 2022.

37 *Game of Thrones*. HBO, 2016.

38 Evil, Battler. "Game of Thrones – S06E09 Knights of the Vale Arrive!" www.youtube.com, 20 June 2016, youtu.be/qA81ewnPEFg. Accessed 24 Aug. 2022.

Index

Printed in the United States
by Baker & Taylor Publisher Services